Beth Strobbe

MAX ← 1 2.00

W9-BWU-267

1509. OKUMO?

motivation 50   or ART Dept
major thesis of book 49,50
def Creative Learn P
                              p. 22
synthesis 91
sociod   def creative process
Brains 79
scamper   F P I S A 78

what makes the difference
GREAT TEACHER -34/92
         ENVIRONMENT 103

openness 54 list guest
timeline 138

Questioning 150 →   A
                      S   ove
                      H T888)
                      E

Under the Advisory Editorship of

LINDLEY J. STILES

Professor of Education for Interdisciplinary Studies
Northwestern University

must accept
respect / 193

Creative Learning and Teaching

A analyzing
S ynthesizing
H ypothesizing
E valuation'

CREATIVE
LEARNING AND TEACHING

E. Paul Torrance
THE UNIVERSITY OF GEORGIA
ATHENS, GEORGIA

AND

R. E. Myers
TEACHING RESEARCH
OREGON STATE SYSTEM OF
HIGHER EDUCATION

HARPER & ROW, PUBLISHERS
NEW YORK   HAGERSTOWN   SAN FRANCISCO   LONDON

Printer & Binder: Vail-Ballou Press Inc.

CREATIVE LEARNING AND TEACHING

Library of Congress Catalog Card Number: 70-108040
ISBN: 0-06-046633-2

To
PANSY and PAT
who provide daily models of creative
learning and teaching

EDITOR'S INTRODUCTION

Creative Learning and Teaching is a unique, much needed, and highly useful book. It brings to teachers the best that is known about creative processes from refined theory and documented research results to practical suggestions for the use of such information in teaching. A strength of the book is its base of new experimentation that the authors have carried out. The ideas have been tested in practice. The reader shares the excitement of seeing creativity used as a central force to improve learning and teaching.

Creativity has long been considered the highest form of mental functioning and human achievement. It has only been in the last decade or so that its relationship to educational processes has been studied. From what has been learned we now realize that available general tests of mental ability do not measure accurately creative capacities or potentialities. The earlier assumption that inclination and ability to respond in novel and useful ways, like native intelligence, were products largely of inheritance, has been refuted. We now know that however creativity is defined—as a novel creation, a divergent yet fruitful process of thinking, or an inspired experience —it is a form of behavior that basically has to be learned. Especially exciting to teachers is the fact that certain instructional strategies are more effective than are others in producing creative responses in students. In fact, as far as creativity is concerned, teaching and learning are closely intertwined—creative teacher performance tends to stimulate creative learning with the result that both teacher and student expand potentialities for creativity. This book mirrors the interactions that take place when teachers teach creatively for creative learning.

This is a book that will help all teachers. The conceptions it makes of creative instructional strategies are applicable, with only minor variations in content and with respect to maturity of learners, to elementary, secondary, and collegiate level schools. The illustrations, although demonstrated on younger children, deal with fundamental factors such as motivation, awareness, reading and communication, inductive questioning, responsive environment, and sequencing. So vivid are the case examples that they stimulate imagination for use in all kinds of learning situations. To read this book is to broaden one's understanding of what creativity is, how it may be nurtured, and to learn ways in which any teacher may live creatively with students.

The authors of this book comprise an unusually talented and creative partnership. Dr. E. Paul Torrance is a preeminent and pioneer scholar of creativity. His basic research in this field and his concern with applying his knowledge to improve practice have made him one of the most quoted and sought-after authorities on this subject. Dr. R. E. Myers complements Dr. Torrance's multiple strengths by insights into and firsthand expertness in creative teaching that have brought fresh documentation to the concepts and strategies presented. To achieve further verification Dr. Myers has worked with hundreds of experienced teachers who were teaching different kinds of students to make certain that any teacher can learn to teach creatively in any educational situation. Together these two men have translated basic research into workable practice and presented the results in interesting and creative ways to help teachers do likewise. The result is a classic resource for achieving creativity in learning and teaching.

LINDLEY J. STILES

PREFACE

This book is intended to be useful to in-service teachers at all educational levels; school administrators and supervisors; college and university teachers of courses in elementary school curriculum, educational psychology, and exceptional children; students enrolled in these courses; and interested laymen. Because its message is so fundamental with regard to the teacher-student relationship, we hope that everyone interested in advancing the intellectual and emotional growth of youth will find it significant.

The theme of the book is *awareness*. Its purpose is to help teachers become better teachers by (1) making them aware of their own creative potentialities; (2) making them aware of the kinship of the teaching-learning and creative processes; (3) making them aware of the wealth of creative talent in every classroom; and (4) making them aware of practical ways of going about the business of enhancing the creative functioning of their students.

To achieve these goals we have tried first to help the reader realize that those who deal most effectively with day-to-day problems are creative and that good teaching is necessarily creative. Secondly, we have tried to help the reader genuinely accept his commitment to aid children and young people develop to the fullest their potentialities.

In its organization and conception, *Creative Learning and Teaching* is modeled after the creative process. The introductory chapters (1 and 2) deal with recognizing and defining a problem upon whose solution much of our future rests: how to develop the creative abilities of our youth at a time when society fosters conformity rather than individuality. The second group of chapters (3 to 5) deals with what is known about the motivating power of creative learning, tested ways of deliberately facilitating creative development and functioning, and the mastery of skills involved in creative teaching. The third group of chapters (6 to 13) is devoted to our hypotheses and their testing. The final chapter presents ideas for facilitating the process of becoming a better, more creative teacher.

Creative Learning and Teaching is designed to influence the behavior of educators. It cannot be assumed that any other group in society will accept the responsibility of seeing that children begin fully to realize their promise.

Many educators nod approvingly when someone seriously advocates that schools consider the expressional aspects of personal growth. They seem satisfied to know that, in recognizing the importance of allowing the child to react to his environment in ways that are uniquely his, they are well on their way to nurturing creativity. Others have already become suspicious of the words "creative" and "creativity." They ask what these words mean—do they mean anything at all? And there are educators who are opposed to the idea of encouraging a child to express his uniqueness, preferring that he model himself after accepted forms. *Creative Learning and Teaching* challenges each of these positions.

In our opinion each of these attitudes is dangerous. Although a problem cannot be solved until it is understood and defined, too many administrators and teachers behave as if they have actually dealt with this complex matter after the identification process has been completed. Although their faith in the screening devices that sort out the talented from the untalented may be misplaced, their real mistake is in thinking of talent as being an entity found only in some children. Assuredly, there are individual differences in all human abilities, including creative abilities. However, *all* normal persons, by their nature, are creative. While children who are exceptionally endowed in artistic or academic areas should be provided appropriate opportunities to develop further their talents, they should not be the only ones to be thought of as creative. All classroom teachers must help children develop a multitude of creative abilities.

We are in sympathy with those educators who are bothered by the indiscriminate use of words such as "creative," "creativity," and "giftedness." On the other hand, those teachers who scoff at the concepts that underlie these words are selling themselves short, and they may well be short-changing their students. Living things characteristically adapt to their surroundings; but man is not content just to adapt to his environment—he has to change it! In changing his world, man changes also. He becomes more capable of changing his environment, and his need to create new forms and new situations becomes stronger. This view of man as a self-acting being who needs to create, who is not functioning fully unless he is creating, is basic to our philosophy.

The third type of educator is probably more firmly entrenched in his ideas than the other two. Educational institutions exert a conservative pressure upon society because they store the accumulated knowledge of a culture and then they endeavor to transmit as much of this knowledge as they can to young people. Educators come to love this knowledge for its own sake; and they come to love the old ways of transmitting it. But the difficulty for the cause of individualism does not end there—when we encourage the child to think creatively we invite him to challenge society and all of its painfully constructed institutions.

It may be too much to expect that conservative educators can be persuaded to welcome criticism of the ideas they revere. However, they can be shown that the world desperately needs new ideas and that our children are the ones who must produce them. The old, beloved ways are not working. There is no other solution: new ideas must be forthcoming!

We are indebted to many people who have encouraged and supported us in the work behind this book. Professor Lindley J. Stiles has been encouraging and patient throughout the eight or nine years that the book has been in the process of becoming. We have been stimulated and challenged by the thousands of students we have taught at the University of Minnesota, Augsburg College, University of Oregon, Colorado State College at Greeley, University of California at Berkeley, University of Georgia, and University of Victoria during this period and the hundreds of thousands of children who have participated in our research and in the field studies of the instructional materials that we have developed. We are also indebted to publishers and authors who have graciously given permission for the use of illustrations and other materials. They include: Ginn and Company, University of Minnesota Press, University of Georgia Anthropology Project, Charles Scribner's Sons, Dr. Sidney J. Parnes, Dr. Pearl Buckland, Dr. Theodore Clymer, Mr. Bert F. Cunnington, and Dr. Marion Rice.

E. Paul Torrance
R. E. Myers

Creative Learning and Teaching

CHAPTER 1 A DIALOGUE

ABOUT THIS BOOK

You pause,
Looking ahead,
Preparing to become
Different—one who touches and
Is touched.

1

Teaching as a Creative Occupation

This book had its genesis in a dialogue between the authors at the University of Minnesota. The interchange of ideas went something like this:

TORRANCE: Both of us have been engaged in research and writing about creative thinking—what it is, how it develops, its value to the individual and to society. Both of us have been creating instructional methods and materials for facilitating creative development and creative functioning. We know that people can learn how to behave more creatively. Do you think we could put in book form what we and others have learned in a way that would help teachers learn how to facilitate creative learning among children?

MYERS: Possibly we could. It would offer a chance to cast teachers in a different light, a light in which they are seldom seen.

TORRANCE: You mean that we could paint a new image of the teaching profession?

MYERS: Exactly. It has always surprised me that people rarely think of teachers as creative professional people. Painters and composers? Yes. Poets, architects, choreographers? Certainly. Dress designers and interior decorators? Perhaps. But teachers? Well, not really—not truly creative persons. Maybe we could present a different picture of teaching especially to teachers themselves. Such a picture might help them to see how they can be creative as teachers—and their jobs might become more exciting and enjoyable as a result.

TORRANCE: If successful, such a book would be as helpful to teachers in service as it would be to those still being trained. But it could be a great benefit to the latter. It might help them get the right start in becoming great teachers. Why do you suppose teaching, which has traditionally been called an art, has never really come to be viewed—by either the general public or teachers themselves—as a creative process? Is it because teachers have used so little imagination and creative thinking in their work? Is it because they do not value creative achievement?

2

MYERS: One reason may relate to the difficulties involved in deciding what human acts or products are genuinely creative. In recent years we have learned a great deal about *how* an original idea is produced. The creative process has been described in various ways. Running through most of the definitions and descriptions about creative thinking is the idea that it is a distinctly human behavior. Since teachers are human, it is puzzling that they have not considered themselves as creative persons. A number of other occupational groups have been studied with regard to their creative characteristics, but little research has been done concerning the creative behavior of teachers.

TORRANCE: Yet learning—real learning, I mean—is creative. Would not the teacher who guides learning be viewed as creative too?

MYERS: Yes, by the very nature of their roles, teachers have to behave in ways characteristic of the creative person. They must be *aware of and sensitive to* what takes place in the classroom. To be effective, teachers must be aware of the needs of their pupils and know what they are motivated to learn and capable of learning.

Teachers must be *flexible*—able to cope constructively with unforeseen events, last minute changes in schedules and plans, and new forces that upset the direction and flow of their pupils' activities.

They must be *spontaneous*—able to react to events quickly and confidently. They must be *original* in their thinking. Since no textbook author, college or university teacher, or supervisor can possibly predict the identity and nature of the almost infinite variety of factors that are present in even the most commonplace teaching-learning situation, teachers cannot follow a course that others have mapped for them. They are constantly forced to adapt materials and create new ones, devise new techniques, and respond to the unexpected.

Moreover, teachers must often be *intuitive* in their judgments, trusting their hunches. So often there just isn't time for careful analysis of the situation that demands immediate action. But I don't have to tell you this. You've been a teacher most of your life and for many years you've observed many kinds of teachers at all educational levels.

Since this book is for teachers rather than for educational psychologists, school psychologists, school counselors, or the like, do you think teachers will take us seriously if we write about "Becoming a Creative Teacher" or "Creative Learning and Teaching"?

TORRANCE: I suppose that depends upon how we decide to interpret "creative teaching." I think we have in mind a kind of teaching that will free children to develop to their fullest and will sensitively guide them in this development. On the other hand, we know that teachers can display a great deal of creativity in their teaching without having any such results. Perhaps we should call this "pseudo-creative teaching." It seems to me society admires more and is more tolerant of this pseudo-creative teaching than the genuine kind of creative teaching that facilitates creative development.

MYERS: Why do you suppose this is true?

TORRANCE: In general, society casts teachers in roles of authorities who must teach by virtue of that authority. Thus, the teacher who arouses children to learn in creative ways has rarely lasted very long because he fails to meet society's expectations. I recall a beautiful account John Steinbeck (1955) once wrote about one of the three "real teachers" that he had encountered. This teacher "breathed" curiosity into the class, and his students brought in facts or "truths shielded in their hands like captured fireflies." The teacher was fired for not teaching the fundamentals.

If the teacher who inspires and guides children and young people to "hold truths shielded in their hands like captured fireflies" has been rare, the one who can at the same time inspire students to "capture fireflies" and acquire the "fundamentals" has been doubly rare.

MYERS: But we know good and well that learning in creative ways and mastering fundamentals or acquiring information are not incompatible. In fact, we know that they can facilitate one another. What then is the real problem?

Acquiring Skills for Facilitating Creative Growth

TORRANCE: One problem has been that there have been such severe taboos against "capturing fireflies" that relatively few teachers ever acquire the skills necessary to do this kind of teaching. A major objective of this book should be to help teachers understand what these skills are—and how they can acquire them and then use them effectively.

I believe that there are subtle changes going on in the objectives of education that will make possible the emergence of an increasing number of teachers who can create an environment in which children can learn in creative ways—that is, to "catch fireflies of truth" and at the same time acquire the "fundamentals." With our explosion of knowledge, we have recognized that it is impossible for children and young people to acquire in school all of the information and skills they will need. The answer seems to be to equip them with the motivations and skills that will keep them learning for the rest of their lives. We are recognizing that a psychology of adjustment is inadequate for our age. Today's children must learn to respond constructively rather than just adaptively or adjustively to change and stress. All of these are things that cannot be acquired by teaching exclusively by authority. Teaching in creative ways is also required. I believe that many people are beginning to sense this and that there is a good chance that sound concepts of creative ways of learning and teaching are already being taken seriously by a great many people.

What Kind of Book Can Help?

MYERS: Yes, I know many teachers who are serious about facilitating the creative development of the children they teach. They lack the skills for doing so, and in their classroom they revert to very dull, ineffective, authoritarian teaching. Can we communicate ideas about teaching to facilitate creative growth by talking *about* them? How can we come closer to insuring that our readers will understand what we're saying *and then actually undergo changes in behavior as a result of having encountered this book?*

TORRANCE: I like your use of the word "encountered" instead of "reading." Such a goal does indeed require more than reading. I think with horror of the idea that some college student will use the book to practice skills of speed reading.

MYERS: Is such behavior really very common, though? Doesn't most of the research show that research data, theories of learning, and education courses have little effect on the way teachers behave in the classroom? I know that one big study about research on teaching children to read (Chall, 1967) maintained that all of the research results in his field actually have had little influence on the teaching of reading.

TORRANCE: Yes, I agree that it has usually been shocking to find how little difference books and courses in education and psychology make in the way teachers behave in the classroom or even in deciding how they ought to act in specific cases. I suppose this concern was what actually made me try to invent more creative ways of teaching and conducting research. I have often suspected that one of the reasons why books don't make any more difference than they do is that they are almost always written in impersonal, objective language and that knowledge is usually presented as being complete, with no open ends. Similarly, I suspect that courses in education and psychology make little difference because they are almost always taught by authority, rarely in creative ways. Facts and ideas may be dismissed, forgotten, or discredited; but it is difficult to dismiss, forget, or discredit an experience—a truly personal encounter with a fact or idea.

MYERS: Perhaps the book's format can help put over the basic concepts. For instance, we might model it after the creative process itself.

TORRANCE: Yes, that kind of format might provide the basis for personal encounters by readers. At the beginning of each chapter, a problem could be stated, together with ideas concerning its solution. Then there could be an examination of the evidence (the testing), following insofar as possible a creative process: something missing or disharmonious, questions, hypotheses and ideas, testing and modification, new relationships, conclusions, and communication of results.

MYERS: How much demand do you think there is for documentation of evidence in a book like this? Many of the things we know to be true will sound unbelievable to many teachers. I realize that some of the more miraculous results are not covered by solid, scientifically-approved research. But many of the ideas that we shall present *are* supported by quantities of very sound research. We know that careful documentation will alienate many teachers, both prospective teachers and experienced ones. How do you think we should handle this problem?

TORRANCE: In mulling this over, I think I agree on the matter of documentation. Three or four ideas have occurred to me in regard to it. One idea is for you to lead the way in each chapter, setting out the first part in a straightforward way, and letting me write the second part using the theme: "How do we know that is true?" The research evidence could be used both to document and reinforce the ideas, as well as to elaborate upon them, adding more substance and pushing our own thinking forward as nearly as possible to the limits.

But then I started thinking about the materials you have been collecting, the anecdotes you have assembled on classroom teaching problems, and the anecdotes both of us have collected from experienced teachers on things they have done that really "made a difference" in the learning of their students. I wondered if it might not be a good idea, instead, to build the entire book around these materials and forget the weighty documentation. The opening chapter could be titled something like "Does Creative Teaching Make a Difference?" In it we could summarize some of the anecdotal materials contributed by teachers and students in order to show that creative ways of teaching *can* make a difference. From these incidents, we can generate ideas concerning what there was about the teachers' behavior that made the difference. Where support for these ideas is available, we could cite the evidence. Where support is lacking, we could present the ideas as ones requiring future investigation. Each subsequent chapter could be devoted to elaborations of one of the ways the teachers behaved to make a difference. Incidentally, I think one of the most fundamental skills for the teacher to develop is increased awareness, and the ability to confront children with learning situations containing missing elements or incompleteness.

MYERS: Yes. I recall that in our original prospectus for this book the statement was made that its basic theme would be awareness. In fact, to quote from the prospectus, the purpose of the book "is to help teachers become better teachers (1) by making them aware of their own creative potentialities; (2) by making them aware of the kinship of the teaching-learning and creative processes; (3) by making them aware of the wealth of talent that exists in every classroom; and (4) by making them aware of how they can go about the business of enhancing the creative potentialities of their students." I think we can still accomplish these objectives by using the format you've outlined.

AWARENESS

Getting Involvement in a Creative Relationship

TORRANCE: If we use this approach, we'll have to decide what are the fresh, provocative ideas we want to elaborate, giving them more detailed treatment and giving the more obvious things very brief treatment. We might summarize in one chapter the usual kinds of things—such as obtaining information through records and through talking with parents—and then devote separate chapters to increasing awareness through seeing relationships, asking provocative questions, observing preferred ways of learning, and permitting oneself to become involved. It seems to me that one of the big social dangers today is that people are afraid to become truly involved in anything. It's a natural consequence of a society that encourages a lack of involvement.

MYERS: Do you think our society has actively encouraged a lack of involvement?

TORRANCE: Yes, in a great many ways, I think we have. We are recognizing some of the dangers of this social illness now, and many efforts have been made recently to treat it. Many young people, in fact, have been screaming for chances to become more actively involved in social problems. Unfortunately there are still many social forces working against genuine involvement with either people or things. There is much fear of automation and other influences that may dehumanize. Teachers too are frightened by ideas of teaching machines, programmed learning books, computer-assisted instruction, and drug-assisted learning. We can understand this fear of automation somewhat when we think of the kinds of experiences that many young people especially have had with lack of involvement. They have experienced it with their overburdened parents, teachers, clergymen, and other leaders. They have been wounded and disillusioned by it.

Just think of the examples that occur almost daily. A woman drops dead at a busy lunch counter in a downtown department store. The customer next to her only moves over a couple of seats and continues eating without comment. The waitresses continue taking orders and serving food. It is some time before anyone even calls the police. A screaming woman is pursued by a rapist or a murderer, while dozens of people passively witness a tragedy that could have been prevented had they not been afraid of becoming involved. Some explain that these things happen because we are changing from a mostly rural past to a mostly urban future. I wonder, however, if a great deal of it has not been encouraged by impersonal, objective, cool, authoritarian teaching—a kind of teaching that has emphasized obedience and acceptance of authority over practically everything else.

MYERS: Is there much evidence that there is now too much obedience and authority acceptance? In the news media we are told only about the rebelliousness and lack of obedience of today's youth.

TORRANCE: At first glance, this appears contradictory. Some of my own research, as well as that of social psychologists such as Milgram (1963, 1965), suggests, however, that while we may have our rebels, most people have become so conditioned to authority acceptance and obedience that they have sacrificed not only creativity and independence of thought, but have permitted this authority acceptance to override moral and religious training, ethics, sympathy, and concern for fellow human beings. It may be that some of the unrest among young people is an overreaction to their conditioning to authority acceptance.

Regardless of what is responsible for the increased tendency to lack of involvement, the fact remains that it makes the facilitation of creative development through teaching difficult. Such teaching requires involvement with learners, co-experiencing. Teachers must be willing to let one thing lead to another.

MYERS: In considering our positions as university teachers, it seems to me that the college or university professor doesn't involve himself with his students because it may be painful to do so; because it is time-consuming; and, what's more, it may be ego-lowering.

TORRANCE: Yes, the university professor who tends to become involved with his students soon finds himself in a very painful dilemma. I really don't know which I find more painful—becoming involved with my students and failing to do research, to respond to correspondents and calls for community service, and to carry out my administrative responsibilities, or *fighting* against becoming involved with my students so that I can accomplish some of these things. Yes, in challenging teachers to become more involved in the learning of their students and to teach in creative ways, we are asking that they make sacrifices, exert very expensive energies, even suffer—but we are asking them also to be more fully alive and to experience joy when students bring in "truths shielded in their hands like captured fireflies."

MYERS: Yes, I know that many professors lead such busy, hurried lives that it is difficult for them to become involved with students. Generally, however, these professors are actually more involved with their students than are those who are not busy. I have known teachers at all levels of education who believe that it is self-demeaning and ego-lowering to spend much time with students.

TORRANCE: Certainly, becoming involved with students and facilitating their creative growth is practically impossible for the teacher who feels that becoming involved with students is ego-lowering. Such a teacher usually likes to feel omnipotent and omniscient, to be an authority—and his security is easily threatened by questions about the unknowns, the incompleteness of knowledge. Again, it goes back to the fact that society expects the teacher to be an authority. He feels that he is failing to live up to society's expectations if he has to admit that there is something that he does not know.

Another important inhibiting factor in American education is that the teacher must grade his students. He has to evaluate their performances and make decisions about their futures. This tends to put teachers and students "on different sides of the battle." In some educational systems, there is external evaluation; and I think this helps to put teachers and students on the same, rather than opposite, sides.

MYERS: This is true at Oxford, where because the teacher is a tutor who prepares the student for examinations originated and graded by others, he and the student are on the same side of the fence. I've always felt—and you've heard me say this many times—that the first thing a teacher should do is to communicate that he and the pupil are on the same team. This is why I think mutual trust is so important. If it's a matter of a contest between the teacher and the pupil, then there will always be a struggle between the two. But if right away the teacher puts himself on the same team, he can't lose.

TORRANCE: That deserves a full chapter in the book—how do

you communicate to a pupil that you are on his side? Once my class in group dynamics devoted four laboratory sessions to creative solutions to this problem. This turned out to be a difficult problem indeed and generated much negative feeling among the members of the class. I think most of them felt that it was a hopeless task.

During the last laboratory session, I asked the small (five-person) laboratory groups to think of analogies that would communicate the qualities of the relationship in which an adult communicates to a child or young person that the adult is on his side. I then asked them to compose cinquains (dwarf poems) to elaborate some of the analogies.

Here is one that reflects something of the feeling of hopelessness that persisted in some:

> Cancer
> No cure
> Erosive as acid
> Ravenous as a wolf
> Hopeless.

There were many cinquains that suggested the writer felt it was too threatening to communicate to a pupil that you are on his side. The following are a couple of samples:

> Boy
> Calm now
> But only as the eye
> Of the hurricane
> Sweeps northeastward
> Threatening.

> Boy
> Explosive
> A fissionable mass
> Waiting, watching, poised, triggered
> Detonation.

MYERS: What are the different ways a teacher can communicate to children that the teacher is on their side? Did your students produce any encouraging ideas?

TORRANCE: Yes, many of their ideas were constructive and hopeful. While many of their proposed solutions were linked to the concept of the teacher as an all-powerful authority, solving the pupils' problems for them, many other solutions stressed openness and awareness. The following are examples of cinquains that reflected this approach:

> Awareness
> Alive, perceiving
> Listening yet active
> Accepted with total love
> Vital.

> Lyre
> Tuned to life
> Sound sympathetic to a troubled mind
> Resonate understanding, warm tones
> Musician.

I know you have emphasized awareness a great deal—and I agree that awareness must occur before a teacher is able to respond to pupils' needs and preferred ways of learning. Inevitably, however, I think one of the tests that demonstrates that the teacher is on the pupil's side is when he "goes to bat" for the pupil and goes out of his way to defend the pupil when he deserves to be defended.

MYERS: That suggests that the teacher is kind of possessive, even somewhat defensive about what his pupils do and say on the playground. I'm sure you don't mean that, do you?

TORRANCE: No, not exactly. Pupils and teachers have to be free to be honest and to search for the truth. But it does mean that the teacher must do what he can to keep his pupils and their potentialities from being destroyed, just as a good lawyer does for his client. The lawyer defends his client from injustices and from the possible harshness and undue coerciveness of the law. And above all, there is a feeling when you hire a lawyer and he accepts your case that he is on your side. I think this same feeling is one of the basic elements of the healthy teacher-pupil relationship—one that must be present if creative potentialities are to be maximized.

MYERS: What about the fiduciary relationship—the confidential nature of a relationship between a lawyer and his client or a teacher and his pupil—is that a part of it? I recall that Hughes Mearns talks about this in *Creative Power* (1958).

TORRANCE: Yes, yes. Once you establish this confidential relationship and the pupil knows that you are on his side, you can afford to make many mistakes in teaching techniques and he will continue learning and growing creatively. You can be critical and he will not be defensive; he will use the criticism constructively. It's essentially the same thing that Moustakas (1959) has in mind in his concept of the creative relationship. The teacher in this relationship is willing to accompany the pupil along untried pathways, not knowing where it will lead but permitting one thing to lead to another.

MYERS: I've noticed too—that once you establish a healthy relationship with a child you can even accuse him unjustly (actually a horrible thing to do), you can bawl him out, you can lose your temper—and the very next day, the relationship is still intact. I have noticed this again and again.

In trying to aid teachers in establishing a creative relationship with children, what kind of assumptions are you making? Are you assuming that teachers really want to become involved with the children they teach, that there is a basic commitment to begin with?

TORRANCE: I suppose I do make that assumption. I honestly believe that most teachers really do desire such a relationship, even though they may deny it and behave in ways that prevent its occurrence. I am sure that I make this assumption when it may not be justified and I have to guard against this tendency. There is a certain joy and excitement in learning creatively, but there is also a great deal of psychological discomfort. There is an essential tension in the curiosity and search for the truth that characterizes creative learning. Much more than a permissive environment is necessary. Teaching in creative ways requires involvement and commitment —the most sensitive and alert kind of guidance and direction, absorbed listening, fending off disparagement and ridicule, and making honest efforts seem worthwhile enough to assure continued effort.

MYERS: Do you think these behaviors can occur, if the teacher does not have a basic commitment?

TORRANCE: A basic commitment must exist! The desire to help must be genuine! The teacher really has to care rather than just "seem to care." But, like Bettelheim's *Love Is Not Enough* (1950), you have to *communicate*—show—that you care. How do you communicate that? In thousands of ways, I suppose, and certainly it takes more than just saying it. If you really care, you are less likely to try consciously to communicate it. You just do!

MYERS: That puzzles me. Would you explain what you mean?

TORRANCE: If a person really cares, he is less likely to do things unconsciously that communicate that he *doesn't* care and more likely to do more things that communicate that he cares. When one only pretends that he cares and tries very hard to show that he cares, many things come forth unconsciously that indicate that he does not really care.

Targets

MYERS: What do you think this book can do? What purposes can it accomplish? Do you see it as a book that might be found in the professional libraries of schools and educators, or do you see it essentially as a college textbook?

TORRANCE: Well, I see it as serving both purposes. As far as its place as a textbook is concerned, I suppose it might be oriented more to elementary education, but it would certainly be applicable to education at all levels from kindergarten through graduate and professional education.

MYERS: We are agreed then that we're addressing ourselves primarily to teachers?

TORRANCE: Yes. Many others could benefit from it, but teachers should be the target audience.

MYERS: Are we running the risk of telling people what they already know but enjoy hearing again? Or, are we giving them new information and challenging their thinking in different ways? When we talk about acceptance and respect, we almost always get a good response from the audience—we get a nodding response—because most teachers enjoy hearing someone advocate "a more humane education" (perhaps it eases their consciences). It's like a good sermon in church, I guess. But on the other hand, do such ideas really affect their behavior?

TORRANCE: The book should emphasize new ideas and fresh information, but not exclusively. Much can be said, in fact, for giving a place of importance to those things that we all know quite well. It helps to come back to these tried and true ideas and see them in a new light and in greater depth. With new information, old truths take on new meaning. We also have to depend upon the anchorings of old truths to place new ideas and fresh information in context. Thus, I would say that we should include enough old ideas to place the new ones in perspective. But we certainly want to take our readers with us in exploring some of the frontiers of knowledge. We don't want them to miss the fun and excitement of this. Besides, we would like to have their company in the future as we continue to explore these frontiers.

MYERS: How can we get the readers involved in the ideas of this book?

TORRANCE: On this point, I think we *are* on the frontiers of knowledge. Generally, it has been relatively taboo to get readers involved in textbooks. From a number of other areas, however, I believe we can find some clues that will be useful in guiding us. Fundamentally, I believe we do it by trying to learn from our own experiences, the experiences of other teachers, existing educational research, and imagination—using these insights and inviting readers to accompany us as we try to push back the frontiers of knowledge in developing a psychology of creative ways of teaching. In addition, I am sure that it will help if we use self-involving language, concrete examples that create vivid and clear but colorful images, and provide enough suggestions for developing the necessary insights and skills to give teachers and would-be teachers a glimpse of some of the things that they can do to develop adequate skills.

MYERS: Do you think we can involve readers by placing problems at the end of chapters? Maybe we can make this section intrinsically worthwhile to readers and in that way not waste space. Actually, I hate to put this kind of exercise at the end of a chapter, where it will often be disregarded, but it seems to be the only place where it can go.

TORRANCE: I suppose such problems could be placed at the beginning of some of the chapters. In *Mental Health and Constructive Behavior* (1965), I wanted to use some problems at the end of chapters instead of summaries. In this approach, the reader is asked to scan back through the chapter and synthesize the material in generating ideas for solutions, evaluating possible solutions, and the like. Here again, though, we run into the problem of social expectations. For a textbook, there is the expectation that each chapter will have a conventional summary of the contents—and this is difficult to escape.

I think we want to conserve as much space as possible for solid content, but I do not think that the use of case problems necessarily results in a sacrifice of content. The problems can communicate content. They can also be used to provide anchorings and illustrations for items of content. Powerfully written incidents that illustrate important dynamics of creative ways of teaching can not only speak for themselves but can go on and on talking and generating new ideas as they are examined in the light of new information and different theories. They are sometimes like experiences. You cannot dismiss them as you can facts. They become a part of you, like an experience, because they engage the intellect, the emotions, the spirit, and generate feelings and attitudes. I realize that this is a goal difficult to achieve but let's make it ours!

REFERENCES

Bettelheim, B. *Love Is Not Enough.* New York: Free Press, 1950.

Chall, J. S. *Learning to Read: The Great Debate.* New York: McGraw-Hill Book Company, 1967.

Mearns, H. *Creative Power: Youth in the Creative Arts.* New York: Dover Publications, 1958.

Milgram, S. "Behavioral Study of Obedience," *Journal of Abnormal and Social Psychology,* 1963, **67,** 371–378.

Milgram, S. "Some Conditions of Obedience and Disobedience to Authority," *Human Relations,* 1965, **18,** 57–76.

Moustakas, C. R. *Psychotherapy with Children.* New York: Harper & Row, 1959.

Steinbeck, J. ". . . like captured fireflies." *California Teachers Association Journal,* November 1955, **51,** 7.

Torrance, E. P. *Mental Health and Constructive Behavior.* Belmont, Calif.: Wadsworth Publishing Company, 1965.

CHAPTER 2 DOES

CREATIVE TEACHING

MAKE A DIFFERENCE?

Frozen,
Fearing failure,
Until warmed and inspired
By their teacher's reassuring love—
Pupils.

The Problem

Concerned teachers frequently ask, "Does my teaching make a difference in the behavior and achievement of the children I teach?" At times, the influences of the family, the community, and the culture seem so strong that the intervention of the teacher makes little difference. This was how Mrs. Platt felt when her fifth-grade pupil, Gertrude, became a serious negative influence in her classroom.

There were several strong leaders in Mrs. Platt's fifth-grade class, but Gertrude was unquestionably the most influential. She was attractive. Her father's status in the community was exceptionally high, even for a prominent physician. And Gertrude was an excellent student. At the first of the school year, Gertrude had also been especially well behaved. But by January she had become quite a problem to Mrs. Platt. Her attitude had changed from ready cooperation and eager zest to stubborn rebelliousness. Gertrude became fond of disagreeing with Mrs. Platt and had little enthusiasm for the activities which the class was guided into. Her reluctance to participate during Spanish (she expressed a great dislike for the television teacher of Spanish) and her decision not to sing during the music period were the big reasons why the class became indifferent to learning Spanish and to being able to sing two-part harmony.

Mrs. Platt asked Gertrude's mother to come to school and discuss Gertrude, but all that came from the conference was that the child was "going through a difficult phase" both at home and at school. At about this time, Mrs. Platt began wondering if her teaching could make a difference in Gertrude's behavior.

Although Mrs. Platt decided that she could not transform Gertrude into a model pupil overnight, she felt she could try to put Gertrude in positions where it would be hard for the child to be dogmatic and negative. Accordingly, Mrs. Platt devised the critical and creative thinking exercise which follows and asked Gertrude to act as moderator. Since the statements were designed to foster controversy and make her pupils dig deeper and think beyond the surface, Mrs. Platt believed that the moderator role would help Gertrude to see that there are many ways of looking at situations.

This is the exercise which Mrs. Platt duplicated and passed out to her pupils. After they had had enough time to make decisions regarding each of the statements, Gertrude invited the class to discuss them.

DOES IT MAKE SENSE?

Place an *S* to the left of the statements below that you believe to be sensible or reasonable. Place a *U* to the left of the statements that you think are unreasonable or illogical. Be careful to understand the terms of each statement before you make a decision. If you have any difficulty with the words, look them up in your dictionary. Give a brief explanation of your answer beneath each statement.

_____ 1. Inasmuch as he was a prisoner and wanted to see some improvements made in his living conditions, Harry decided that he would run for County Supervisor of Prisons.

_____

_____

_____ 2. Since Nancy was discovered to be cheating during the test, all of the children in the class should be punished.

_____

_____

_____ 3. No inanimate things grow.

_____

_____

_____ 4. A blank page is more easily read than a page of small type.

_____

_____

_____ 5. If the earth orbits around the sun, then it is a satellite.

_____

_____

_____ 6. The silence was suddenly broken by a hush.

_____

_____

_____ 7. If something is beautiful, it is also valuable.

_____

_____

_____ 8. In spite of a fatal accident in his youth, Ned went on to become one of the country's top racing drivers.

_____

_____

_____ 9. All in all, Jerry has two sisters and three brothers-in-law.

_____

_____

_____ 10. Since Mr. Green is a Republican, his son is also a Republican.

_____

_____

_____ 11. Blind children often have difficulty in learning to speak.

_____

_____

_____ 12. An object either has color or it has no color.

_____

_____

_____ 13. The Jackson twins were seen riding to town alone in their car, with Phil in the middle.

_____

_____

_____ 14. Some birds do not build nests.

_____

_____

_____ 15. A six-legged animal with wings may be an insect.

_____

_____

Do you think Gertrude became more open-minded as a result of acting as moderator for the discussion? If so, what was there about the experience that made the difference?

What other devices might have been tried to help Gertrude become more constructive?

Would you have done some more investigating to determine the causes of Gertrude's attitude about class activities?

Might the trouble have been partly Mrs. Platt's fault?

Most of the items in Mrs. Platt's exercise grew out of recent experiences of the children in connection with their studies in science and social studies. She had used a similar exercise once before in order to help her pupils to develop dictionary skills and also to encourage them to be more thoughtful in making judgments. *Which statements, in your opinion, occasioned the most debate? Which most likely stimulated further study?*

Mrs. Platt must be given credit for trying to improve a situation that was not improving and that might well have become worse. It is not unusual nowadays to find a teacher occasionally occupying one of his pupil's seats. Teachers who have adopted this perspective, if only for a brief time, have usually learned something about the pupil's position in their classroom, and about their own teaching methods. Similarly, we hope that when Gertrude led the discussion she was able to obtain several insights about some of the problems which confront a teacher.

At least a part of Gertrude's discontent at school probably stemmed from her indifference to or dislike for Mrs. Platt, who was doing little to help Gertrude transform her resistance or negative will to creative energy. The fact that Gertrude did not like Mrs.

Platt was undoubtedly difficult for the latter to accept. One of the most difficult barriers for a young teacher to learn to cope with in order to become effective is the strong desire to capture and hold the love of every child in his classroom. Being liked is a valuable reward for the teacher who cares about his pupils—there are few satisfactions in his life that equal the pleasure from a throng of enthusiastic children crowding around his desk in the morning. But it should not be the motivating factor in the teacher's interactions with his pupils.

We have observed numerous situations like the one just recounted: a teacher is discouraged and feels that his teaching makes no difference in the behavior and achievement of his pupils; then out of this discomfort he begins trying to define the problem and comes up with a creative solution that engages the creative processes of the child. Changes that seem almost like magic take place! Creative teaching and learning have made the difference. As a result of these observations, we began wondering how frequently these phenomena occur and what useful conclusions might be derived from them.

Creative Learning and Teaching

Since this book is about "creative learning and teaching"—and the terms "creative learning" and "creative teaching" have already been used—perhaps it would be a good idea to state what those terms mean to us.

In this book, the terms "creative teaching" and "creative learning" will be used to refer to what happens when the teacher and the pupil become involved in the creative learning process. We have defined the "creative learning process" as one of becoming sensitive to or aware of problems, deficiencies, gaps in knowledge, missing elements, disharmonies, and so on; bringing together available information; defining the difficulty or identifying the missing element; searching for solutions, making guesses, or formulating hypotheses about the deficiencies; testing and retesting these hypotheses, and modifying and retesting them; perfecting them; and finally communicating the results. This definition describes a natural human process. Strong human motivations are involved at each stage.

In school, sensitivity to problems, gaps in information, deficiencies, disharmonies, and the like may be aroused by a sequence of learning experiences designed and directed by a teacher, or may be aroused by the self-initiated activities of an individual learner or group of learners. Regardless of the source of the arousal, sensing an incompleteness, disharmony, or problem arouses tension. When this happens, the learner is uncomfortable. We may say that he is "curious," has a "divine discontent," or "recognizes a need." Whatever label we use, the learner wants to relieve his tension. If he has no adequate learned response or if habitual ways of responding are inadequate, he searches both in his own memory storehouse and in other resources such as books, the experiences of others, and the like for possible answers. From these, he may be able to define the problem or identify the gap in information. This done, he searches for possible alternative solutions, trying to avoid commonplace and obvious (also erroneous or unworkable) solutions by investigating, diagnosing, manipulating, rearranging, building onto, and making guesses or approximations. Until these guesses or hypotheses are tested, modified, and retested, the learner is still uncomfortable. He is still motivated to continue trying to perfect his solution until it is aesthetically as well as logically satisfying. The tension remains unrelieved, however, until the learner communicates his results to others.

We have called this the "creative learning process" because it involves the production of information or development of skills that are new to the learner and are to some extent original. If we apply criteria of originality such as those of Selye (1962)—suggesting that the answer must be true, generalizable, and surprising in the light of what was known at the time of the discovery—or the criteria of statistical infrequency and length of the mental leap away from the obvious and commonplace, we arrive at an indication of the degree of creative energy involved in the process.

To recapitulate now, we see that the process involves such strong, impelling human motivations as the following:

Involvement in something meaningful.
Curiosity and wanting to know in the face of wonder, incompleteness, confusion, complexity, disharmony, disorganization, or the like.

Simplification of structure or diagnosing a difficulty by synthesizing known information, forming new combinations, or identifying gaps.

Elaborating and diverging by producing new alternatives, new possibilities, etc.

Judging, evaluating, checking, and testing possibilities.

Discarding unsuccessful, erroneous, and unpromising solutions.

Choosing the most promising solution and making it attractive or aesthetically pleasing.

Communicating the results to others.

What Happens When Creative Learning and Teaching Occur?

Studies of the influence of creative teaching (Torrance, 1965ab; Torrance, Fortson & Diener, 1968; Crutchfield, 1966; Parnes, 1967) have almost always been concerned with the immediate effects upon entire classroom groups, schools, or school systems. We know from these studies that creative teaching usually results in increased creative growth, involvement and participation in creative activities, liking for school, and the like.

Group changes significantly greater than chance have occurred even though some of the learners involved in these experiments did not show progress. In fact, some of the pupils of even the most creative teachers failed to show creative growth. Moreover, these studies do not tell us what differences creative teaching makes in individual lives over extended periods of time.

Some critics say that the studies we have are of no value because they do not indicate whether or not the influence of creative teaching persists. On the other hand, it might be argued that children accustomed to learning by authority experience temporary disorganization when they encounter creative teaching and would not show improvement in behavior until there has been sufficient time to master the skills for learning creatively.

To obtain raw data from which some of these problems can be explored, we asked some of our students to recall instances in which they allowed children, young people, or adults in their classes to become involved creatively and then observed that the experience made a difference in achievement and behavior. These students included teachers, administrators, and school psychologists at all levels of education from nursery school to college and adult education. Almost all of them were relatively experienced teachers. In one group, 165 students were present when this request was made and 135 were able to recall such instances either in their own educational experiences or in their teaching. These responses were solicited at the end of a two-week course taught at the University of California at Berkeley on "Creative Ways of Teaching."

The raw data supplied by these 135 students provide many provocative clues concerning the difference that creative teaching makes and what there is about creative teaching that makes a difference. An attempt will be made here to synthesize and summarize some of these clues.

Only a few of the respondents denied that creative teaching *can* make a difference. In these rare instances the denial seemed to stem from the mistaken notion that all changes that occur in children are of a developmental nature and are independent of teacher influence. For example, one teacher wrote as follows:

"Right now, I can't really remember any particular child whom I've encouraged and where there has been a noticeable change. I have always felt that any change at the end of the kindergarten year was due mainly to the natural developmental growth for the five-year old. . . ."

This attitude is encountered rather frequently among teachers and developmental psychologists who have accepted the view that development is genetically determined and that the developmental process is unchangeable. We believe that this view results from a misinterpretation of developmental studies that show what kinds of development generally take place at certain ages when children experience *only* what the environment just happens to provide. Studies of disadvantaged children by Bloom (1964) and others show that patterns of development established during the first five or so years of a child's life are rarely reversed and indeed may be irreversible. On the other hand, the incidents recalled by the 135 respondents in the class on "Creative Ways of Teaching" suggest that such developmental patterns *can* on occasion be reversed.

The following are the reversals in patterns of development these teachers mentioned most frequently:

From nonreader to average or superior reader.

From vandalism, destructiveness, and lack of school achievement to constructive behavior and improved achievement.

From emotionally disturbed and unproductive behavior to productive behavior and outstanding school achievement.

From estrangement and lack of communication to communication and good contact with reality.

From social isolation and rejection to social acceptance and productive group membership.

From fighting and hostility to improved speech skills and lack of fighting.

From bitter, hostile sarcasm to kindly, courteous, thoughtful behavior.

From apathy and hate of school to enthusiasm about learning.

From lack of self-confidence and self-expression to adequate self-confidence and creative self-expression.

From mediocrity of achievement among gifted pupils to outstanding performance.

From inattention and short attention span to absorbed attention and sustained performance.

From diagnoses of mental retardation to diagnoses of normal or superior mental functioning.

From troublesome behavior to outstanding job performance.

Some of the respondents even indicated that it is the knowledge that teaching can make a difference that sustained them in their teaching roles.

We realize full well that the above summary leaves us open to two major criticisms: (1) that we are proposing creative teaching and learning as a panacea and (2) that we are talking about miracles. We would have liked to have investigated more fully these accounts of "miracles."

Generally, teachers do not expect "miracles" concerning the reversibility of an earlier established developed pattern. In fact, they may even unconsciously, perhaps, work against the occurrence of such "miracles." Just such a phenomenon was observed by Lichter, Rapien, Seibert, and Sklansky (1962) in their study of intellectually capable students who dropped out of high school. These authors worked with the school dropouts and reached a point where they thought these students had reversed unfavorable developmental trends and would achieve satisfactorily in high school. They found, however, that the teachers expected them to behave according to their old patterns. In fact, it seemed as though the teachers almost forced these students to resume their old patterns and to abandon their new ones.

On the other hand, encouraging findings have been reported by Rosenthal and Jacobson (1968) in their controversial Pygmalion study. In this experiment, teachers were told to expect certain children, randomly chosen, to show unusual spurts of intellectual growth during the forthcoming year. Most of these children were disadvantaged and from Mexican-American backgrounds. At the end of the year, both the "Pygmalion" children and their controls were retested. A gain of 20 or more total I.Q. points was achieved by 47 percent of the randomly chosen children, while only 19 percent of the control group achieved gains this great. The younger children (first and second graders) showed greater gains than the older ones (third, fourth, and fifth graders) during the experimental year, but the older ones retained their gains more successfully.

We do not, in fact, propose creative teaching and learning as a panacea, nor as the mainspring of miracles. We do maintain that— under genuinely concerned, imaginative, and hard-working teachers —children generally will grow creatively and will solve many learning problems that otherwise defy solution. We also maintain that most of these apparent "miracles" have quite understandable and logical explanations and are reasonably predictable. It is our hope that the material presented in this book will increase the reader's own ability to help bring about such miracles.

FROM NONREADER TO READER

The most frequent change described by the 135 respondents is from nonreader to reader, a change usually accompanied by generally improved behavior and achievement. Some of these changes occurred in the primary grades, while others did not occur until the intermediate grades or the junior high school years. The following incident concerns such a change:

"In second grade we do lots of creative writing and I usually type the children's stories and let them illustrate them. John, a dreamy lad, artistic, sloppy, and a very slow reader, disturbed me by never getting more than a sentence or so written. Usually that was lost in the crumpled welter in his desk by the time the next chance to work on it came around. John was a "poor listener" and took offense over nothing. He often cried because he thought he was being slighted. (The sociogram showed him not so much rejected as ignored.)

"One day I let him dictate to me and I typed his story as he talked. He wanted to tell the story of the *Spider*—from a TV horror story. I was tempted to censor this, but fortunately kept my mouth shut. John's story was long. It was a problem to take the time to do it all, but I did, while the class carried on. His choice of words, sentence structure, use of suspense, etc. were very vivid, imaginative, mature. When I read the story to the class, the reaction was one of wild enthusiasm. John was starry-eyed. He learned to read the story, did many more, and learned to read other things. His behavior improved and he made friends."

It takes a great deal of concern, courage, and tolerance of one's own anxiety for a teacher to do what this one did. This story is reminiscent of the account Jesus gave of the shepherd's unhesitating willingness to leave the ninety-nine safe sheep to search for the one lost one and of the rejoicing that occurred when that sheep was found. Most teachers are understandably afraid to help an individual child who is not learning and to vary their teaching for him for fear that the majority will suffer from neglect. Similarly, there is opposition to special services for exceptional children because this may result in the neglect of "the average child." It is quite probable, though, that the ninety-nine will continue learning while the teacher is helping the single child who does not learn in the same way as the others and that they will rejoice when that child learns in his own way and produces something unique and precious.

FROM DESTRUCTIVE BEHAVIOR TO CONSTRUCTIVE BEHAVIOR

Destructive behavior on the part of a child or adolescent is especially disturbing to teachers, classmates, and administrative and custodial personnel. Students describing the consequences of creative teaching indicate, however, that destructive behavior can be transformed into positive, creative energy and generally constructive behavior. The following is an account of one such instance:

"The principal, the janitor, the teachers all worked on the problem of John, the vandal. He was reported as being the culprit of many a weekend shambles at our school, but no one could prove anything. He couldn't stay still very long; his iron muscles seemed to need to move every minute; he was as strong, at twelve years, as most grown men. He was almost a permanent fixture in the office because of undesirable behavior. He was skilled, a *natural,* in things mechanical. He liked to boss and was often swaggering and bully-like in his playground behavior. The consensus, as a result of brain-storming, was that John did not feel he belonged. The problem was how to make him feel he *did* belong.

"He was appointed by the Student Council (in which he could never be an officer, because of their strict code of grades and behavior) to be chairman of the lunchroom committee. He organized a team of boys; they spent half their noon recess cleaning, moving tables, helping the janitor. He began to notice the litter which collected in certain windy corners of the schoolyard. His 'gang' cleaned it up. He helped park cars for Back-to-School-Night. One woman ran her car into a deep ditch, when she did not wait for John to show her the way. The way he directed her, telling her how to cramp the wheels and when, was a marvel. She would have had to have a tow-away, except for his know-how. He had organized the entire parking area without a hitch; the drivers followed his directions; and all this done as well as an adult could have done it.

"Happily, as John became 'part' of the school, the vandalism became less and less. Reports came to us that he threatened (and coming from this boy that was no mean threat) others who tried to destroy school property. Happily, he began to take an interest in schoolwork. His father told us that John had at last said, 'I like school.' He said John had learned to read things around the house, in the neighborhood, at the store, and on trips for the first time in his life. His art work (racing cars, engines, and antique cars) was excellent. We all hope some of this progress will continue when he leaves us this fall to go to junior high school."

The transformation of John the vandal took a teacher of unusual sensitivity to potentialities. She had to see John's mechanical genius, his unusual talent for organizing and leading people, and his artistic ability, instead of being blinded by his misbehavior. Perhaps as important was her courage to have enough confidence in her awareness of his potentialities to see that he had a chance to use them in a responsible way that would serve the school. Her concern was with developing potentialities rather than punishing misbehavior.

FROM TROUBLEMAKER TO STAR LEARNER AND TEACHER

In the case of John, ability for verbal learning is perhaps limited—although his capacity for art, mechanics, and leadership are outstanding. Thus, the development of his potentialities took a direction quite different from that reported for David, a younger learner:

"David had been a problem in kindergarten. He knew it and acted it out in the first and second grades. He had thoroughly convinced everyone he was a problem by the time he entered my third grade.

"A thatch of yellow hair, crystal clear blue eyes—as he walked along the path to school all he needed was a fishing pole over his shoulder to be the perfect Huckleberry Finn! He intrigued me and interested me beyond words—there must be a key to David, and I must try to find it.

"I set the stage in every possible way so he would do a few things at least that we could praise—this was a shock to him and he didn't know quite what to do with praise!—By Christmastime we had arrived at the point of mutual respect for one another.

"At Christmas in our room we take a trip around the world and explore the Christmas customs of the children in other countries. This year we had decided to go by plane. We had a representative from the airlines as a guest speaker—telling about tickets, traveling by plane, and showing some slides of various countries.

"The day came when each child was to make his ticket for the country he wished to visit. I was surprised as I watched David— usually he was one of the last ones to start, but this time he was well on his way immediately. As I 'toured' the room, I noticed David's ticket would be for Sweden. This surprised me as he had brought many things from Mexico in for Sharing Time, and I had rather thought his ticket would be for Mexico. The 'Captain' for the trip arranged his 'passenger' list by countries. David was the only one for Sweden. This seemed to please him, and as time passed we were all amazed at the responsibility he assumed in finding things to present about 'his country.'

"We found that he had chosen this country because his favorite grandmother had come from Sweden. . . . He found it necessary to write five or six letters to her for various items of information. I was surprised at the neatness and the care with which he did the job— would that he had done many of his other papers in like manner!

"He wrote some wonderful factual stories about Sweden. His Swedish fairy tales were really something! He often found expression at the easel—and such vivid colors.

"The day when the class were his 'guests' in Sweden he told of the customs and even taught us a game the Swedish children play. He also taught us to make the little "goodie" baskets they hang on their Christmas trees.

"Our children come to school by bus, but the two weeks before Christmas David walked nearly every morning because he wanted to get there early so he could get extra painting or writing done. As he was telling me goodbye on the last day of school before the holidays, he said "Gee, Miss T, this is the neatest Christmas I've ever had—I feel like I've almost been to Sweden."

"I had found my 'key' to David. He needed to find out things and tell them, sometimes do a bit of embroidery on them, sometimes do a bit of dreaming and make-believe on them. He liked his real world much better too.

"This did change David. He no longer needed to be the 'bad boy.' He adjusted to the praise and found it 'fun' (as he said) to write stories, draw pictures, etc. of his 'secret world.' He was so busy doing this he didn't have time to revert to the 'old' David."

FROM ESTRANGEMENT AND RETARDATION TO ADJUSTMENT AND ACHIEVEMENT

A number of the anecdotes related by the respondents involved children who seemed to be estranged and out of contact with reality and who were regarded as mentally retarded. The following account of Jamie at the time he was in the fifth grade falls into this category:

"Jamie lived on another plane. He seemed to feel no need to relate to the world around him. As he entered the fifth grade, the children thought of him as a 'dumb kid.' In a flexible individual reading program I was able to let him skip around in the book as the spirit moved him and report in the way he was able through drawings. He completed one fourth-grade and two fifth-grade readers during the year and I feel he is ready to face any sixth-grade reading material.

"At the same time in a 'slow' math class he was exposed to an imaginative teacher. By allowing him to use his interest in motors to develop a math project he was able to show a real flair for teaching others and his classmates discovered Jamie had brains!"

FROM BITTER SARCASM AND HOSTILITY TO KINDLINESS AND SUCCESS

Encouraging the creativity of a bitter, sarcastic and hostile youngster and transforming such negative feelings into positive creative energy is indeed a trying task, as described by the teacher who wrote the following anecdote:

" 'You have no children, have you, Miss Murdock?' As I read, I wanted to laugh, but I did not flicker an eyelash. This tall, reserved ninth-grade boy was offering me his most precious possession, a short story.

"Looking back, I wonder how I lived through the next four years. Here was a boy driven by an inner compulsion to write (no 'motivation' needed here, just responsiveness). But his home life was desperately unhappy, and the boy was considered bitter, sarcastic, and hostile. For those years it seemed to be my fate to serve as a sounding board, critic, refuge, rescuer, and inspiration. People who write of the ideal student-teacher relationship surely do not mean this. He took out his frustrations on me, and I continually sought some better solution to his problem.

"At last he had a poem accepted by *This Week* and then came a time when nearly every poem he sent to *The Saturday Evening Post* or *Ladies Home Journal* was accepted. As success came, his nature changed. He became kindly, courteous, thoughtful. . . ."

FROM FIGHTING AND UNCOMMUNICATIVENESS TO IMPROVED SPEECH

Similar difficulties are presented by younger children who are uncommunicative and seem to be able to communicate only by fighting. Such was the case of Gary in the following incident reported by a kindergarten teacher:

". . . Soon it became apparent that he was a very silent boy. His most effective way of communicating was with his fists. Gary was referred to the nurse (who talked with the doctor), the guidance worker, and the speech therapist. Gary still remained almost speechless. . . . The real breakthrough came when Gary wanted to make a truck. The imagination, planning, and problem-solving in this project forced him to talk. This intense interest helped him persist until the project was completed. The concentrated effort in using the tools did not give him time or energy for fighting. His speech skills showed improvement for the remainder of the year. . . ."

FROM AN UNLOVING AND UNLOVED CHILD TO A LOVING AND LOVED CHILD

Perhaps one of the most difficult feats for many teachers is to love an unloving and unloved child. This was one of the problems involved in the story of Rick, a big third-grade boy:

"Rick was a big third-grade boy who worked with the slow group in arithmetic, reading, and spelling. He annoyed the other children in the room too much until I supplied him with materials to use when his work was finished. Both his behavior and his written work improved. With black yarn he crocheted and measured many yards of single crochet. Later he used a stapler and in cursive writing made a big caption at the top of the bulletin board.

"All of our feelings improved toward Rick near the end of the year. I honestly like him."

What Made the Difference?

The anecdotes already presented may have suggested to the reader a number of hypotheses concerning what there was about the experience, way of teaching, or relating of teacher to child that made the difference. Although these must be regarded as hypotheses for further testing, we find a number of them recurring throughout the accounts. In some way, the teacher in most instances provided a responsive environment—an environment which included a sensitive and alert kind of guidance and direction, the creation of an atmosphere of receptive listening, responding to children as they are or might become rather than as they have been told that they are, fighting off ridicule and criticism, and making their efforts to learn worthwhile. The following are the factors most frequently mentioned or which come through strongest in the hypotheses derived from these anecdotal materials:

Recognizing some heretofore unrecognized potential.

Respecting a child's need to work alone.

Inhibiting the teacher's censorship role long enough to permit a creative response to occur.

Allowing or encouraging a child to go ahead and achieve success in an area of interest in a way possible for him.

Permitting the curriculum to be different for different children.

Giving concrete embodiment to the creative ideas of children.

Giving a chance to develop responsibility and to make a contribution to the welfare of the group.

Encouraging deep involvement and permitting self-initiated projects.

Reducing pressure, providing a relatively nonpunitive environment.

Approving the pupil's work in one area to provide courage to try the others.

Voicing the beauty of individual differences.

Respecting the potential of low achievers.

Showing enthusiasm for the pupil's ideas.

Supporting the pupil against peer pressures to conformity.

Placing an unproductive child in contact with a productive, creative child.

Using fantasy ability to establish contacts with reality.

Capitalizing upon hobbies, special interests, and enthusiasms.

Tolerating complexity and disorder, at least for a period.

Permitting oneself to become involved with pupils.

Not being afraid of bodily contact with children.

Communicating that the teacher is "for" rather than "against" the child.

Giving stimulating or provocative examinations.

The reader can doubtless think of other factors in his own experiences that have made a difference and can find other factors both in the cases already described and in the ones which will be presented in this section.

PERMITTING CHILDREN TO WORK ALONE AND IN THEIR OWN WAY

In learning and doing creative work, many people are unable to function very well in a group. They seem to need to "march to a different drumbeat" or "sing in their own key." Much in established ways of teaching creates a set which makes this divergency difficult. Even beginning teachers find it possible, however, to permit such divergent behavior. The following story illustrates this point and suggests a number of other ideas as well:

"Last year was my first year of teaching. I had a student, Mark, whom I immediately recognized as an extremely creative student, and someone for whom I had an enormous respect.

"The study of Latin America is a required part of our social studies curriculum for the sixth grade. I followed every step of what I had been taught in 'Teaching Social Studies in the Elementary School' . . . , letting the class decide what you need to learn about people and a country to understand them and their needs. A secretary wrote the names of the various Latin American countries on the board, so that the children could select the country's committee they would like to be on to prepare written reports. We decided that the major countries would need more on a committee. . . . Ecuador came up, and two people volunteered and were given that country to research and do a project on. After all of the countries had been spoken for, I noticed that Mark had not made a choice.

"Talking with him, I learned that he had wanted Ecuador, as he had been reading Darwin's journals and was fascinated by the Galapagos Islands, but he hadn't wanted to work with anyone, so hadn't held up his hand. Well, I said that was all right, and that he could make up a separate report on the Galapagos Islands, which he agreed to do.

"Three weeks later Mark had not begun his report, in the sense that he had nothing on paper. He was just too busy reading books, interviewing anthropologists at the University of California, and thinking. I tried very hard to help him get something on paper, but when I saw that he was just too interested in Darwin's discoveries and their implications and the evidence of it that remains to this day on the Islands, I decided Mark's assignment would be changed to an oral report. He reacted very favorably to this, delivering a magnificent account of what kind of person Darwin was, an account of the voyage of the *Beagle,* and then a very instructive lecture on the various forms of a single species as they appear on the different islands, drawing pictures of the variants on the chalkboard—complete with describing the different environment a different island would offer and asking the other students in the class to guess what variant they would imagine would result!

"Mark got such a good feeling out of this experience, I was able, when the next report came up, to talk with him in terms of being able to operate in more than one manner and thus be prepared to be flexible and able to choose. I put it to him in terms of baseball: that a player might be a righthander but it would be to his advantage to also learn to bat left-handed so that he could be a switch-hitter. He decided he would prepare a written report, which he did—a very good one—and in on time and beautifully done, even as far as presentation, right down to the bibliography.

"This point is, I think, that in honoring his involvement at a particular time in research, he learned to respect me enough to consider the advantages when the next report came around of knowing how to prepare and get in on time a written report."

If we examine the teacher's report of this episode closely, we find several factors involved. One of the more salient factors contributing to the teacher's success in working with Mark was her willingness to change or bend her planned sequence of experiences to permit Mark to function in such a way as to achieve his potentialities. He was able to function in terms of his abilities and interests, without actually upsetting the curriculum or the classroom organization. We find, however, that the teacher had already recognized Mark's creative potential and that she had an enormous respect for him. She recognized that she would be bucking a strong force to divert him at this time from his interest in the Galapagos Islands; furthermore, she saw how he might be able to contribute meaningfully to the curriculum for the entire class. She had not counted upon his absorption being so great that he could not find the time to write his report. She remained open and flexible, however, and saw that he might contribute most by giving an oral report, a challenge which he met with unexpected skill. Having achieved success and respect from his teacher, he was then ready to learn some of the more conforming ways of behaving in the educational environment. In fact, he was even able to include a very proper bibliography documenting his report. In this way he has learned adaptive and constructive ways of behaving which will doubtless stand him in good stead throughout his educational career.

CURRICULAR VARIATIONS FOR DIFFERENT CHILDREN

The "democratic" concept that all children should be taught the same things and that the curriculum should be the same for all children has long stood in the way of achieving individualization of instruction. It also stands as a barrier to creative ways of teaching. Once a teacher is committed to creative teaching and the encouragement of children to learn creatively, the curriculum becomes different for each child, at least to some extent. This occurs in a variety of ways. The following account describes how it occurred in one nursery school:

"A three-year-old on a walk with the class was shown a snail. Completely fascinated, he spent the remaining school time (one and one-half hours) observing and touching the snail, rather to my annoyance, but I let him alone while the rest of us went on with crafts, etc. The child consequently became so interested in nature's small creatures that at age five he is quite an authority on small creatures. He approaches them stealthily. While looking for lizards once, he practically looked a rattlesnake in the eyes. He immediately recognized it and retreated just as quietly and was unharmed."

With some children it is necessary to permit deviations in subject matter as well as method or format of reporting. This is one of the discoveries apparent in the following excerpt:

"The teacher began by saying to Diane, 'You seem to be creative, so now create.' Assignments were given to Diane to produce poems on the subjects about which other students were writing reports. Generally these results were far from creative. Finally, the teacher and I decided not to stipulate what special thing she should do, or even the date upon which it should be done. The result has been a much more steady flow of interesting—occasionally unique —stories, poems and pictures."

The following anecdote describes how curricular deviations can be encouraged when needs and interests arise:

"Fred, at the beginning of the third grade, was an average student, afraid of standing out before the class. I suspected there was more to him than was apparent on the surface. He worked quickly and accurately.

"He liked science, so I asked him to be my assistant during experiments. He was expert in the use of batteries and radio equipment, but still very shy.

"One day his mother asked me if I opposed his taking an adult correspondence course in radio. He started the course with the help of a neighbor. I encouraged him to share his inventions with the class. Soon other children were bringing him radios to repair and collecting spare parts for his 'business.' His reading improved, his language work and arithmetic improved, and we discovered that he even had a sense of humor—the result of encouraging him to engage in creative learning experiences."

You will note that Fred's improved performance spread to other areas—reading, language arts, and arithmetic. Many other respondents reported similar spreads of effects. If such phenomena are as common as they appear to be, teachers will need to reexamine the common assumption that permitting a child to spend time on something different from the remainder of the class will result in disabilities that will never be overcome in fundamentals.

A NONPUNITIVE ENVIRONMENT

It is apparent that the teachers who described the incidents reported in this chapter relied heavily upon a real, warm, positive involvement in responsible creative behavior rather than upon punishment or other external pressures. When children fail in school, teachers and parents rather generally try to motivate them through some type of external pressure although such attempts have already failed repeatedly. Glasser in *Schools Without Failure* (1969) points out quite dramatically that guns, force, threats, shame, and punishment have been proved by history to be poor motivators. He reminds his reader that such motivators work only as long as the gun (force, threat, etc.) is pointed and as long as the person is afraid. If fear disappears, or if the gun is put down, motivation ceases. Educational research has shown repeatedly that external motivation must be repeated again and again and does not engender the sustained motivation necessary for continued effort to learn.

Children who prefer to learn in creative ways frequently are unable to learn or behave in constructive ways because they anticipate that any effort they make will be punished. For a child who has undergone a long period of this kind of conditioning, a great deal of patience and waiting may be required before he is able to learn at all. The following account will illustrate how this expectation can be changed gradually:

"In September, last year, one of my third-grade students, a boy, appeared to be so emotionally disturbed that he was unable to do any of the usual school activities. He would frequently hide his head in his desk or cover his ears and eyes when asked to do written work. He seemed to expect a lot of punishment. Gradually as he found he was not being punished he began working on various unusual projects of his own which he kept in his very untidy desk. For instance, although he would do no art activities with the class, he would make diagrams of various machines and science projects. I admired and enjoyed his work and gradually he was able to write stories and reports about the numerous things that interested him. The words he asked to have spelled for him were more difficult and unusual than those asked for by anyone else in the room. Although he and I were the only ones able to read his papers, I felt we had made real progress."

The retarded child who is an original thinker is especially likely to experience a great deal of punishment, and it may be necessary for the teacher to work with parents to develop reasonable expectations so that they will not be highly punishing and will be willing to reward him for the original contributions that he is able to make.

The following case illustrates this point:

"One experience that I shall always remember concerns a boy I had in kindergarten two years ago. Tim was limited in mental ability . . . and was repeating the year in kindergarten. For the first semester I got little response from him. . . . After Christmas, we began a program of creating our own books as an approach to beginning reading. I made plans with the children, gave them blank books made of double newsprint pages and bright covers. They could choose their own subjects and work on them as long as they wanted or when they wanted. After they finished the pictures I would write the stories they told me. To my surprise, Tim was the first one to finish a book, and his was very exciting. As we had planned, we read the books during the story time and put them in our class library. He was thrilled and proud when his was read and watched to see when other children would read his book in the library. . . . He made much more effort to contribute, and his last year's teacher asked what had happened to Tim—'He had never looked so happy before.' His mother showed a similar reaction and I was able to discuss his limitations with her, showing that successes were possible and the great value of accepting his contributions and rewarding his achievements with praise and encouragement."

CHANGING THE PERCEPTION OF THE GROUP

To create a nonpunitive environment it is often necessary to change the perception that the group has of a particular child or young person. Such problems may arise even with exceptionally gifted children, as we see in the following incident:

"Last year in my gifted class I had two girls who became immediate friends. Prior to the fourth grade they had been in different schools. They engaged in silly, isolated play during recess. All of the teachers were aware of them and their behavior. One girl was extraordinarily tall. They were becoming 'odd balls' to the rest of the class. I suspected they were possibly the most creative. I offered them many possible experiences for self-initiated projects. One girl wrote five- to ten-page stories outside of class. . . . After reading several of her stories aloud the children began to appreciate and respect her. By the end of the semester she became an important person in the class. She organized activities and stimulated much creative learning among her classmates. . . . She could easily have become a permanent object of their ridicule. . . ."

At times, children lack confidence to learn creatively because the things that they are expected to do require skills that they have not achieved; meanwhile, they do not use the very fine skills that they do possess. It is only when they have opportunities to use the skills that they possess that they are able to gain the respect of their classmates and move forward. Such was the case of Donald, related by his first grade teacher:

"Last year I had a little boy in my first grade who was a very good reader and a fine student. He was, however, extremely shy and lacked confidence in self-expression. For some of our reading activities, the children chose Donald for the storyteller or the puppet show narrator. Since the children expressed confidence in him he accepted and found that we all enjoyed the way he told stories. He then began to write original stories and he has written some of the most enjoyable, humorous stories. And he began writing stories any time he could outside of school. He showed a great deal of originality and elaboration in his drawings also. I think now that Donald has confidence in his ability and I hope that he will not be daunted by over-criticism of his messiness in his writing."

The case of Dana, related below, had been allowed to become much more serious than either of the foregoing. This incident illustrates that the perceptions of a class can be changed and that progress can be achieved, even if the teacher cannot control the total environment enough to make possible sustained progress.

"When Dana entered my fourth-grade class, the principal gave me a bulging cumulative folder and much information about Dana's previous undesirable behavior and nonlearning experiences. He had been retained in the third grade and had run away from school on frequent occasions. He had a severe speech problem; he stuttered so badly that he was most difficult to understand. As expected, reading was a problem but arithmetic was average.

"It was difficult at the beginning because the children didn't accept him and they were tempted to mimic him. I decided not to push the reading skills and let Dana enter the discussion group in reading at his own choice. (He later asked to read and take part in puppet shows.) I talked the principal out of any extra help except for the speech therapist who was a kind man and was a good male relationship for Dana.

"I discovered Dana had talent in art through a hand puppet show. He became art director for the reading group, and this later developed into the position of the art consultant for the classroom. Dana's self-respect and prestige blossomed. He created many new ideas for the class. He never missed a day of school and worked diligently in every subject.

"But the greatest half-hour in every student's life that fall was when Dana enthusiastically but laboriously read (stammered) his two-page report on snakes while the whole class listened respectfully and quietly. It was really a thrill for everyone in the room because we all felt a part of Dana's great achievement. We had all learned so much. (Dana moved a month later and was expelled from the new school for being a behavior problem.)"

Teachers cannot play God to their pupils and it is sometimes difficult to determine the extent to which teachers should intervene in the lives of their pupils. In Dana's case it was heartbreaking to see what seemed to be genuine growth stopped when, perhaps for the first time, Dana had found a classroom environment in which he felt safe enough to learn. His teacher could only hope that at some future time Dana would be able to build upon the brief period of growth he experienced in the fourth grade.

Many investigators (Clark, 1965; Glasser, 1969; Pressman,

1969; Riessman, 1962; Rosenthal & Jacobson, 1968) of the learning problems of disadvantaged children have concluded that the main reason why such children fail is that teachers have such low expectations of them. Moreover, Pressman forcefully asserts that the expectations teachers have of substandard performance from children in slum schools is not only the most important reason for the failure of poor children, but also the most difficult to change. He observes that this expectation of substandard performance seems to pervade the entire atmosphere of slum schools.

To illustrate how this happens he cites an example from Kohl's *36 Children* (1967). Kohl reported that when the children he taught in a Harlem school began to come out of their tough shells, they showed sustained curiosity in the classroom. Some of the boys had made a volcano with vinegar and baking soda and wanted to try more experiments. Kohl went to the school's assistant principal and asked for science supplies. He was told that there were none. When Kohl reported this to his class, they snickered and insisted that there were plenty of science supplies but that they would never get to use any of "that stuff because the school was just a 'bean school' in Harlem." He challenged them to show him, and the boys led him to a locked closet that turned out to be filled with brand-new scientific equipment. The principal then allowed Kohl to use the equipment, but wondered seriously if the youngsters were capable of getting anything from it. *problem*

Experienced and Inexperienced Teachers

Since the sensitivities, imagination, and teaching skills reflected in the above incidents are of high order and not easily developed, some may feel that it is not possible for them to achieve such skills. While a majority of the incidents narrated in this chapter were written by young teachers with only one to three years of experience some of them were provided by older teachers. Some of these older teachers also described how, for them, creative teaching is still a slow process but one they regard as realistically possible. The following account concerns one such example:

"I have taught for fourteen years, starting in quite a stereotyped, authoritative fashion and discipline, but I thought all was fine because of colorful, versatile presentations. I liked to observe quiet absorption in work. Gradually I became dissatisfied and experimented more. . . . Two years ago I began a buddy system in math that I've revised, experimented with and am very excited about. So in my "old age," I find myself becoming more flexible and inventive. It surprises me. Shouldn't the opposite be true? Another fifteen years should see me a fine teacher!"

We believe firmly that each teacher's way of teaching is a unique invention that takes place just like any other invention or creative production. All inventions, however, are built upon failures, imperfections, and little successes and the insights that come from them. It is our hope that from our own experiences, those of our students, and existing theory and research, we will be able to provide some guides and clues that can be used in your own invention. Reading this chapter, we hope that you have become reassured that creative teaching, though it may require expensive energies, does make a difference in lives and is immeasurably rewarding. In the next chapter, we will try to help you lay the groundwork for understanding the motivating power of creative teaching and learning and some of the major characteristics of educational experiences that result in creative learning.

Making Your Own Summary

Before going to the next chapter, you might find it useful to try the following problem in an effort to synthesize and apply the ideas in this chapter:

WHAT CAN BE DONE ABOUT THE UNCOMPLIMENTARY COLLEAGUE?

Your seventh-grade pupils inform you one day that the teacher next door has just said some uncomplimentary things about your teaching. According to one of the volunteers of this unwelcome news, your colleague, an English teacher, said something like this:

"Why, you people don't even know who the presidents were or where the states are located! She has you doing all those silly games instead of really learning geography and history. It's about time she taught you something in that class and quit all that foolishness. I've noticed that her pupils never are informed about the things they should know."

Aside from the fact that your colleague's outburst was very "unprofessional," you are shocked by it because you had no idea that your teaching methods were being criticized by any of your fellow teachers. Although you have not met socially with your colleague in the three years you have had adjoining rooms, the two of you have been on amicable terms throughout that time.

What should you say to the pupils who have conveyed this upsetting news? How can you respond to the teacher? Or should you respond in any way? Should you merely ignore the entire incident?

Filling in the Picture. There are twenty-two teachers in your building, which is located in an older residential section of a large city. The teacher who was critical of your teaching is a veteran of some fifteen years or more. Your teaching experience has been limited to the three years you have spent in your present classroom. Although there is a great deal of divergency in the teaching methods of the individual faculty members, for the most part your fellow teachers are tolerant of viewpoints and attitudes which are at odds with their own. Your principal has other responsibilities in the district, and so is not always available to his teachers during the day. The teachers' professional organization has a professional relations committee which meets monthly. In general, the teachers are not enthusiastic about their organization.

REFERENCES

Bloom, B. S. *Stability and Change in Human Characteristics.* New York: John Wiley & Sons, Inc., 1964.

Clark, K. B. *Dark Ghetto.* New York: Harper & Row, 1965.

Cranston, R. *Miracle of Lourdes.* New York: McGraw-Hill Book Company, 1955.

Crutchfield, R. S. "Creative Thinking in Children: Its Teaching and Testing." In O. G. Brim, Jr., R. S. Crutchfield, and W. H.

Holtzman. *Intelligence: Perspectives 1965.* New York: Harcourt, Brace & World, 1966. Pp. 33–64.

Glasser, W. *Schools Without Failure.* New York: Harper & Row, 1969.

Kohl, H. *36 Children.* New York: New American Library, 1967.

Lichter, S. O., E. B. Rapien, F. M. Seibert, and M. O. Sklansky. *The Drop-Outs.* New York: Free Press, 1962.

Parnes, S. J. *Creative Behavior Guidebook.* New York: Charles Scribner's Sons, 1967.

Pressman, H. "Schools to Beat the System." *Psychology Today,* March 1969, **2(10),** 58–63.

Riessman, F. *The Culturally Deprived Child.* New York: Harper & Row, 1962.

Rosenthal, R. and L. Jacobson. *Pygmalion in the Classroom.* New York: Holt, Rinehart & Winston, Inc., 1968.

Selye, H. "The Gift of Basic Research." In G. Z. F. Bereday and J. A. Lauwreys (eds.). *The Gifted Child: The Yearbook of Education.* New York: Harcourt, Brace & World, 1962. Pp. 339–408.

Torrance, E. P. *Rewarding Creative Behavior.* Englewood Cliffs, N. J.: Prentice-Hall, Inc., 1965a.

Torrance, E. P. "Exploring the Limits of the Automation of Guided, Planned Experiences in Creative Thinking." In J. Roucek (ed.). *Programmed Teaching.* New York: Philosophical Library, 1965b. Pp. 57–70.

Torrance, E. P., L. R. Fortson, and C. Diener. "Creative-Aesthetic Ways of Developing Intellectual Skills among Five-Year Olds." *Journal of Research & Development in Education,* 1968, **1(3),** 58–69.

CHAPTER 3

BUILT-IN
MOTIVATION
IN CREATIVE LEARNING

Create—
A revelation—
Exposing oneself to
Understanding, pain, growth, rebirth—
To BE.

The Problem

Mr. James thought he had a tough job. Teaching English seven periods a day to groups of seventh-graders was not what he had thought it would be. For one thing, the youngsters were not predictable. One class would respond enthusiastically to a lesson, and another class would demonstrate an indifference to the same lesson that bordered on apathy or hostility. The girls were especially hard to figure out. Some were entering teenhood and pubescence with élan; others were confused by the changes in themselves and by their new routine at junior high school. The boys seemed to be quite immature to Mr. James. They were interested in sports, stamps, pets, cars, war, clothes, music, television, and business—but somewhat superficially. It seemed to Mr. James that none of the boys really dug deeply into anything. A few were very interested in girls, but most of the dating in the school was done by the ninth-graders. Taken as a whole, his seventh-graders were hard to teach —especially English.

After trying a number of devices that he hoped would spark some interest about the construction of sentences and paragraphs and the roles that certain kinds of words play in the English language, Mr. James concluded that the exercises and games he had found in professional books and magazines were ineffectual. He decided then to adopt a technique that has been popular with teachers for centuries, that of posting examination scores. Mr. James reasoned that if the scores on the weekly quizzes he gave were recorded for all to see the youngsters would be motivated to try harder. They would not wish to have a low score posted which their friends could see; and, since they appeared to be competitive young people, they would try to outdo each other in obtaining high scores.

For several weeks Mr. James thought he saw in some of his pupils a slightly greater desire to understand their lessons, and he could see improvement in many of their performances on quizzes. Posting grades seemed to be the answer to his problem. Then, the old indifference returned stronger than ever. Mr. James was disconcerted. Nothing he tried had any effect for very long. After a few days, the idea of having a schoolwide spelling bee with a big prize for the winner occurred to him.

Do you think the spelling bee motivated a majority of the pupils of the school?

Which pupils do you think would be most enthusiastic about this kind of competition?

Which pupils would be least interested in the spelling bee?

Do you think Mr. James would have encountered so much indifference if he were teaching transformational grammar?

Did any of Mr. James's motivational strategies described above cause his pupils to really want to know, to find out things, or even to make use of what they learned?

Motivating Power of Creative Learning and Teaching

A major thesis of this book is that creative ways of learning have a built-in motivating power that makes unnecessary the application and reapplication of rewards and punishment, as we find Mr. James doing. It is our contention that if teachers keep alive the creative processes of their pupils and sensitively guide them, there will be plenty of motivation and achievement.

Research in social psychology (Lewin, 1947; Torrance, 1965a) has shown that we can usually improve almost any kind of human functioning—increase rates of learning, improve undesirable behavior, and the like—by increasing or decreasing motivation in the form of external pressures (rewards or punishments). As noted in the previous chapter, however, such improvements are generally temporary in nature. Nevertheless, most people seem to think of motivation almost entirely as external pressure.

We have observed that many children are almost totally unresponsive to external pressure, whether in the form of reward or punishment. In fact, it seems that the more they are rewarded the worse they behave and the less they learn, and likewise the more we punish them the worse they behave and the less they learn.

Even when reward and/or punishment succeed temporarily, they do not supply the inner stimulation necessary for continued motivation and achievement. Such motivation is short-lived and requires continuous reapplication. The inner stimulation and involvement from creative ways of learning make the reapplication of rewards and punishments unnecessary. Although rewards are less erratic as motivators than punishment, they are still quite erratic in motivating learning. In another source, Torrance (1965b) tried to show that children with school learning problems can be motivated by:

giving them a chance to use what they learn as tools in their thinking and problem solving;
giving them a chance to communicate what they learn;
showing an interest in what they have learned rather than in their grades;
giving them learning tasks of appropriate difficulty;
giving them a chance to use their best abilities;
giving them a chance to learn in their preferred ways;
recognizing and acknowledging many different kinds of excellence;
and giving genuine purpose and meaning to learning experiences.

In this chapter, we will attempt to show why creative ways of learning have a built-in motivation for achievement and attempt also to identify some of the most essential characteristics of educational methods for facilitating creative ways of learning.

The motivating power of creative ways of learning could perhaps be explained on the basis of the evidence concerning the importance of man's cognitive and aesthetic needs. It is widely acknowledged that man is an inquisitive, exploring being, who cannot keep his restless mind inactive even when there are no problems to be solved. He seems to be unable to keep from digging into things, turning ideas over in his mind, trying out new combinations, searching for new relationships, and struggling for new insights. These things result from the power of man's cognitive needs—his need to know, to find out. Man's aesthetic needs are almost as relentless as his cognitive needs. Man's search for beauty is not always expressed in a painting or in a sonata, however. Maslow (1954) reports that he learned from a young athlete that a perfect tackle could be considered as aesthetic a product as a sonnet and could be approached in the same spirit of creativity and achievement. From a housewife, he learned that a first-rate soup is more aesthetic and represents a higher level of achievement than a second-rate painting.

It could be argued that stimulus-response psychology with its rewards and punishments actually creates obstacles to the genuine kind of motivation that results in self-initiated and continuing learning. Usually, motivation of achievement by external rewards and punishments is actually motivation by fear. So much energy goes into coping with the fear, and the accompanying learning requires such expensive energy, that motivation to continue learning cannot be sustained. The drill that seems necessary in much stimulus-response learning and adequate reinforcement of desired responses is frequently so monotonous that we have the same effects as occur in fatigue and exhaustion. Many children also regard such learning as drudgery. There is a lack of intrinsic interest. There is no fun. Again, learning under such conditions requires expensive energy and leaves little energy available for continued learning, especially self-initiated learning. Frequently stimulus-response learning requires unquestioning acceptance of customs and traditions, conventionality and uncritical imitation of contemporaries, subjection to authority and to books, and slavery to details without attention to ability to organize and systematize the information acquired. Again, such learning leaves little energy for continued learning. Thus, there is little wonder that external rewards and punishments have to be reapplied continuously in order to keep the processes of learning and achievement going.

A simpler and more natural process than any of the foregoing alternatives is the creative learning process, defined in Chapter 2 (p. 22). There it was noted that underlying the creative process itself are very powerful, healthy human motivations. It is our contention that these motivations are ready to be activated in all reasonably healthy children, young people, and adults. When learning activities give reasonably good chances of satisfying these motives, zestful learning usually occurs.

Now let us try to identify some of the educational methods which seem to be most successful in activating the creative learning process, showing how powerful motivations enter into them to sustain continued learning and achievement.

Educational Methods That Facilitate Creative Learning

Many of the inventors of educational methods throughout the history of education have tested and described methods possessing built-in kinds of motivation. The basic elements comprising these methods may be observed in the efforts of young children to learn before they are given any instruction. Alfred Binet (1909), in fact, asserted that "all, or almost all, children before being given any instruction show a taste for singing, drawing, story telling, inventing, manipulating objects, moving them about, using them to construct others." He urged that educators build their instruction on these "natural activities" and benefit from "the start already made by nature." Nature furnishes the activity and the teacher intervenes only to direct it.

Froebel (1879) also suggested that educators take their cues from the early learning activities of children. He urged them "to comprehend the earliest activity of the child, the impulse to spontaneous and personal activity, to encourage the impulse to self-culture and self-instruction through self-shaping, self-observation, and self-testing." He considered knowing, feeling, and willing as the three activities of the mind and argued that the child's self-activities were a good guide to the kind of encouragement and practice needed. He observed that attention to differences in sound is one of the first awakenings of children and argued that instruction in song was one of the most effective means of education with young children. Similarly, he emphasized the importance of rhythmic sound and movement in cognitive development; the cultivation of the beautiful in sound and movement; and the use of the child's hands in shaping, modeling, drawing, painting, and pointing. He believed that "nothing is more contrary to nature than to forbid a young child the use of its hands." Thus, his educational methods made extensive use of the child's hands in riveting the child's attention and in connecting all of the instruction given the child. In fact, he emphasized the total involvement of the child's body, mind, and spirit.

An early American educator, Forbush (1900), emphasized the child's strong play instincts as sources of cues for educational method. He argued that play is the natural way by which the child finds out things. There is now a renewed interest in the role of play in facilitating cognitive development among children. Nina Lieberman (1967) has recently suggested that playfulness may also be important in the cognitive development of adolescents.

Using our definition of the creative learning process, we have tried to identify some of the most essential characteristics of educational methods possessing built-in motivation and to illustrate them with examples in different subject matter fields.

INCOMPLETENESS, OPENNESS

Perhaps the most essential characteristic of self-motivating learning experiences is incompleteness or openness. Many outstanding creative people have commented upon the power of incompleteness in motivating achievement. Ben Shahn (1959), in discussing his creativity in painting, describes how he traps images like some inventors trap ideas. He explains that these images are not complete, saying, "If I had a complete image I think I would lose interest in it." To him, the most rewarding thing about painting is the sense of exploration and discovery that he finds in it.

A pupil may encounter incompleteness outside of school which may motivate his achievement, or he may encounter it in the classroom. The incompleteness may be encountered in pictures, stories, objects of instruction, the behavioral settings of the classroom, or in structured sequences of learning activities. In current work with five-year-olds, Torrance has been encouraging children to see all knowledge as incomplete. He shows children a picture or reads them a story, asking them then to think about all of the things that the picture or the story does not tell about the events described and finally to ask questions about these things.

In answering the children's questions, information is frequently given as incomplete. The incompleteness and changing nature of the objects presented are emphasized. Early in the year, a beautiful zebra plant with three blossoms—a big blossom, a middle-sized one, and a little one—was presented to the children. They were asked to guess how many days it would take the little blossom to grow to be the size of the big one. Their guesses were recorded. The size of the large blossom was established by holding a piece of paper behind it and tracing its size. Day after day, checks were made to find out whether the little blossom had become the same size the big blossom was at the time of the first observation. On the tenth day it happened, and there was great glee among those who had guessed "ten days."

There are many teacher strategies for creating and/or using incompleteness in motivating achievement. We have attempted to identify the strategies that might be used for this purpose before, during, and after a reading lesson, a science lesson, an art lesson, or whatever. The following strategies are usually effective prior to a lesson, assignment, or other learning activity:

1. Confrontation with ambiguities and uncertainties.
2. Heightened anticipation and expectation.
3. The familiar made strange or the strange made familiar by analogy.
4. Looking at the same thing from several different psychological, sociological, physical, or emotional points of view.
5. Provocative questions requiring the learner to examine the information in new ways.
6. Requiring predictions from limited information.
7. Tasks structured only enough to give clues and direction.
8. Encouragement to take the next step beyond what is known.

During the process of a lesson, assignment, or other learning activity, the following strategies seem to be useful:

1. Continued heightening of anticipation and expectation.
2. Encouragement of the creative and constructive, rather than cynical acceptance of limitations.
3. Exploration of missing elements and possibilities made systematic and deliberate.
4. Juxtaposition of apparently irrelevant or unrelated elements.
5. Exploration and examination of mysteries and puzzles.
6. Preserving open-endedness.
7. Ongoing predictions from limited information as new data are acquired.
8. Heightening and deliberate use of surprises.
9. Visualization of events, places, etc.

The following teacher strategies seem especially appropria__ following a lesson, assignment, or other learning activity:

1. Playing with ambiguities and uncertainties.
2. Calling for constructive response (a better way, a more beautiful effect, etc.).
3. Digging deeper, going beyond the obvious.
4. Elaborating some element through drawings, paintings, dramatics, imaginative stories, dramatizations, and the like.
5. Searching for elegant solutions (i.e., solutions that take into account the largest number of variables).
6. Experimentation and testing of ideas.
7. Encouraging future projection.
8. Entertaining improbabilities.
9. Encouraging multiple hypotheses.
10. Reorganization or reconceptualization of information.
11. Syntheses of diverse and apparently irrelevant elements.
12. Testing and revising predictions.
13. Transforming and rearranging information or other elements.
14. Taking the next step beyond what is known.

Some of the illustrations given by Bruner (1959) for history and geography in the intermediate grades provide fairly good models for using incompleteness in motivating achievement.

Bruner describes a lesson in history, for instance, in which the teacher encouraged the class to organize and use minimal information to draw a maximum number of inferences. The teacher apparently modeled his technique on the tried method of the story teller. He presented the beginnings of the Whiskey Rebellion and said to his pupils, "You now have enough information to reconstruct the rest of the story. Let's see if we can do it." As Bruner commented, this teacher was urging his pupils to cross the barriers from learning into thinking. They had been "hooked." Thinking such as this exercise required, however, is the reward for learning. Thus, these pupils were not cheated of their reward.

Bruner (1959) also describes a fifth-grade geography unit which capitalized upon the incompleteness of the information supplied. One class was presented blank maps, containing only tracings of the rivers and lakes of the North Central states, along with notations of the natural resources. The pupils were asked first to indicate where the principal cities, railroads, and main highways would be located. At this point, books and maps were not permitted. Upon completing this first exercise, the class discussed their productions and each child attempted to justify why the major city would be here, a large city there, or a railroad on this line.

According to Bruner, the discussion was a hot one and after an hour and much pleading, permission was given to consult the rolled-up wall map. He writes that he will never forget one youngster, as he pointed his finger at the foot of Lake Michigan, shouting, "Yipee, Chicago is at the end of the pointing-down lake!" And another replying, "Well, O.K.; but Chicago's no good for the rivers and it should be here where there is a big city (St. Louis)." He reports that the children were slightly shaken-up transportation theorists when the facts were in, but that what they learned had become important to them personally.

Torrance has experienced similar unforgettable experiences observing five-year-olds learn mathematics. After children have figured out the value of an unknown (the number of blocks under a box) in an equation and then checked their accuracy, the resulting wild glee is something to behold. Torrance has also observed the urgent pleas of kindergarteners or first graders to be taught how to use rhythm band instruments, following the first wild exploration of looking, smelling, feeling, sounding, and tasting the instruments. Until this exploration is completed, efforts to teach the proper use of the instruments are wasted.

PRODUCING SOMETHING AND THEN DOING SOMETHING WITH IT

A favorite strategy of the authors for building in motivation in a learning activity through creative processes is to have the learner produce something—a drawing, a story, a papier-mâché animal, etc.—and then do something with what he has produced. This strategy is a central feature of the ideabooks for elementary and junior high school pupils created by the authors (1964, 1965ab, 1966ab) and of the Imagi/Craft materials (Cunnington and Torrance, 1965).

In the ideabooks, there are three levels of involvement. The initiating activity allows the pupil to work with his classmates in producing ideas. He then thinks more deeply about the subject on his own. At the third level, he is encouraged to do something with what he has produced.

In the Imagi/Craft materials, a variety of techniques are used to accomplish this purpose. In *Sounds and Images,* the child is asked to record the word pictures of the images generated to each of four sounds. He is then asked to listen to these same four sounds a second and third time, each time stretching his imagination further and further. Finally, he is asked to select his most interesting image and use it as the basis for a painting, story, or song. In several of the recorded dramatizations, the recording is stopped at strategic points for problem solving, guessing of consequences, and consideration of various possibilities. These possibilities are then used as the basis for further inquiry, research, or such productions as dramas, poems, stories, or songs.

In some "Just Imagine" exercises now being developed by Torrance, a variety of techniques are used for getting children to produce something and then to do something with what they have produced. Let us examine a fairly typical pattern. In one of these exercises, the children are shown an attractive picture of a pond with frogs, lily pads, and insects. The children are asked to just imagine that they could enter into the life of the pond and become anything in the pond that they wanted to be. Each child was then asked to choose what he wanted to be. As a result, we had frogs, alligators, fish, mosquitoes, water, sticks emerging from the pond, tree roots at the bottom of the pond, and even the fog that comes over the pond early some mornings. Then we created the drama of the pond. The frogs jumped, croaked, and sang their song. When the alligator entered the pond, the jumping and croaking ceased; and we stopped to wonder why. The fog came over the pond, and we stopped to wonder how this made the frogs, the fish, and the other living things feel.

Immediately after this dramatic creation of life in the pond by a group of twenty-four children, the children were asked to draw some event that might occur if they could enter the life of the pond. Later, the experience was used for writing songs and stories which were then placed on reading charts and used as reading materials, as well as for singing and creative movement. The experience was also used for teaching number facts. "If there are three frogs on the bank, three frogs on the lily pads, and three frogs on the log, how many will there be in the pond if they all jump in? If three of them jump out, how many will be left in the pond?" After such explorations as these, one class was encouraged to make more elaborate paintings of something that happened in the pond. In another class, a giant mural of the pond was painted. Each child then constructed, painted, and placed in the pond something of interest to him. Paintings of life in a pond presented the children with difficult problems. For example, how do you draw and paint the animals in the pond and then add the water so that it does not cover up the animals and hide them?

Educational and psychological literature is filled with successful experiences in which creative writing has motivated still other kinds of learning. Maya Pines (1967), after surveying the leading programs for teaching pre-primary children to read, concludes that all of the most successful ones had one thing in common. They all elicit the child's creativity by letting him make up his own words and stories almost from the beginning. Such methods harness the child's own drive, and standard primers are avoided like the plague.

Alta Boyer (1959) describes a method for use in first grade in which, first, the children draw something. They then tell the teacher about it. After she writes down what they have said, they want to read it and also what their classmates have said. Boyer tried this method first with a group of children who were not learning to read. The following year, she began using this method the first day and, through it, seems to have avoided many of the usual reading difficulties. When children are encouraged and permitted to write creatively, this seems to provide all of the motivation necessary for learning the skills of writing. If their writings are shared and enjoyed rather than corrected and kept secret, high-level skills seem to emerge. June D. Ferebee (1950) describes a problem boy whose first story gave him such great pleasure that he began writing copiously. Through such generous activity, his stream of creative power must have clarified itself because before the end of the school year he was writing in rhythmical prose.

These and similar experiences are an interesting contrast to the theme-a-week experiments in which students are required to write a theme each week to be corrected and graded by the teacher. In almost all of these experiments (Heys, 1962), little or no improvement has resulted in spite of enormous expenditures of energy by both teachers and pupils. Writing no themes seems to produce just as good results. As early as 1902, Colvin reported studies which indicated that formal correction and criticism inhibit development in creative writing. He found that progress was made when appeals were made to the fundamental interests of the pupils, when compositions were written to be read in class and enjoyed (not corrected), and when originality was encouraged.

Just why educational methods in which pupils produce something that leads to doing other things are so powerful in motivating additional learning and creative achievement is not altogether clear. Some people maintain that the power of such methods comes from the fact that human life is meaningless without creativity and that consequently creativity excites creativity. Truly creative poetry can stimulate the scientist, and the creative insight of the scientist can stimulate the poet. Others (Flanagan, 1959) have explained that the more creative acts we experience, whether they are our own or those of others, the more we live, and anything that makes a person more fully alive is likely to facilitate creative achievement. Some creative products, however, are far more powerful than others in motivating achievement. Mary O'Neill's (1961) *Hailstones and Halibut Bones*, for example, seems almost always to impel children to write poems about color, experiment with color, and find out things about color. The creative productions of one child also seem to impel others to similar efforts. Perhaps this is because these productions present a challenge that is within attainment. It may be that their very imperfections (incompletenesses) motivate achievement. It would certainly be unwise to rely entirely upon creative masterpieces whatever their nature.

Perhaps the most fundamental explanation is that producing something produces involvement and out of this involvement comes creative learning.

HAVING PUPILS ASK QUESTIONS

The child's "wanting to know" is reflected in the number and kinds of questions he asks. The number of questions a child asks generally increases during the second and third years of life, coinciding with his spurt in language development. Early questions are of the "what is that?" variety. The child who points to objects in books and magazines, asking, "what is that?" is learning how to read a picture. The child who is brought up in a home without books and pictures or who is not permitted to ask such questions finds it difficult, therefore, to learn to read or interpret pictures. After the "what" questions, the "why" and "how" questions come. Thus, by the time a child enters school for the first time he is on his way to learning the skill of finding out by asking questions. When he enters school, however, the teacher begins asking all the questions and the child has little chance to ask questions himself. Furthermore, the teacher's questions are rarely asked to gain information. The teacher almost always knows the answer. Real questions for information are rare. Questions asked in the classroom are usually to find out whether the child knows something that the teacher knows.

Just imagine how stimulating it would be if teachers really asked children for information! If teachers did this, children would ask questions far more freely and with greater skill and excitement. Pupils and teachers would be kept busy finding out what they want to know.

Both parents and teachers are probably unaware of many of the things they do to discourage children from asking questions. Parents say too frequently such things as these (Patri, 1931):

"Go away. Can't you see I'm busy?"
"Ask your teachers and stop bothering me."
"Oh, never mind what it is. It doesn't concern you."
"Mind your business. I do wish you would keep your nose out of what does not concern you. Take out the garbage."

Many teachers who say that they encourage children to ask questions, insist that the questions be asked properly, that the questioner be recognized and stand up properly, that questions be on the proper subject (one to which the teacher knows the answer), that questions not be silly ones, and so on and on.

Asking questions that the teacher cannot answer should be accepted as normal and desirable, coming out of a mutual searching for the truth. Too frequently, teachers become angry and punitive when asked questions that they cannot answer. During Thomas Edison's brief school career, the teacher never liked the kind of questions he asked. Poor Tom seemed to be unable to stop asking such questions and as a result spent many mornings sitting on the low stool in the corner. The climax came one morning when Tom noticed a river in Ohio that ran uphill. Tom asked the teacher how could water run up a hill. It was then that the teacher pounded on his desk and shouted, "Thomas Alva, you always ask entirely too many questions! You are addled!" (Guthridge, 1959). That was Thomas Edison's last day at school. Albert Einstein was also asked to withdraw from school because he asked so many questions that his teachers could not answer (Hammontree, 1961). Children need guidance in learning the skills of asking questions that enable them to find out the truth about things. In recent years, research and development projects have yielded findings that are helpful in accomplishing this task. For example, Suchman (1962) has developed and tested materials for teaching better inquiry skills. Maw and Maw (1966) have developed materials for understanding and encouraging curiosity among children. Torrance is currently experimenting with the use of pictures, stories, puppets, and other materials to develop higher-level questioning skills among pre-primary children.

Fundamental to the development of better questioning skills is the teacher's ability to be respectful of the questions children ask and to help them achieve the skills for finding the answers. Nothing is more rewarding to the child who asks a question than to find the answer. This does not mean that the teacher must answer the question immediately or answer it at all. Perhaps it would be a good rule never to tell a child something he can find out for himself. This does not mean that answering questions should be postponed. Teachers should learn how to enrich the moments between the asking of the question and finding an answer. The answer to good questions rarely comes all at once in a single fact. Usually, it comes in small facts. Before the question can be answered, these small facts must somehow be put together like a detective puts facts together to solve mysteries. This can be an exciting process, filled with built-in motivations. This is doubtless the reason why Crutchfield's (1966) use of mysteries to teach problem-solving skills to disadvantaged children has been so successful.

Making Your Own Summary

The following problem will give you a chance to summarize for yourself and apply the ideas presented in this chapter.

APATHY TOWARD READING IN THE FIRST GRADE

You are the teacher of twenty-six first-grade children who seem to have little enthusiasm for learning how to read or print. The youngsters are interested in numbers, and they enjoy any kind of bodily activity such as playing games or dancing; however, they appear to be usually indifferent to acquiring language skills. Inasmuch as the majority of your pupils come from lower income homes in which television is almost the only medium for obtaining contact with people outside the neighborhood, there is probably a good reason why your pupils do not see the urgency of learning to read and write. On the other hand, you have taught classes of six-year-old children in this neighborhood for five years, and your present class is by far the most apathetic group you have encountered.

In late September you had told yourself that the youngsters were not progressing as well as you had expected them to because they were "immature." Now it is the beginning of November and you are becoming somewhat dismayed by their indifference to the business of becoming literate. Most of the children simply are not excited about the prospect of being able to read. While they take pride in keeping the room neat and attractive and in caring for the animals and plants in the room, your pupils form letters carelessly and are obviously not fascinated by the mechanics of printing.

What plan of action might be followed to engender some enthusiasm for reading and writing in your class? First, though, what do you think the real problem is? What additional facts do you need? List on a separate sheet of paper the questions you would like to ask. On the basis of the above description, predict the answers to your questions.

Now, compare your predictions with the following additional information:

Your school is located in an industrial city whose population is estimated to be about 30,000. The building was originally designed to accommodate five hundred pupils, but there are over six hundred enrolled at present. There are four first-grade classrooms.

A number of energetic people spark your staff, but the turnover each year is rather high. Many teachers find it difficult to work in the school because a majority of the parents are indifferent about their children's education. Most of the parents are working-class people. A few children have fathers or mothers who are white-collar workers or proprietors of small businesses; none of the children has a parent whose occupation might be labeled professional. Your principal has a fine reputation for supporting his teachers and cooperating with them in their efforts to make them instructional programs more effective. He gets along well with the members of the community; his success in public relations, it is said, is the result of a realistic approach to his school's problems.

Given these facts, what do you think the problem really is?

Now try to develop at least twenty ideas for solving the problem as you have restated it. List them on a separate sheet of paper, drawing from the ideas presented in this chapter.

On what basis will you make your decision among the twenty ideas? Draw up a list of at least three criteria by which you will evaluate your ideas.

On the basis of your evaluations, which idea do you think has the best chance of engendering enthusiasm for reading?

Now, draw up a plan for carrying out this idea.

Finally, predict as accurately as you can what will happen if your idea is implemented.

REFERENCES

Binet, A. *Les Idées Modernes sur les Enfants.* Paris: E. Flammarion, 1909.

Boyer, A. "Reading and Creative Writing in a First Grade Classroom." In *Claremont College Reading Conference.* Claremont, Calif.: Claremont College, 1959. Pp. 23–33.

Bruner, J. S. "Learning and Thinking." *Harvard Educational Review,* 1959, **29,** 184–192.

Colvin, S. S. "Invention versus Form in English Composition: An Indicative Study." *Pedagogical Seminary*, 1902, **9**, 393–421.

Crutchfield, R. S. "Creative Thinking in Children: Its Teaching and Testing." In O. G. Brim, Jr., R. S. Crutchfield, and W. H. Holtzman. *Intelligence: Perspectives 1965*. New York: Harcourt, Brace & World, 1966.

Cunnington, B. F. and E. P. Torrance. *Imagi/Craft Series*. Boston: Ginn & Co., 1965.

Ferebee, J. D. "Learning Form through Creative Expression." *Elementary English*, 1950, **27**, 73–78.

Flanagan, D. "Creativity in Science." In P. Smith (ed.). *Creativity*. New York: Hastings House, 1959. Pp. 103–109.

Forbush, W. B. "The Social Pedagogy of Boyhood." *Pedagogical Seminary*, 1900, **7**, 307–346.

Froebel, F. (translated by H. Barnard). *Papers on Froebel's Kindergarten, with Suggestions of Principles and Methods of Child Culture*. Syracuse, N.Y.: C. W. Bardeen, Publisher, 1879.

Guthridge, S. *Tom Edison, Boy Inventor*. Indianapolis: Bobbs-Merrill, 1959.

Hammontree, M. *Albert Einstein: Young Thinker*. Indianapolis: Bobbs-Merrill, 1961.

Heys, F., Jr. "The Theme a Week Assumption: A Report of an Experiment." *English Journal*, 1962, **51**, 320–322.

Lewin, K. "Frontiers in Group Dynamics: Concept, Method and Reality in Social Science; Social Equilibria and Social Change." *Human Relations*, 1947, **1**, 5–41.

Lieberman, N. J. "Personality Traits in Adolescents: An Investigation of Playfulness-Nonplayfulness in the High School Setting." Brooklyn, N.Y.: Brooklyn College, 1967. Mimeographed.

Maslow, A. H. *Motivation and Personality*. New York: Harper & Row, 1954.

Maw, W. H. and E. W. Maw. *Personal and Social Variables Differentiating Children with High and Low Curiosity*. Newark, Del.: University of Delaware, 1966.

Myers, R. E. and E. P. Torrance. *Invitations to Thinking and Doing*. Boston: Ginn & Co., 1964.

Myers, R. E. and E. P. Torrance. *Can You Imagine?* Boston: Ginn & Co., 1965a.

Myers, R. E. and E. P. Torrance. *Invitations to Speaking and Writing Creatively*. Boston: Ginn & Co., 1965b.

Myers, R. E. and E. P. Torrance. *For Those Who Wonder*. Boston: Ginn & Co., 1966a.

Myers, R. E. and E. P. Torrance. *Plots, Puzzles, and Ploys*. Boston: Ginn & Co., 1966b.

O'Neill, M. *Hailstones and Halibut Bones*. Garden City, N.Y.: Doubleday & Co., 1961.

Patri, A. *The Questioning Child*. New York: Appleton-Century-Crofts, 1931.

Pines, M. *Revolution in Learning*. New York: Harper & Row, 1967.

Selye, H. "The Gift for Basic Research." In G. Z. F. Bereday and J. A. Lauwreys (eds.). *The Yearbook of Education*. New York: Harcourt, Brace & World, 1962. Pp. 399–408.

Shahn, B. "On Painting." In *The Creative Mind and Method*. Cambridge, Mass.: WGBH-FM, 1959. Pp. 20–21.

Suchman, R. J. *The Elementary School Training Program in Scientific Inquiry*. Urbana, Ill.: School of Education, University of Illinois, 1962.

Torrance, E. P. *Guiding Creative Talent*. Englewood Cliffs, N.J.: Prentice-Hall, Inc., 1962.

Torrance, E. P. *Mental Health and Constructive Behavior*. Belmont, Calif.: Wadsworth Publishing Company, 1965a.

Torrance, E. P. "Motivating Children with School Problems." In E. P. Torrance and R. D. Strom (eds.). *Mental Health and Achievement*. New York: John Wiley & Sons, 1965b. Pp. 338–353.

Torrance, E. P. *Torrance Tests of Creative Thinking: Norms-Technical Manual* (research ed.). Princeton, N.J.: Personnel Press, 1966.

CHAPTER 4 MUST

CREATIVE DEVELOPMENT

BE LEFT TO CHANCE?

Aware
Of their struggle
To win respect and grow,
You search for ways to help—for you
Care.

The Problem

Imagine that you are a fifth-grade teacher. A parent of one of your pupils complains to you by telephone that her daughter cannot spell. The parent protests that you are spending too much time on problem solving and creativity and not enough on spelling. She says, "Everyone knows that if a child is going to be creative it will come out anyway, so what's the use of trying to teach that?"

From what you know of the children in your previous classes and of the pupils of other teachers, both your class and the child are average in their spelling skills. When you look into the matter more deeply on the following day, you learn that your pupils are doing somewhat better than the average fifth-graders in the country. The girl about whom the complaint was made is actually achieving at a superior level in spelling. If standardized achievement-test norms are appropriate criteria, there is nothing to be alarmed about. Although the spelling of your pupils certainly might be improved in their written work, you just cannot see how you can spend more time on spelling since there are so many other things the children want to learn—things you believe are important for them to learn.

In which direction would you turn? Would you try deliberately to improve the quality of your pupils' spelling by devoting more time to spelling and let other things go? Or, would you try to think of ways of improving spelling without cutting down on other parts of your program? How could you make parents aware of the improvement in spelling, if it does occur?

ADDITIONAL BACKGROUND INFORMATION

Perhaps more ideas will occur to you, if additional information about the school is considered.

Your school is located in a suburb of a moderately large city. The parents of the children who attend the school, almost without exception, expect their children to enter college. They are very anxious that their children show evidence of high achievement in school. Recently many parents have expressed great dissatisfaction with the school system. Most of their complaints center around the contention that the minds of the children in elementary school and junior high school are not being trained adequately. The more outspoken of the parents maintain that their children's lack of skills in spelling and arithmetic is shocking. Your principal is a person who has ridden out other storms with equanimity and patience, but he is obviously concerned about the criticisms which have been directed at the nature and quality of the instruction in his school. Your fellow teachers are somewhat upset by the attacks, and most of them are confused about what they should do to improve their instructional programs. Almost all of them believe that one important goal is to develop in children the motivations and skills for lifelong learning and creative thinking.

CAN SKILLS OF CREATIVE THINKING BE TAUGHT?

Do you think that these teachers are justified in their stand? Can the skills of creative thinking be developed, or is this something that should and must be left to chance: Is it possible to teach the skills of creative thinking?

Some of the Issues

Just a few years ago, it was commonly believed that creative thinking, the production of original ideas, inventions, and scientific discoveries had to be left to chance. Indeed many people still think so! However, deliberate methods of creative problem solving (Osborn, 1957; Clark, 1958; Gordon, 1961; Parnes, 1967) have amassed an amazing record of inventions, scientific discoveries, and other creative accomplishments. Experiments involving these deliberate methods of improving creative behavior have likewise been convincing (Maltzman, 1960; Parnes and Meadow, 1960; Torrance, 1961; Ray, 1967). In our own work we have consistently found that deliberate methods of creative thinking can be taught from the pre-primary through the graduate school years. Almost always students have improved markedly, sometimes dramatically, their ability to produce original and useful solutions to problems. As we see it, the evidence is strong that creative thinking does not have to be left to chance!

Since the major objective of this book is to help teachers in their efforts to aid children in achieving their full potentialities, we feel that we must come to grips with this issue: "Must creative development be left to chance?" Furthermore, much of this book is predicated on the conviction that creative development *does not* have to be left to chance. Therefore, we feel that we should set forth some of our reasons for this conviction.

For years, students of creative development and behavior have observed that five-year-olds lose much of their curiosity, imagination, and excitement about learning; that nine-year-olds become greatly concerned about conformity to peer pressures and give up many of their creative activities; and that beginning junior high students show new kinds of concern for conformity to behavioral norms with the result that their thinking becomes more obvious, commonplace, and safe. In 1930, Andrews published data to document the drop at about age five. As early as 1900, the drops at about ages nine and thirteen had been documented and have been further supported in *The Minnesota Studies of Creative Thinking: 1958–66* (Torrance, 1967a).

Those who have commented on the drops in creative thinking ability and creative behavior in general have almost always assumed that these were purely developmental phenomena. For example, Wilt (1959) observes that creativity may all but take a holiday at about age nine or ten and, after the crisis has passed, returns only for a few. She concludes that about all that can be done is to keep open the gates for its return. Rarely, however, has anyone taken a contrary stand until recently. One of these rare individuals, Susan Nichols Pulsifer (1963), takes such a stand concerning the abandonment of creativity at about age five. She maintains that it is not a natural developmental change but is due to the sharp man-made change which confronts the five-year-old and impels him by its rules and regulations.

Torrance has also been unwilling to accept the assumption that the severe drops in measured creative thinking abilities are purely developmental phenomena which must be accepted as unchangeable. In his longitudinal studies (1968), it seemed obvious that many children needlessly sacrificed their creativity, especially in the fourth grade, and that many of them did not recover as they continued through school. It also seemed that many problems of school dropouts, delinquency, and mental illness have their roots in the same forces that cause these creativity drops.

Some of the Evidence

CLASSES WHERE CREATIVITY DOESN'T TAKE A HOLIDAY

It will certainly take a great deal more research than is now available before many people will be convinced about this matter. Personally, we consider the accumulated evidence rather convincing. One of the first positive bits of evidence—small, but impressive —came from experiences in studying the creative development of two fourth-grade classes taught by teachers who are highly successful in establishing creative relationships with their pupils and who give them many opportunities to acquire information and skills in creative ways. There was no fourth-grade slump in these classes, either in measured creative-thinking abilities or in participation in creative activities.

These two teachers, one a man and the other a woman, manifested many qualities which we believed might possibly account for their results. Both of them clearly found great joy in teaching and in interacting with children. They both showed an amazing understanding of the thinking of their pupils. They knew some of the most intimate details of the children's strivings and stresses, apparently without making special efforts to obtain such information. Furthermore, they could see immediately the relationships between their pupils' creative productions and their strivings and stresses. At times, these two classes would become quite noisy, but both teachers could obtain quiet and order almost instantly. In fact, one of them used the word, "Freeze!" to obtain instantaneous quiet and stillness whenever the situation called for it. She could then give instructions and reorganize the task of the group with little waste of energy.

DIVERSE PATTERNS OF DEVELOPMENT

Although the cues derived from observations concerning these two outstanding teachers were useful in learning how to foster creative development at any age, they were not sufficient. We did not grasp some of the most powerful meanings of this experience until we began analyzing data obtained from several cultures outside the United States and from a segregated Negro school (Torrance, 1967b). For some time, Torrance had felt that he had to know how the creative-thinking abilities develop and express themselves in other cultures. Meanwhile, he had continued to try to find out in just what ways children continued to grow at the various stages at which declines in creativity occur. For one thing, he found experimentally that during the fourth grade most children stop relying upon adults for judgment and information and start relying upon their peers. In another study, he found that their interest in judging and evaluating increases. In an experiment to evaluate the relative effectiveness of different ways of stimulating children to compose songs, one of Torrance's students (Weideman, 1961) found that fourth-graders produced fewer songs than children in any other grade from first through sixth. However, the fourth-graders were more interested than any other group in judging songs which the other grades had composed. Furthermore, their judgments agreed more closely with those of the music experts than did those of any other class.

Torrance was still anxious, however, to find out whether there is the same pattern of development in other cultures that had been found in the United States. He believed that this information would help to indicate whether or not the drops in creativity, such as the one at the fourth grade, are natural or man-made. He had reasoned that if the drop in the fourth grade is due largely to increasing peer pressures to conformity that he would find a different pattern of development in less peer-oriented cultures.

As results were obtained from studies in different cultures (Torrance, 1967b), the developmental curve was found to take on a different shape in each culture. Furthermore, the characteristics of the developmental curve can be explained logically in terms of the way the culture treats curiosity and creative needs.

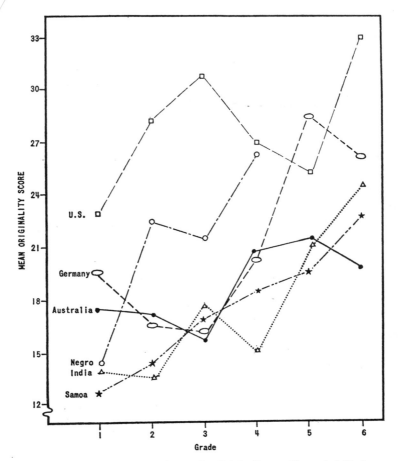

Figure 1. Developmental Curves for Originality on Nonverbal Tasks for Six Cultural Groups. From E. P. Torrance, *Education and the Creative Potential* (Minneapolis: University of Minnesota Press, 1963), p. 76.

For purposes of illustration, let us examine in Figure 1 the developmental curves for figural originality in the United States, United States (Negro), Western Samoa, Australia, Germany, and India. There are no drops in the developmental curve for Samoan subjects. The level of originality begins in the first grade at the lowest level of any of the cultures studied but the growth is continuous from year to year. The second greatest continuity in development is shown by the United States Negro sample. Through the fourth grade, German and Australian children seem to show about the same level and pattern of development. Pressures towards standardization and conformity apparently occur quite early and continue for the Australian child but not for the German one. The overall pattern of growth among the children in India is much the same as in the United States, especially in the mission schools and public schools. (Incidentally, the level of the children of India is considerably higher on the verbal than on the figural tasks, while the reverse is true of the United States Negro sample and of the Western Samoan sample.)

Since the development of originality of thinking shows greater continuity in Western Samoa than in any of the other cultures studied, let us look further at these data. Margaret Mead's (1939) pioneering work in the 1920's, reports of modern observers, and our data support a picture of high cultural continuity and suppression of creativity and independence of thought almost from birth and especially during the early years.

According to Mead, "keep still," "sit still," "keep your mouth shut," and "stop that noise" are thoroughly ingrained into the Samoan child. He is not even permitted to cry! He cannot even experiment with his voice to find out what sounds he can make. The older children have responsibility for disciplining the younger ones, so conformity is taught almost from birth. Even today, Samoan teachers value quietness greatly. Mead points out that Samoans were imitative and reproductive in their crafts rather than creative. Likewise, Samoan children today excel in the craftsmanship of their drawings, when given the Goodenough Human Drawing Test or Buck's House-Tree-Person Test. Their drawings are reproductive rather than creative. The characteristic MOST valued by Samoan teachers in their pupils is REMEMBERING WELL.

Both Mead and modern observers of Samoa have stressed the role in their culture of the extended family, the participation of all ages in the life of the community and the mixing of all ages even in school. Mead used these facts and the continuities in regard to sex in explaining why Samoan adolescents did not experience the periods of emotional upset and personality disturbance common among adolescents in the United States. In today's Samoan schools, there is no strict age segregation, and a wide range of ages is found in a single grade, especially in the remote government schools.

The characteristics ranked highest by Samoan teachers on the Ideal Pupil Checklists are these: remembers well, healthy, and always asking questions. "Always asking questions," however, has quite a different meaning for the Samoan teacher than for the United States teacher. The Samoan teacher does not have in mind the searching, inquiring kind of question, but the dependency kind of question, "Is this what you want?" "Is this right?" It was even difficult to administer the tests of creative thinking. Samoan pupils continually asked, "Is this all right?" "Is this what you want?" and the like.

Samoan teachers ranked the following characteristics LOWER than did the other cultures: adventurousness, initiative, curiosity, determination, energy, independence in judgment, industriousness, self-confidence, self-sufficiency, sincerity, thoroughness, and versatility. They placed a HIGHER value than did teachers in other cultures on such characteristics as these: being a good guesser, competitiveness, promptness, haughtiness, physical strength, quietness, and liking to work alone. In general this pattern of values may logically be expected to support cultural continuity and a generally low degree of creativity.

In the remote villages of Samoa, the school is somewhat modified but the culture of the village remains almost untouched. *There is little discontinuity in life and development even in the schools, however, but a number of discontinuities are beginning to creep into Samoan culture through the mission schools.* Many of the taboos introduced by the mission schools are in conflict with the traditions of the culture.

The effects of these emerging discontinuities are reflected in the developmental curves for creative thinking, if the data from the more urban mission schools are separated from those of the more remote government ones. Although the degree of creativity is lower in the more remote village schools, there is no break in the continuity of creative development. In the mission schools, there is a higher level of creativity but a sizeable drop at about the end of the third grade. Thus, the introduction of cultural and educational discontinuities seems to be associated with a higher level of creative functioning, discontinuity in creative development, and personality disturbance.

REDUCING DISCONTINUITIES IN EDUCATION

Since many of the ideas that will be presented in this book involve the reduction of discontinuities that interfere with creative development at all stages of growth, let us review some of the common discontinuities at the most critical stages and examine a few instances in which these discontinuities have been reduced. An understanding of many of the discontinuities in personality development can be obtained from a review of almost any text in developmental psychology which attempts to set up stages of development. At each new stage, new demands are made and new patterns of behavior are required in order to cope with them. A number of additional discontinuities have become evident through our own research.

Among the five- and six-year-olds, we have observed that concerns about sex appropriateness and emphasis on sex differences become tremendously inhibiting. For example, boys at this age frequently refused to offer suggestions for improving a nurse kit and some girls similarly refused to offer any suggestions for improving a toy fire truck. Some of the more creative boys, however, first transformed the nurse kit to a doctor's kit. After this, it was quite acceptable and respectable to think of ideas for improving it. Some children similarly refused to read materials which they considered inappropriate to their sex role. Thus, whole areas of experience become taboo, and thinking is thereby inhibited, even paralyzed.

Many kindergarten and first-grade children are inhibited in thinking because they have been warned harshly by parents and teachers that they must eliminate fantasy. Although we are interested in developing a sound type of creativity, we believe that it is necessary to keep fantasy alive until the child's mental development is such that he can engage in this sound type of realistic, truth-searching creative thinking. Frequently, in individual testing, it becomes apparent that a child has thought of an idea. He will smile or grin broadly and begin to speak, only to let the smile change to a pained frown or sad look and the eager utterance to fade into silence.

We have given more attention to the discontinuities that occur at about age nine when the child reaches the fourth grade than to any other stage of development. Indeed, we have discussed this problem with a number of gifted sixth-graders who pointed out many influences which they feel caused them to become less imaginative, curious, and original in their thinking at about this time. They would usually begin something like this: "Well, when we went into the fourth grade, we were half-through elementary school and they expected us to act more grown up." As such a discussion would continue, they would almost always point out that in the fourth grade they had to begin sitting in orderly rows in the classroom and keeping their feet on the floor. Classroom activities immediately became more organized and formal. They received credit only for what they put on paper. The animals in their stories no longer talked. Usually, they had to go to another building, upstairs in a two-story building, or to a different wing. They had to start doing written homework and their papers were expected to be neat with no smudges. The subject matter became different; they began having lessons in geography, history, and the like. They began participating in student government and serving as monitors of their fellow students' behavior.

As Torrance tested children of this age, he was impressed by their inhibiting preoccupation with safety, prevention, and fear of making mental leaps. The problem, "What are all of the possible things Mother Hubbard could have done when she found no bone in the cupboard for her dog?" was easy for younger children but quite difficult for the nine-year-old. The nine-year-old is so preoccupied with the idea that Old Mother Hubbard should have prevented this predicament that he is unwilling to think of how she could have gotten herself out of it. They want to stick close to the stimuli and are extremely guarded in making mental leaps. In the Product Improvement Task this tendency seemed to stem from inhibitions concerning cost, in many cases. Uncertainty expressions became frequent. These phenomena have been observed and documented by numerous investigators. For example, L'Abate (1957) found that nine-year-olds showed a greater use of "uncertainty expressions" than younger children. Professional workers in the field of remedial vision also tell us that they have observed this uncertainty in their work with children of this age. When given the Rorschach Ink Blot Test, these children will say that they are not as imaginative as other children and that they cannot make anything out of the blot. They will practice visual-training exercises endlessly but fail to make progress, continuing to be unsure, hesitant, and slow in their perceptions.

In working with intermediate teachers, it has also become apparent that many intermediate-grade teachers live in quite a different world from their colleagues in the primary grades. Their education in college has been different, and their methods of instruction are different. Many intermediate teachers admit frankly that they have no idea about what goes on in the primary grades.

In our studies of the ways in which teachers talked with children about their creative writing, teachers in the intermediate grades differed markedly from their colleagues who taught in the primary grades. The intermediate-grade teachers were far more preoccupied with correctness and form and were less willing to sacrifice these for creative values than the primary teachers.

As a youngster enters junior high school, he usually has to go to another building, frequently in another part of the town or city. The school is usually larger, and there are different teachers for each subject. There is much emphasis on promptness, and tardy slips have to be dealt with. Extremes in dress and appearance are discouraged—that is, deviations from what "all of the others" are wearing. There are new pressures and anxieties concerning the approval of the opposite sex. Pressures to be well-rounded socially and athletically are also intensified.

For most youngsters, the transition from junior high to senior high school is marked by greater continuity than from elementary school to junior high school. Apparently, however, there are some discontinuities introduced into the senior high school at about the senior year. Since high school seniors are faced in their senior year with the immediacy of the transition to college, work, or military service, the imminence of these may introduce discontinuities. There are new demands for grown-up behavior, sanctions against regression to childish thinking and behavior, and new uncertainties.

As, with imaginative, creative teachers, we have explored the problems associated with the discontinuities in creative development, we have found that many of them have devised ingenious ways for reducing the educational and cultural discontinuities of the particular group with which they work. Frequently, however, they have had to violate existing school rules and policies in order to carry out these procedures.

Deliberate Methods of Creative Problem Solving

In recent years, a number of deliberate, disciplined methods of creative problem solving have been developed for use in groups. Much experimentation and practical experience have now accumulated concerning some of these methods. The application of these deliberate, disciplined methods increases the chances, but does not guarantee, that truly original, creative solutions will be produced. However, when such methods are not used, rarely does anything more than marginal improvement result. It has also been shown that it is possible to teach these deliberate, disciplined methods of creative problem solving.

Here are brief descriptions of three of the generally most successful and widely used of these disciplined methods of group problem solving.

Creative Problem Solving

The disciplined, deliberate method known as "creative problem solving" is undoubtedly the most widely used of these methods. This method was originated by Alex F. Osborn (1948, 1957) and further developed by Parnes (1962, 1967) and other members of the Creative Education Foundation. The method is sometimes associated with "group brain-storming," one of the several aspects of the creative problem-solving process as formulated by Osborn and Parnes. The process actually follows quite closely the definition in Chapter 2 (p. 22).

SETTING THE CONDITIONS

It has become increasingly clear that even highly educated adults frequently do not possess either the skills or the attitudes necessary for the successful application of creative problem solving. In fact, these skills and attitudes sometimes appear to come more naturally to children than to adults. Training programs, however, seem to be fairly successful in developing essential attitudes and skills in adults. Among the more important of the facilitating conditions are these: warm-up and involvement in the problem, an innovative attitude, a search for new implications, procedures for removing the "brakes" on thinking and idea production, a creative climate with psychological safety and freedom, inhibition of impulsive action, breaking habit-responses, and the like.

STEP 1. SENSING PROBLEMS AND CHALLENGES

The first deliberate step in the disciplined approach to creative problem solving is the sensing of problems and challenges. This step of the process is set in motion by encountering a perplexing situation. Sometimes the perplexing situation is encountered by the group or by certain members of the group. At other times, it is necessary for someone to make the group aware of the perplexing problem and recognize it as a challenge. In the classroom, children may encounter perplexing situations, ambiguities and uncertainties, paradoxes, gaps in knowledge, and the like. Or, it may be necessary for the teacher to make children aware of these puzzling phenomena and to develop and heighten concern about the problem.

STEP 2. RECOGNIZING THE REAL PROBLEM

The second step in the creative problem-solving process is recognizing the real problem. Involved in this step is the search for facts about the problem or puzzling situation. Usually this produces what Parnes (1967) calls the "big mess"—a confusing array of facts, difficulties, and gaps in information. Sometimes, the search for additional facts is necessary. Then efforts are begun to synthesize "the mess" by redefining the problem. This is done by asking what the basic objectives are, searching for broader and broader restatements of the problem, changing the wording of the statement of the problem, trying to get at the essence of the problem, and finally breaking the problem down into subproblems for solution.

In the classroom, this step may involve pulling information from the experiences of the children, information contained in the textbook, searching for additional information in reference sources, or even in experimentation. It may involve the collection of original data or any other method of fact finding. During this period, it is difficult to maintain openness and maintain the deferred judgment necessary for a thorough job of fact finding and problem definition.

STEP 3. PRODUCING ALTERNATIVE SOLUTIONS

The next step in the creative process is the production of a large supply of alternative solutions. During this phase, it is especially important to defer judgment and remove the various blocks to creative thinking—habits, convention, and conformity. Group members must recognize that "silly" ideas can be very useful and should follow the four well-known rules of group brainstorming:

Criticism is ruled out. This does not mean that criticism is ruled out altogether. It simply means that criticism is suspended during this phase of the process. One of Osborn's fundamental contentions was that creative thinking and evaluative thinking cannot occur very effectively at the same time.

Free-wheeling is welcomed. The wilder the ideas the better. Offbeat, impractical, silly ideas may trigger in other group members a practical, breakthrough idea which might not otherwise occur.

Quantity is wanted. This rule is supported by data indicating that the greater the number of ideas produced, the greater the likelihood of useful, original ideas.

Combination and improvement are sought. Group members are encouraged to hitchhike on the ideas of others in the group, to suggest how ideas offered by other group members can be turned into better ideas, or how two or more ideas can be combined into a still better idea, and the like.

In addition, the production of ideas is further spurred by the use of questions, free association, analogies, systematic scanning and combination of possibilities, as well as by deliberately going beyond the obvious, forcing relationships, using all of the senses, and the like.

The following is an example of one list of idea-spurring questions:

PUT TO OTHER USES? New ways to use as is? Other uses if modified?

ADAPT? What else is like this? What other ideas does this suggest?

SCAMPER

MODIFY? Change meaning, color, motion, sound, odor, taste, form.

MAGNIFY? What to add? Greater frequency? Stronger? Larger? Plus ingredient? Multiply?

MINIFY? What to subtract? Eliminate? Smaller? Lighter? Slower? Split up? Less frequent?

SUBSTITUTE? Who else instead? What else instead? Other place? Other time?

REARRANGE? Other layout? Other sequence? Change pace?

REVERSE? Opposites? Turn it backwards? Turn it upside down? Turn it inside out?

COMBINE? How about a blend, an assortment? Combine purposes? Combine ideas?

STEP 4. EVALUATING IDEAS

When the members of a group are able successfully to defer judgment, all kinds of ideas are usually produced; and their evaluation becomes a major task. To select the best ideas, it is necessary to develop evaluative criteria—objective standards for selecting the most promising ideas. These may include such things as cost, time required, usefulness, practicality, social acceptance, and other considerations. The most elegant solutions take into consideration a variety of criteria. The development of criteria is itself a creative challenge, according to Parnes (1967).

The application of criteria enables the group to select its most promising ideas. In some cases, several of the most promising ideas can be applied. In other cases, it is necessary to select one idea and then implement it.

STEP 5. PREPARING TO PUT IDEAS INTO USE   *selling ideas*

The evaluation of ideas and the selection of the most promising idea or ideas for solution does not end the creative problem-solving process. After a promising idea has been found, there is a challenge to make it acceptable. In the process of implementing the idea, further changes may be necessary. Idea production is called for again in developing plans for carrying out the idea, and for selling or promoting it. It may be necessary to tailor the idea for special groups to make it attractive to them and to gain acceptance for it. It is necessary to think of the possible consequences of the application of the idea, as well as the possible obstacles to its implementation. All of these considerations should result in a successful plan of action.

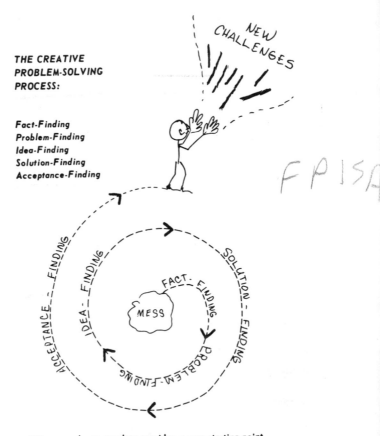

THE CREATIVE
PROBLEM-SOLVING
PROCESS:

Fact-Finding
Problem-Finding
Idea-Finding
Solution-Finding
Acceptance-Finding

"Every goal man reaches provides a new starting point, and the sum of all man's days is just a beginning."

Lewis Mumford

Figure 2.   Typical Flow of the Creative Problem-Solving Process. Used by permission from S. J. Parnes, *Creative Behavior Workbook* (New York: Charles Scribner's Sons, 1967).

Figure 2 summarizes the typical flow of the creative problem-solving process as conceptualized by Parnes (1967).

SKILLS REQUIRED

A variety of intellectual and nonintellectual skills are necessary for the successful operation of the creative problem-solving process and these are learned largely through practice, with guidance usually necessary. Among the necessary skills are making accurate observation, becoming sensitively aware of surroundings, fully utilizing all senses, shifting points of view, questioning, making both deliberate and random association, making predictions, organizing and reorganizing patterns, taking careful inventories, manipulating ideas, and making use of analogy.

We have found that these methods are quite successful with disadvantaged children. It is important, however, that work be done in small groups and that the creative problem-solving experiences have meaningful consequences.

Sociodrama as a Creative Problem-Solving Process

Sociodrama at its best is a group creative problem-solving approach, and the problem-solving process in sociodrama can be as deliberate and as disciplined as any other problem-solving approach. The general principles of sociodrama were formulated by Moreno (1946) and have been elaborated and refined by Moreno himself, Haas (1948), Hansen (1948), Klein (1956), and others.

Sociodrama can be carried on in the ordinary classroom or in practically any other physical setting, if the director or teacher can create the proper atmosphere. Some children find it easier to identify with a role if they are furnished with a single, simple, stage prop. Some teachers accumulate a variety of old hats, caps, bonnets, helmets, shoes, coats, and the like. The director must be imaginative in transforming one desk and a chair into a ship, say, and the same desk and chair at another time into a jet aircraft.

The objective is to examine a group or social problem by dramatic methods. Multiple solutions may be proposed and tested out sociodramatically. As new insights are developed, these too can be practiced and evaluated.

A number of things can be done to produce readiness for sociodrama. It is frequently a good idea to use several periods prior to any mention of sociodrama for free and open discussions of common problems. Generate as much spontaneity as possible in these discussions. This is a part of the process of becoming aware of puzzling situations, conflict situations, and the like. The problem selected for sociodramatic solution should be one that the children have identified as important to them or at least one that has direct implications for most of the members of the class.

The steps in the problem-solving process in sociodrama are quite similar to those outlined in the preceding section on creative problem solving.

STEP 1. DEFINING THE PROBLEM

The director or teacher should explain to the children that they are going to try an unrehearsed skit. It's a good idea to begin by asking a series of questions to help define the problem and establish the conflict situations. At this point, the teacher does not accept any responses as answers but asks other questions to stimulate or provoke further thinking.

STEP 2. ESTABLISHING A SITUATION (CONFLICT)

Out of all of the responses, the teacher or the group describes a conflict situation in objective and understandable terms. No indication is given as to the direction that the conflict resolution should take.

STEP 3. CASTING CHARACTERS (PROTAGONISTS)

Participation in roles should be voluntary. The director, however, must be alert in observing the audience for the emergence of new roles and giving encouragement to the timid child who really wants to participate. Rarely should roles be assigned in advance. Several members of the class may play a particular role, each trying a different approach to the solution of the problem.

STEP 4. BRIEFING AND WARMING UP OF ACTORS AND OBSERVERS

It is usually a good idea to give the actors a few minutes to plan the setting and to agree upon a direction. While the actors are out of the room, the director or teacher should warm up the observers to the possible alternatives. When the actors return, they can be asked to describe the setting and establish more fully their role identities. This warms up both the audience and the actors. This procedure, however, should be rather brief.

STEP 5. ACTING OUT THE SITUATION

Acting out the situation may be a matter of seconds or it may last for ten or fifteen minutes. As a teacher gains experience as a sociodrama director, he will be able to use supplementary production techniques for digging deeper, increasing the number of alternatives, getting thinking out of a "rut," and getting children to make bigger mental leaps in finding better solutions. The director should watch for areas of conflict among the children, not giving clues or hints concerning the desired outcome. If the acting bogs down because a child becomes speechless, the director may encourage the actor by saying, "Now, what would he do?" or turning to another actor and saying, "What happens now?" If this does not work, it may be necessary to stop or "cut" the action.

An effort should be made to maintain a psychologically safe atmosphere and to give freedom to experiment with new ideas and new behavior. It is in this way that children "see and feel" other ways of "behaving."

STEP 6. CUTTING THE ACTION

The action should be stopped or "cut" whenever the actors fall hopelessly out of role, or block seriously and are unable to continue; whenever the episode comes to a conclusion; or whenever the director sees an opportunity to stimulate thinking to a higher level of creativity by using a different production technique or moving to a different episode. A list of some of these production techniques and brief descriptions of them will be given later in this section.

STEP 7. DISCUSSING AND ANALYZING THE SITUATION AND BEHAVIOR

There are many approaches to discussing and analyzing the situation and behavior in the sociodrama. Applying the creative-thinking model, it would seem desirable to formulate some criteria to use in discussing and evaluating the situation and the behavior among the actors and observers. In any case, this should be a rather controlled type of discussion wherein the director tries to help the group redefine the problem and/or see the various possible solutions indicated by the action.

STEP 8. MAKING PLANS FOR FURTHER TESTING OF IDEAS FOR NEW BEHAVIOR

There are in use a variety of practices concerning planning for further testing of ideas generated for new and improved behavior resulting from a sociodrama. If there is time or if there are to be subsequent sessions, the new ideas can be tested in a new sociodrama or a continuation of the original sociodrama. Or, the plans may be related directly to applications outside of the classroom.

In addition to developing creative-thinking abilities and developing skills in problem solving, sociodrama may result in other desirable outcomes such as:

1. Profiting from experience without "paying for it" or suffering unduly from mistakes.
2. Presenting socially accepted solutions, additional alternatives.
3. Clarifying distorted concepts, developing social skills and attitudes, and the like.
4. Developing oral language.
5. Giving the teacher insight into the thinking and learning problems of the children.

Some children who have great difficulty in demonstrating their creativity in writing, or any of the expressive arts, may find in sociodrama a method in which they can show their ability. Many people who work with disadvantaged children believe that sociodrama is an especially good medium for such children. It is especially adapted to their physical, concrete way of learning.

SOCIODRAMA PRODUCTION TECHNIQUES

A variety of production techniques have been developed by Moreno (1945) and his associates. Some of them are especially good in freeing actors and observers to produce more creative ideas for solutions. The following production techniques have been especially useful in our own work:

Direct Presentation Technique. The children are asked to act out some problem situation, new situation, conflict situation, or the like related to the statement of and/or solution to the problem under study.

Soliloquy Techniques. One actor may engage in a monologue concerning his silent, unverbalized reactions in the situation. Or the technique may involve a portrayal by side dialogues and silent actions, of hidden thoughts and feelings, parallel with overt thoughts and actions. Soliloquy techniques are especially useful in producing original solutions when thinking is blocked by emotional reactions.

Double Technique. One of the actors in the conflict situation is supplied with a double who is placed side by side with the actor and interacts with the actor as "himself." The double tries to develop an identity with the actor in conflict. By bringing out the actor's "other self," the double helps the actor achieve a new and higher level of creative functioning. New and better solutions frequently arise from this interaction. The Actor-Double situation is usually set following the use of the Direct Presentation Technique after the actor has withdrawn from the conflict. He may be imagining himself alone in his room, walking alone in the woods, walking alone on the street, or the like.

Multiple Double Technique. This is an especially useful technique for bringing different points of view to bear on a conflict situation. The actor in the conflict situation is on stage with several doubles of himself. Each portrays another part of the actor in conflict (as he is now, as he was when he was younger, etc.).

Mirror Technique. In this technique, another actor represents the original actor in the conflict situation, copying his behavior patterns and showing him "as if in a mirror" how other people experience him. This technique may help the actor leap emotional blocks to produce better solutions to the conflict situation.

Role-Reversal Technique. In this technique, two actors in the conflict situation (the protagonists) exchange roles—a mother becomes a child and a child becomes a mother; a teacher becomes a pupil and a pupil becomes a teacher. Distortion of "the other" may be brought to the surface, explored, and corrected in action, and new solutions may be evolved.

Future Projections Technique. The actors show how they think the conflict will shape up in the future.

Auxiliary-World Technique. The entire world of the actor in conflict is restructured through a series of "acts" or portrayals of episodes in his world. Each of these acts should represent some part of his world that influences his behavior and has consequences for the resolution of the conflict situation.

Riessman (1964) and others who have studied the learning problems of disadvantaged children have observed that they are quite articulate in role-playing situations, in spite of the fact that they are quite inarticulate in the usual formal school situations. If the deprivation has been serious, however, it may be necessary at first to make certain modifications in the standard production techniques described in this chapter.

A special form of the creative problem-solving sociodrama for use with disadvantaged preschool children has been reported by Smilansky (1968). She calls it sociodramatic play and has found that it has aided severely disadvantaged children in coping with the demands of the school. In sociodramatic play, as in most other creative ways of learning, the child is able to draw upon whatever experiences he has had. In doing this, he plays a role with his peers. His social experiences and observations are combined in an interaction with other children. Some of the verbal interaction is imitation of adult talk and an integral part of role playing. Some of it involves the discussions necessary to plan and sustain the cooperative play. Thus, it includes both imitative and imaginative elements.

Smilansky found that one of the most striking things about the behavior of disadvantaged children is the lack of sequence in their activities and conversation. She reports that such children tend either to stick to one activity without elaborating it or to jump from one activity to another disconnected one. They seemed to be unable to develop a theme, a thought, or game. Smilansky's research reveals growth in these and other aspects of behavior through the use of so-ciodramatic play.

Torrance, in his work with disadvantaged black children, has developed a special form of psychodramatic play called "Magic Net" and has used it with children ranging from age five to age thirteen. In using a fairly traditional approach to creative dramatics with these children, he had found that they exhibited strong feelings of fear, either refusing to attempt roles or unable to take roles with any degree of reality and imagination. The "Magic Net," which consists of pieces of 36 x 72-inch nylon net in various colors, was then used to create an atmosphere of magic in which the children could imaginatively become whatever they wanted to become. They were asked in turn to stand, walk, and dance like the person, animal, or supernatural being that they wanted to become.

In the "Magic Net" game, about ten children were given pieces of net and invited to choose whatever role they desired. They were then asked to "feel" themselves into these roles in various ways. Next, the entire group would be invited to make up a story, using the roles chosen by the actors wearing the "Magic Net." The story is enacted as it is told by the audience. Usually, one story teller begins a story and others continue it. In some cases, it has been found helpful to give the story teller a "Magic Net" to overcome his self-consciousness and to identify him clearly.

A notable characteristic among both the younger and older disadvantaged children was the tendency to choose the same role that their peers had chosen. If one girl chose to be a queen, the other girls would also choose to be queens and the boys would choose to be kings. They seemed to have an extremely strong need for the support of their peers, for a co-experiencing of roles. Thus, stories were created with five queens and five kings, or with five witches and five old men. Even when a child dared to choose a unique role, it was sometimes necessary to reinforce him with other children in the same role. On one occasion, Pamela, an extremely timid six-year-old, chose to be a bear in a princess story. Neither the magic of the net nor the director's encouragement were powerful enough to enable her to play the role of the bear. The magic came when the director assigned three aggressive boys to be bears and to support her in her role. Then she became a bear with zest. The graduate student who was working with Pamela commented as follows concerning her behavior on that day:

"Pamela had been so quiet and had not been a part of the creative drama, dance, song, or play until today. Then she was given a magic net and decided to be a bear. She was too timid and withdrawn to be a good bear, even with encouragement. Dr. Torrance, realizing this, reinforced her with some more bear children. She became an excellent bear. She overcame some of her shyness and began to interact with the group, not just in play acting. Her success seemed to change her whole self-image. Pamela in her quiet voice entered into the group problem-finding game and gave some very intelligent problems. She was anxious to participate and contribute to the group. . . . I saw a sense of achievement in her approach.

"Earlier I could not get her to concentrate and study the picture when she did the Picture Interpretation Test. She would answer questions without studying the picture. But, today, she would look at pictures and study them. She was able to make up an entire story of 'Smokey Bear' from the pictures. I was amazed that she knew so much. . . .

"Her self-image is very poor, maybe because of her sense of failure in the first grade. But the one feeling of success at being a bear and Dr. Torrance's congratulations changed her self-opinion. She was much more self-assured after that in her discussions with me. I found today that she is far more intelligent than I had dreamed. She lacks confidence and being unsure and inhibited can be taken for signs of a low I.Q. But when the inhibition is broken, you can see that she is not dull but too afraid to exert and show her abilities."

For use with pre-primary children Torrance has recently devised an extension of the "Magic Net" technique to the use of puppets and the puppet theater. The children are asked to assign roles to their puppets and the story teller is supplied with a "Magic Net." The first story teller relates an episode which is enacted immediately. The next story teller takes up the predicament where the first one left it and this in turn is enacted. During the early stage, mimicry is used without speech. Later, dialogue can be used.

Synectics Group Approach

The synectics group approach to creative problem solving has been described by W. J. J. Gordon (1961), George M. Prince (1968), and others. The term "synectics" is from the Greek and means joining together of different and apparently irrelevant elements. The synectics group approach seeks to integrate creatively a number of diverse individuals into a problem-stating and problem-solving group. Its purpose is to increase the chances of success in problem-stating, problem-solving situations.

The developers of this approach maintain that creative efficiency can be markedly increased if people understand the psychological processes by which they operate. They further maintain that emotional components are more important than the rational in creative production. Thus, it is these emotional, irrational elements that must be understood in order to increase chances of success in a problem-solving situation. They admit that ideas must stand the test of logic but that genuinely creative, breakthrough ideas do not occur as the result of logical reasoning.

In the early experimentation of the synectics groups, the experimenters found that useful, original, breakthrough ideas occurred when certain psychological states existed in the members of the group. The experimenters identified such psychological states as involvement-detachment, deferment, speculation, play, and the like. Although they experienced difficulty in teaching groups to develop these psychological states, they did learn, however, that these states occurred when they did things to make the strange familiar or the familiar strange. Three mechanisms of play seem to be especially useful for this purpose:

Play with words, with meanings and definitions. Gordon (1961) offers the example of playing with definitions of "open" in inventing a can opener.

Play with pushing a fundamental law or basic scientific concept to its limits. For example (Gordon, 1961), in one instance, a synectics group postulated a universe in which water runs uphill. This might be described as a "just suppose" technique.

Play with metaphor. Of the three mechanisms of play, play with metaphor has proved to be most useful. In the synectics approach, metaphor is defined as an expressed or implied comparison

H needs metaphor ANALOGY

which simultaneously produces intellectual illumination and emotional excitement. Metaphor seems logical and scientific since it focuses on a similarity of relations or of functions. Much of its value in generating original ideas comes from the richness of associations that arise from it. Through its empathic quality it involves one personally and gives him a new feeling about or understanding of an object or state.

Synectics groups depend primarily upon the following four kinds of metaphor for making the familiar strange or the strange familiar:

Personal Analogy. Personal identification with the elements of a problem releases the individual from viewing the problem in terms of previously analyzed elements. A statistician translates a human relations problem into concepts of probability, analysis of variance, factor analysis, and the like. A chemist translates the same problem into equations combining molecules and the like.

Direct Analogy. The mechanism of direct analogy describes the comparison of parallel facts, knowledge, or technology. One of the most historically famous inventions from direct analogy is Alexander Graham Bell's invention of the telephone from a direct analogy to the human ear, with which he was intimately familiar as a teacher of the deaf.

Symbolic Analogy. The mechanism of symbolic analogy uses objective and impersonal images to describe the problem. Groups effectively use this analogy in terms of poetic response. Once the analogy is stated the effect is immediate. There is a spurt of associations and the effect is there complete.

Fantasy Analogy. This mechanism involves the mechanism of wish fulfillment. The group creates fantasies, magical solutions, and then tries to bring them down to earth by finding ways of making them practical.

The problem-solving steps or flow may vary from problem to problem, depending upon the success of the group in finding analogies that pay off. Prince (1968) has outlined a typical flow of steps as follows:

1. *Problem as Given*. A general statement of the problem is given to the problem-solving group by an outside source.

2. *Analysis and Explanation by Expert*. The expert restates the problem, trying to make the strange familiar.

3. *Purge.* Group members air their immediate, off-the-top-of-the-head solutions. The primary purpose is to help the group understand the problem better.

4. *Generation of Problems as Understood.* Each group member writes a restatement of the problem as he understands it.

5. *Evocative Question.* This is a question that requires an analogical or metaphorical answer.

6. *Examination.* A selected example is examined factually, and played with. This includes both descriptive facts about the example and statements that are more speculative and strange.

7. *Force Fit.* The analogies produced in Step 5 are "force-fitted" to the problem. This may produce strain but in the process the problem is stretched, pulled, and refocussed and can thus be seen in a new way. Attempts are made to make the irrelevant relevant. The forced fit provides the raw material for new lines of speculation.

8. *Viewpoint.* The potential solutions that emerge from the forced fit lead to a new viewpoint and new lines of speculation.

9. *Excursion.* The foregoing eight steps constitute an "Excursion." If one Excursion does not produce a new Viewpoint, another Excursion is initiated.

The principles of synectics and the skills involved in using them are being incorporated into various kinds of instructional materials. Gordon and his associates (1966) have devised an experimental creative writing course for children in the intermediate grades. This course emphasizes the development of skills for "making it strange" and uses this kind of play for generating ideas and a mood for creative writing. The Imagi/Craft materials by Cunnington and Torrance (1965) give a great deal of attention also to analogizing and elaborating analogies. Through some of the dramatizations, children are shown how inventors use analogies for getting their "big ideas" and for working out their inventions. For example, the story of Alexander Graham Bell shows how the direct analogy of the human ear and the telephone was used in making an invention. One new reading program gives a great variety of exercises in analogy play both in the readers themselves and in the guides for teachers. Figure 3, showing a page from one of these readers (Clymer and Gates, 1969), illustrates one way in which this kind of skill development is encouraged.

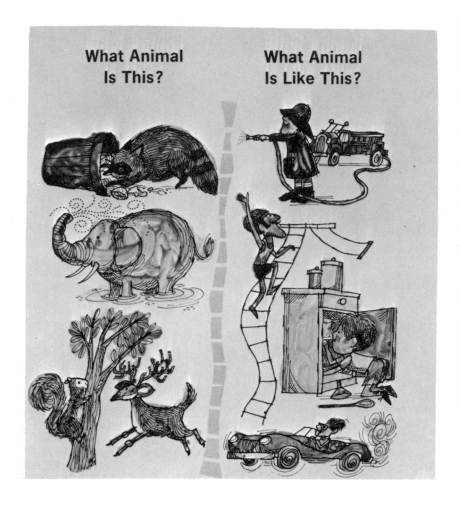

Figure 3. Example of Analogy Exercise in Reader. From T. Clymer
and D. Gates, *May I Come In?* (Boston: Ginn and Company, 1969), p. 35. Used by permission.

Making Your Own Summary

Use the ideas presented in this chapter to produce possible
solutions to the problem described below.

THE ASSIGNMENT

The teacher used a local happening as the basis for an assignment in creative writing. The report in the evening paper read:

"Dead sparrows lay everywhere yesterday on the small city park at _____. . . . 'They were everywhere. . . .' said the gardener in charge of the park today. 'It was a terrible thing. . . .' The birds might have 'drunk from a puddle formed by spillage of detergent.' . . ."

The teacher read the extract from the paper to his class and a short discussion was held about it. He was quite pleased when he found that many of the children had seen the picture and the article. He then made the following comments to his class before asking them to write a story:

"We've all seen the picture from last night's paper. I want you to imagine yourself as (a) one of the sparrows that survived or (b) a person who accidentally spilt the detergent, or (c) you may even imagine yourself as the workman arriving to clear away the many dead sparrows."

SAMPLE COMPOSITIONS

The following are examples of two compositions written in response to the above assignment.

The first was neatly written with no errors in spelling or grammar by a child of very high ability:

"The gardener found some dead sparrows in the city park. He thinks they died from drinking some detergent."

The second was written by a child of very, very low ability:

"When I came to work that morning I conted blev my iys, I felt that my hart had shrivveled up with the spirits insiad me pecking the flsh and cring out and I sow my self nelling and prang prang for them to say something to me but a las they bind even morer than I asket if I cood go home for a day and I wept I would never firgive myself."

Corrected, the composition would read as follows:

"When I came to work this morning I couldn't believe my eyes. I felt that my heart had shrivelled up, with the spirits inside me, pecking the flesh and crying out. And I saw myself kneeling and praying—praying for them to say something to me. But alas, they didn't even murmur. Then I asked if I could go home for a day—and I wept. I would never forgive myself."

YOUR TASK

Your task is to develop a plan or strategy for talking with each of these two children concerning their compositions. Use one of the problem-solving approaches described in this chapter to increase your chances of developing an effective plan for talking with each of them. The usual procedures used by teachers are known to be very ineffective in accomplishing the goals of this teacher. Thus, something other than the usual ones is needed.

Even better, you might give each of the three problem-solving approaches a trial through role playing or sociodrama and see which serves you more effectively in this instance. Or, you might want to try these approaches on a classroom problem of your own.

REFERENCES

Andrews, E. G. "The Development of Imagination in the Pre-School Child." *University of Iowa Studies in Character*, 1930, 3(4).

Clark, C. H. *Brainstorming*. Garden City, N.Y.: Doubleday & Co., 1958.

Clymer, T. and D. Gates. *May I Come In?* Boston: Ginn & Co., 1969.

Cunnington, B.F. and E.P. Torrance. *Imagi/Craft Series*. Boston: Ginn & Co., 1965.

Gordon, W. J. J. *Synectics: The Development of Creative Capacity*. New York: Harper & Row, 1961.

Gordon, W. J. J. and Associates. *Making It Strange*. Cambridge, Mass.: Synectics, Inc., 1966.

Haas, R. B. "The School Sociatrist." *Sociatry,* 1948, **2,** 283–321.

Hansen, B. "Sociodrama, A Methodology for Democratic Action." *Sociatry,* 1948, **2,** 347–363.

Klein, A. F. *Role Playing.* New York: Association Press, 1956.

L'Abate, L. "Sanford's Uncertainty Hypothesis in Children," *ETC.: A Review of General Semantics,* 1957, **14,** 210–213.

Maltzman, I. "On the Training of Originality." *Psychological Review,* 1960, **67,** 229–242.

Mead, M. *From the South Seas.* New York: William Morrow, 1939.

Moreno, J. L. *A Case of Paranoia Treated Through Psychodrama.* Beacon, N. Y.: Beacon House, 1945.

Moreno, J. L. *Psychodrama, Vol. I.* Beacon, N.Y.: Beacon House, 1946.

Osborn, A. F. *Your Creative Power.* New York: Charles Scribner's Sons, 1948.

Osborn, A. F. *Applied Imagination* (rev. ed.). New York: Charles Scribner's Sons, 1957.

Osborn, A. F. *Applied Imagination* (3rd ed.). New York: Charles Scribner's Sons, 1963.

Parnes, S. J. "Can Creativity Be Increased?" In S. J. Parnes and H. F. Harding (eds.). *A Source Book for Creative Thinking.* New York: Charles Scribner's Sons, 1962. Pp. 185–192.

Parnes, S. J. *Creative Behavior Workbook.* New York: Charles Scribner's Sons, 1967.

Parnes, S. J. and A. Meadow. "Evaluation of Persistence of Effects Produced by a Creative Problem-Solving Course." *Psychological Reports,* 1960, **7,** 357–361.

Prince, G. M. "The Operational Mechanism of Synectics." *Journal of Creative Behavior,* 1968, **2,** 1–13.

Pulsifer, S. N. *Children Are Poets.* Cambridge, Mass.: Dresser, Chapman & Grimes, 1963.

Ray, W. S. *The Experimental Psychology of Original Thinking.* New York: The Macmillan Company, 1967.

Riessman, F. *The Culturally Deprived Child.* New York: Harper & Row, 1964.

Smilansky, S. *The Effects of Sociodramatic Play on Disadvantaged Pre-School Children.* New York: John Wiley & Sons, 1968.

Torrance, E. P. "Priming Creative Thinking in the Primary Grades." *Elementary School Journal,* 1961, **62,** 34–41.

Torrance, E. P. *The Minnesota Studies of Creative Thinking: 1958–66.* Greensboro, N.C.: Richardson Foundation, 1967a.

Torrance, E. P. *Understanding the Fourth-Grade Slump in Creative Thinking.* Final USOE Report, Cooperative Research Project 994. Athens, Ga.: Georgia Studies of Creative Behavior, 1967b.

Torrance, E. P. "A Longitudinal Examination of the Fourth Grade Slump in Creativity." *Gifted Child Quarterly,* 1968, **12,** 195–199.

Weideman, R. A. "An Experiment with Grade Children in Making Creative Songs with Varied Stimuli." Master's research paper, University of Minnesota, Minneapolis, 1961.

Wilt, M. E. *Creativity in the Elementary School.* New York: Appleton-Century-Crofts, 1959.

CHAPTER 5 ACQUIRING
SKILLS OF FACILITATING
CREATIVE LEARNING

Ignite
And feed
The flame within me
With your younger lights of
Understanding.

The Problem

In the first chapter, we discussed teaching as a creative occupation, as well as some of the problems of acquiring the skills of facilitating creative learning among children. In the second chapter, we presented the case for creative teaching and learning, attempting to show that teaching *can* make a difference in behavior and learning even in what might appear to be "hopeless cases." In the third chapter, we developed the idea that creative ways of learning have a built-in motivation that does not require the application and reapplication of reward and punishment. In the fourth chapter, we argued that creative behavior does not have to be left to chance and described some deliberate, disciplined methods for increasing the chances that creative behavior will occur in the classroom.

By now, you may be asking, "Can I become the kind of teacher you are talking about? Can my teaching make a difference in the learning and behavior of my pupils? Can I design and direct learning activities that have built-in motivation? Can I increase the chances that my pupils will behave in truly creative ways?"

At times even the best teachers wonder about these things, especially when they are able to observe the teaching of another truly skilled teacher. This was Mrs. Harter's problem.

Mrs. Harter had mixed feelings about being assigned the classroom next to Mrs. Bolling's. Of all the teachers in the large suburban school, Mrs. Bolling was considered the most original and inspirational. Mrs. Harter knew that her new neighbor would generously provide her with a number of ideas for making a classroom stimulating if she were asked. The veteran teacher had a reputation for helping younger teachers. Mrs. Harter, who had spent four years teaching fifth-graders, was well aware of the attractiveness of Mrs. Bolling's room before she moved from a building on the other side of town. She became increasingly conscious of the murals, mobiles, papier-mâché animals, and pets next door as the weeks passed.

Before Thanksgiving Mrs. Harter became aware that many of Mrs. Bolling's pupils were visiting her room before school and during the recesses and that very few of her own pupils bothered to visit Mrs. Bolling's room. On two or three occasions, when she had kept a couple of her pupils after school to practice their mathematics skills, they were joined by several of Mrs. Bolling's pupils. In spite of these indications that her classroom was appealing, Mrs. Harter felt uneasy because she knew that the principal always brought visitors to Mrs. Bolling's room and had never brought anyone to see her classroom. Her pupils were doing some interesting things, too. However, they were not the kinds of activities that result in displays. The children held debates, put on skits, conducted a variety of experiments, and enjoyed visiting other classes. Mrs. Harter encouraged her pupils to invite architects, surgeons, city officials, mechanics, and farmers to visit their class and to discuss their work. She was enthusiastic about her pupils' ideas, and occasionally allowed a pupil to spend almost all of his time at school on a subject or project that particularly interested him. Mrs. Harter herself enjoyed learning about nature, sports, space travel, famous people, food, and almost any other subject worthy of investigation. Her cheerful manner and sincere concern for her pupils' welfare made her classroom a comfortable and supportive place for all of the youngsters in the class, but especially for three children who were from broken homes. Mrs. Harter realized that her pupils liked her, but she wondered if she should admit her feelings of inadequacy and ask Mrs. Bolling's advice about how to conduct some exciting art activities.

How would you analyze Mrs. Harter's dilemma?

What things might have supplied Mrs. Harter with security?

What is the difference between the kind of security that Mrs. Bolling claimed and the kind that Mrs. Harter might have claimed?

Think of the person that you consider the greatest teacher you have known personally. *In what did this teacher find his security?*

What are the things that give you security in your teaching?

How a Teacher Invents His Way of Teaching

The teacher who teaches creatively and facilitates creative learning among his pupils cannot find his security in a textbook, in dominating the classroom, in being all-knowing, or in having a quiet class and a neat, orderly classroom. He must be willing to find his security in indications that his pupils are interested and deeply involved in learning and are excited about school. He must find security in his ever-emerging invention—"his way of teaching," his unique invention. But, how does one arrive at his invention?

The techniques, strategies, materials and methods, and relationships used by a teacher in creating conditions for creative behavior and growth must be that teacher's own. You can reproduce the techniques, strategies, materials and methods used by some outstanding teacher. You can even say all of the correct words and do all of the correct things, but they won't mean a thing unless you recombine them to make your own unique invention. They simply will not ring true!

This unique invention of the teacher emerges through the creative process of trying to accomplish important goals. As you fail or succeed in these goals, you become aware of your deficiencies, defects in your techniques and strategies, and gaps in your knowledge. You draw upon your past experiences. You intensify your search for clues in your ongoing experiences. You try to apply creatively the scientifically developed principles you have learned in your professional education or through your reading. Then, you read and study some more. You see things of which you have hitherto been unaware. You make or formulate hypotheses concerning ways of teaching. You test and modify these hypotheses and tell others what you have learned. Through the pain and the ecstasy which accompanies this process, your personal invention evolves!

Since your ways of teaching must be your own invention, no one can present you with a precise prescription for creating the conditions most favorable for creative growth. Your own personality resources and skills, the needs and abilities of your pupils, and the expectations of the community in which you are teaching all interact to determine what ways of teaching will be most productive. It *is* possible, however, to derive from experience and research some general principles which increase markedly the chances of your creating such conditions. It is possible to create teaching procedures and sets of instructional materials which have built into them many of these tested principles. It is the teacher's creative task to weave all of them into a new combination which meets the needs and abilities of the class, and is in harmony with the needs and abilities of the teacher.

In this chapter, we will identify and discuss briefly some of the most pervasive and powerful principles for acquiring the skills of facilitating creative learning.

Examples of Fundamental Principles

WARM-UP

Perhaps the most fundamental condition for creative behavior is that of adequate "warm-up," a case of creativity begetting creativity. One thing must be permitted to lead to another. This warm-up occurs when we produce something and then produce something else from what was created earlier. It also occurs when we in some way extend, stretch, or limber up our minds.

An example of this principle is found in the work of Irving Maltzman (1960) at the University of California at Los Angeles. In his experiments, Maltzman used a list of twenty-five words which he read to subjects five times. Each time a word was read, the subject had to respond with a word which he associated with the stimulus word. Each successive time, he had to push his imagination further to come up with a different association. Following such a "mind-stretching" exercise, Maltzman found that his subjects produced a larger number of original ideas or solutions to test problems, including practical, real-life problems. Using a technique known as "Sounds and Images," Cunnington and Torrance (1965) used recorded sound effects in much the same way that Maltzman used lists of words.

PROGRESSIVE WARM-UP

Various types of shock effect have been used to call forth inventive and ingenious responses. Shock, however, is almost always accompanied by some delay in response and must be used with some risk. Some individuals will usually be overwhelmed by the shock and be paralyzed in their thinking. Thus, progressive warm-up is likely to be more reliable than sudden and/or intense shock. The

"Sounds and Images" technique of Cunnington and Torrance provides a good example of this principle. The sound effects range from simple to complex and from commonplace or familiar to unusual or strange. The first sound effect in one form of the records, for example, is a rather easily recognized thunderstorm. The fourth consists of six different, relatively unfamiliar and unrelated sounds. The first places little burden upon the respondent's ability to synthesize and organize into a single, cohesive image the elements composing the sound effect. The fourth, however, imposes a terrific load on ability to synthesize.

Progressive warm-up may also be achieved through verbal instructions. Both Maltzman's word-association technique and the "Sounds and Images" record make use of this method. In "Sounds and Images," pupils are asked first to imagine something—any visual image which can be put into words—which might be associated with the sounds. Next, he is asked to be even more imaginative. Having gotten "out of his system" some of the more obvious, commonplace images, and having "warmed up" his mind, he is prepared to permit his imagination to leap. Finally, he is urged to let his imagination swing wide, to leap all barriers. This, of course, sometimes makes adults feel uncomfortable. At certain stages of development youngsters also feel uncomfortable by the time they reach the third stage. A majority of adults tell us that they like best their responses to the second repetition of the sound effects. Responses to the first presentation are seen as being too dull and obvious and give little pleasure. The third set of responses, however, contain too many "wild and way out" responses. Respondents are afraid that they have perhaps lost touch with reality or that others will think so. Secretly, however, many of them seem rather proud that they were able to produce such surprising responses, and are able to laugh over them.

DIVERGENT THINKING MADE ACCEPTABLE

Children are afraid to think any except the most obvious ideas, if they do not feel that it is safe. Again, "Sounds and Images" provides a good example of a set of materials through which this principle is applied. Instructions contained in the records and the structure of the materials make it acceptable for the respondent to think divergently, to produce original, even wild, ideas.

We have tested this principle in a number of experiments. For example, in one experiment with sixth-graders, we varied the reward (Torrance, 1965). In one condition, we offered a prize of $2.00 to the pupil who produced the largest number of ideas, regardless of quality, and a prize of 25 cents for the pupil who produced the largest number of original, unusual ideas for improving a toy dog so that it would be more fun for a child to play with. In the other condition, the reward was reversed, with the highest reward for the largest number of original, unusual ideas. The average number of original responses under the first condition was 6.2 and under the second, 12.2—almost double. The difference in sheer number of ideas (23.0 to 20.4), however, was not statistically significant (could have occurred by chance in more than 5 cases out of 100). The small difference was in favor of the group rewarded on the basis of sheer number of responses.

In another experiment, we staged a similar contest in the writing of imaginative stories. Under one condition, the prize was awarded on the basis of originality and interest; under the other, it was made on the basis of correctness. We found that those who were rewarded for originality, compared to their classmates who were rewarded for correctness, wrote stories which were longer, more original, and more interesting but which contained more errors.

In some classes above the third grade it may be difficult to create conditions under which it is acceptable to think divergently or differently from the remainder of the class. It may not be enough that it be acceptable in the eyes of the teacher. It must be acceptable also in the peer group. When this occurs, the teacher may have to make a deliberate, conscious effort to modify the group norms.

FREEDOM FROM THREAT OF EVALUATION

External evaluation is threatening and as a result tends to shut off from awareness some area of experience. This reduces a person's ability to think beyond the obvious, the safe, the familiar. With young children in kindergarten and the primary grades, this is a powerful force. In one experiment, Torrance (1965) found that unevaluated practice compared with evaluated practice is followed by a more creative performance in similar tasks requiring creative thinking. By the fourth grade, children are apparently so accustomed to being evaluated on everything that the instructions freeing them from the threat of evaluation had little effect.

INVITATION TO REGRESS

"Sounds and Images" contains a built-in invitation to regress, to have fun, to laugh, and to enjoy one's self. The recorded instructions and the nature of the task itself both invite regression. Some college groups attack the task in a very grim manner. Even such grim groups usually begin laughing before the end of the third stage of the task.

Many students of the creative process have concluded that creativity—even the serious, scientific kind—is facilitated when one is able to regress occasionally—to laugh, to be childlike, to be dependent, to fantasy. Very early in the development of testing procedures for assessing creative potential, Torrance discovered the importance of the invitation to engage in the tests "just for fun." He made this discovery when he found that some apparently timid children were unable to produce any responses. Frequently he would say, "Come on, just for fun! This doesn't count." At this point, responses frequently would start tumbling forth. How well this device will work with older groups is not certain.

The teacher in the United States, however, labors in a cultural environment with a work-play dichotomy. This makes it "sinful" to have fun when we should be working or not having fun when we are supposed to be playing. Since school is supposed to be work, activities that involve laughter or fun are generally discouraged, punished, or at best held in low esteem.

FREEDOM FROM INHIBITING SETS

Many kinds of conditions inhibit or paralyze thinking. When we ask people in a test to think of unusual uses of tin cans, it is difficult for them to think of a tin can as anything other than a container. In fact, schizophrenics in one study (Hebeisen, 1959) gave container uses in 87 percent of their responses. Healthy adults usually make about 40 percent of their responses container uses, while only about 15 percent of the responses of children are of this type. Thus, age and experience, illness, and the like all create sets which bind our thinking, making us less flexible. It becomes necessary deliberately to create conditions that will free individuals from such sets.

Two devices are used in "Sounds and Images" to help free persons from sets that might interfere with their creative thinking. First, they are asked to fold their paper back so that they cannot see their previous responses. Thus, they symbolically put out of their minds the earlier responses and can start anew. Some individuals, however, are unable to put aside these earlier responses and only elaborate upon them or think of minor variations from them. Second, the narrator of the record refrains from giving examples. In an experimental version of "Sounds and Images," examples of more and more imaginative responses were given at each stage of the warm-up to facilitate the warm-up. It was found, however, that these examples created sets from which many respondents were unable to free themselves.

This latter principle has also been tested in a variety of other situations. From two art classes, we were shown samples of puppets made by pupils. The products from the first class were nice but unexciting creations. Technically they were excellent. The products from the second class were varied and exciting. They differed along many dimensions. Only one variable differed in the conditions created by the teacher. In both classes, she showed the same model. In the first class *she* suggested several possible variations. In the second class, she asked the *pupils* to suggest possible variations. Thus, the pupils in the first class rejected the teacher's suggestions of variations and stuck to the original model. Their minds had not been sufficiently warmed up to break out of the mold, or set, created by the teacher's model. In the second class, having to think of other variations themselves, their minds became warmed up and they were able to produce an interesting and exciting variety of puppets.

OTHER CONDITIONS

Many other conditions for facilitating creative functioning could be identified. The purpose of this chapter is to identify a few facilitating conditions and to show how various pieces of information can be recombined to create instructional materials, teaching techniques, or relationships.

In creating favorable conditions for learning and thinking, care should be exercised to see that pupils are reasonably comfortable, both physically and psychologically. If individuals are too cold, too hot, too fatigued, too hungry, too sleepy, too frightened, or too uncertain about what is expected of them they are not likely to do much thinking. This does not mean that hungry or fatigued people have not at times reached great heights in their thinking. The fact is, however, that it takes an enormous amount of motivation to overcome the effects of any of these discomforts.

The relationship of the teacher to the pupils is extremely important and much will be said in this book concerning teacher-pupil relationship. In the creative teacher-pupil relationship, the teacher must be willing to permit one thing to lead to another, and should not be disturbed when a pupil asks an unexpected question or proposes a surprising solution. The relationship is dominated by love and kindly concern. Discipline may be strict and certain but not punitive or cruel. The pupil must feel that the teacher is "on his side." Otherwise, things can go badly awry.

How Teachers Arrive at Their "Inventions"

Throughout the rest of this book, we will give thumbnail sketches of how teachers arrive at their "inventions" or unique ways of teaching. In many of them, you will be able to identify some of the errors and defects which entered into the process. In each case, you will be asked to push further the thinking generated by the cases described. We will identify some of the theoretical issues involved and cite some of the research evidence that might be useful in evaluating solutions. It will be your task to apply creatively any insights you may achieve.

A MATTER OF TRUST

For the first two months of the school year, Mr. Stein played a game, reluctantly, with the members of his sixth-grade class. The youngsters continually interrupted their work to ask him if they might go to the lavatory, make an important telephone call, or retrieve a jacket on the playground. They thought of a great number of reasons for being elsewhere. Some of their excuses were well-founded, but most of them were conceived in the spirit of an old contest which they had been waging with their teachers for years. Sometimes Mr. Stein assented. Sometimes he brushed aside the request with a brief explanation as to why it was unreasonable. He was usually annoyed, as were the teachers who had been engaged in this game in previous years. Finally, when several pupils had asked to be excused from the room for a variety of near-urgent reasons, Mr. Stein responded to a two-o'clock telephone request with the statement that if any member of the class were restless or bored he was free to go outside and amuse himself on the playground. He assured his pupils that they need not ask his permission—they could just go.

Thereafter, it was Mr. Stein's custom to announce at the beginning of each school year that any member of his class could go outside at any time of the day, if he were so inclined. The only restriction he placed upon the offer was that no more than two children leave the room at a time, to decrease the likelihood that other classes in the school would be disturbed. Mr. Stein's attitude was that in order to develop a sense of responsibility in children an adult must demonstrate his trust in them. Although he enjoyed talking to his pupils about such ideas as responsibility, trustworthiness, and honesty, he did not preach to them. He waited for an opportunity to arise before making his feelings about these matters explicit.

Do you think Mr. Stein's technique was successful with all of his classes year after year? Would you be willing to make such a "deal" with your pupils?

Many teachers purposely leave their classes unsupervised (even when it is against the policy of their schools) in order to provide opportunities for the children to prove themselves responsible and trustworthy. *Do you think the risks involved in this practice outweigh any possible gains? Would you ever deliberately leave your class unsupervised? Should we test children in such ways—or are we really tempting them unnecessarily?*

Now that you have made your evaluations of Mr. Stein's teaching "invention," how would you justify the evaluations and the decision you made? What are the issues involved?

Let us take a look now at the process that Mr. Stein used in his own attempt to perfect his ways of teaching.

MR. STEIN'S CREATIVE PROCESS

As with any invention, the first step in Mr. Stein's creative process was his discomfort. He had reluctantly entered into the old game of teacher versus pupil. Even entering into this game was apparently uncomfortable for him. As the game progressed he became even more uncomfortable, until he could no longer tolerate the tension being produced. Suddenly, he decided to reverse the procedure. Teacher and pupil would play on the same side. This was a solution definitely off the beaten track and possibly in violation of some school regulation. Apparently Mr. Stein tested and modified the procedure which he conceived. His big ideas occurred, as most new ideas do, all of a sudden after he had been struggling for a solution.

RELATIONSHIP TO CONDITIONS FOR CREATIVE GROWTH

Some of you may have difficulty in seeing the relationship between Mr. Stein's solution to his classroom discipline problem and the conditions for creative growth. Actually, many important conditions for creative growth are at stake in Mr. Stein's theory. There was little that was really creative in the condition which existed during the first two months of school in Mr. Stein's class. The techniques used by these sixth-graders were apparently primitive ones that children have used to control and coerce their elders for ages. Furthermore, all of their energies were being dissipated in the struggle between the teacher and the class. Little energy was left for intellectual achievement.

Perhaps one of the most important conditions for creative growth is that pupils feel that *their* teacher is on *their* side. Due to prior conditioning, it is frequently difficult to communicate to youngsters that you actually are on their side. The teacher's problem is usually one of deciding how far he is willing to go in order to communicate this fact. This decision usually involves risk on the part of the teacher—and this illustrates another important aspect of Mr. Stein's behavior. It took courage. Perhaps this was made possible by his confidence in the worth and dignity of his pupils. Mr. Stein was willing to enter with them into a new relationship. He could not know where it would lead. He had to trust in his own skills, his own capacity for establishing relationships with boys and girls, and his faith in them.

A number of other features in Mr. Stein's case which probably contributed to the creation of conditions for creative growth should be mentioned, if only briefly. There were times when he freed his pupils from the threat of immediate evaluation. He didn't monitor their behavior; neither did he have them monitor one another's behavior. He established reasonable limits and gave them enough structure to make them comfortable in their new relationship. Finally, he recognized that there were times when, as shown by their restlessness and boredom, they needed relief from their tensions. Most important perhaps was Mr. Stein's own creative approach, his helping his pupils to learn creatively from their own experiences at appropriate times, and his creative relationship with them.

INVOLVING CHILDREN IN A CREATIVE TASK

In April, Mr. Goetz had the uncomfortable feeling that his pupils were bored. Since most of them had recently reached their eleventh birthday, he thought that their boredom was unusual. The fifth-graders he had taught in the past did not sag so badly in the spring. Mr. Goetz decided that there must be something wrong with his ways of teaching. The thought that his pupils were bored with school and had lost the excitement of learning was intolerable!

One night, as he searched his mind for an idea which would shake his pupils loose from their lethargy, Mr. Goetz's eyes fell upon a book which he had purchased recently, *Teenagers Who Made History* by Russell Freedman (1961). It occurred to him that his pupils might enjoy reading biographies of individuals whose genius revealed itself at an early age. Perhaps they could more easily identify themselves with famous people who had won acclaim at an age close to their own.

On the following day, Mr. Goetz suggested to his class that

they might like to learn about young people who had made important contributions to human progress. He talked a little about three of the persons featured in *Teenagers Who Made History*. The children were fascinated by his stories of Louis Braille, Samuel Colt, and Galileo. They were also genuinely eager to find out about other persons who had accomplished great deeds as teenagers. The youngsters decided, furthermore, that it would be a good idea to share what they had discovered about the prodigies whom they had studied, so they gave reports to the class when they had completed their research. As it happened, the last of the children to give a biographical report was a boy who talked about Louis Braille. When the boy had finished his report the class seemed particularly interested in the process by which young Braille had produced the raised dots which were such a wonderful substitute for printed words. Mr. Goetz volunteered to obtain as much equipment for writing in braille as he could. He was able to bring to class a Braille Writer, a stylus, and some special paper which is used in braille writing. As a result, the children learned to write a few words in braille by finding a reference book which described and pictured the braille alphabet.

Mr. Goetz was pleased with the way in which his pupils had become interested in historical figures, and even more pleased by the way they had gone ahead on their own and investigated these persons. He felt that he should not let their enthusiasm slip away again—since they were beginning to dig in and do things on their own. He wanted to encourage them to continue to learn independently. During the year his pupils had demonstrated their love for games and contests, and they greatly enjoyed using their imaginations when given opportunities to do so. So he improvised a follow-up lesson on Louis Braille. This is approximately how he presented it to the class:

"Did you know that every day of your life you make use of signals and symbols—just as Louis Braille did? For instance, when a bell rings here at school, you know what that signal means—especially when the bell rings at 3:00. When you come to a traffic light which shows a red color, you also know what to do. (If you did not understand the signal, you might lose your life!) The X you make when you do arithmetic problems is a sign which tells you to multiply, and you recognize it immediately. When you swallow milk which tastes peculiar or sour, you have a different kind of signal—a very important one, for you can become very sick by drinking milk which has spoiled. And every time you talk or write to someone you are using symbols—things which tell other people how you feel, what you want to know, or what they should do. Just the word "Help!" when shouted by a boy or girl in the water tells you a lot in a hurry. Louis Braille would have recognized some of these signals, but the meaning of others—the visual symbols and cues—would have escaped him.

"Today I'm going to ask you to make up your own signs and symbols. They won't be true symbols, of course, until many people understand what they mean, but if they are used they can have a meaning which is recognized by all of the people who are familiar with them. First of all, I am going to give you a blank piece of paper. You can do some experimenting on this paper to see how imaginative and clever you are. Try to invent as many signs or symbols as you can for the things we do in school. For example, can you think of a sign or symbol which would tell us it's time for lunch? (Remember, a symbol doesn't have to be a *picture* of something; when Braille made his system of dots, the dots stood *for* letters and punctuation marks.) Then, after you have worked awhile inventing symbols for the events which occur during the day, I'll go to the chalkboard and write the times when we do different things, starting with the first event, flag salute, and so on until the last event, dismissal. When I have finished writing the times on the board, we can have each of you write in chalk your symbol for what happens at that time of day. We can then try to decide which of the symbols does the best job of indicating to us what the event on our schedule is. I guess we'll have to make up our minds how we'll decide which are the most suitable symbols. In other words, we'll have to think about why we think one symbol is better than another. When we are all through, we'll have created a whole new set of symbols which can be used by us—and understood only by us—to tell us what we're going to do during the day."

Was this lesson contrived or forced? Do you think it went over? One of the difficulties which Mr. Goetz anticipated was in helping his pupils set up some criteria for judging the symbols which would be most suitable. They had not had much experience in setting up criteria and objectively evaluating products, and he was afraid that his pupils might be swayed by the popularity of the children who presented the idea. *If this were the case, why did Mr. Goetz go ahead with the contest? If you were in his place, would you have avoided possible trouble by giving equal status to all of the symbols which were offered?*

We hope that you have gone ahead and made the judgments and decisions called for by the questions above. Doing so involves one kind of hypothesis making. You can test these hypotheses on the basis of the experiences which you have already had and those which you will have in the future. You can also test them against what you know from reported research and against your future readings. Some of you will object to making the kinds of guesses or predictions called for at the end of these cases. You have been taught that you must keep an "open mind" and to some this means not thinking. If you think about these matters seriously, however, you can hardly restrain yourself from making guesses, from having opinions. The openness that counts is that which operates when you examine honestly the data which enables you to reject, accept, or revise your hypotheses.

MR. GOETZ'S CREATIVE PROCESS

A variety of dimensions of the creative process is illustrated by Mr. Goetz's behavior in this episode. First, he was uncomfortable. He sensed that something was wrong. He recognized the existence of a problem. One of his first hypotheses was that his pupils were bored. He strengthened this hypothesis by comparing the behavior of his present class with that of previous fifth-grade classes. Thus he did what must always be done before any kind of creative or adaptive action can take place. He identified the problem: his deficiencies in teaching these pupils. On the other hand, tough-skinned people who never see any problems never do any creative thinking and fail to take adaptive action. In a study of mathematics teaching (Torrance, 1965), it was found that it is the teacher who accepts his responsibility for unsuccessful results who is able to do the most creative thinking. The teachers in the study were asked to describe each month what they considered their most and least successful lessons and to advance hypotheses concerning the factors which made them successful or unsuccessful. Almost all the teachers ascribed success to something that the teacher had done. Only a small percentage ascribed the *lack* of success to anything that the teacher had done. Those who did, however, knew of a larger number of alternative ways for teaching a mathematical concept and were able to think of a much larger number of unfamiliar methods of teaching the concept than their colleagues.

You will remember that Mr. Goetz's tension over the situation with his pupils became intolerable. Such tension may motivate creative behavior on the part of some teachers, but others will be overwhelmed by it and see no creative solutions. Mr. Goetz continued to search for some solution, however, even at night—then, suddenly, the sight of a book sparked an idea. Such an idea would not have come had he not been concerned about the problem and had he not continued to expose himself to new materials and sources of ideas.

You will also note that Mr. Goetz hypothesized that his pupils would enjoy the materials which he intended introducing. Although it should not be the goal of teaching to entertain children, learning and creative problem solving can be fun. In fact, many new ideas and creative learning frequently occur when an individual seems to be "playing around." Another valid hypothesis that Mr. Goetz made was that his pupils would identify with teenagers who had made outstanding creative contributions while they were still teenagers. Boys and girls need models of creative behavior, models with whom they can identify and from whom they can learn. Youngsters also learn to value their own ideas in this way.

Like Mr. Stein, Mr. Goetz also made use of sound warm-up techniques and permitted one thing to lead to another. Of the numerous possibilities, he capitalized upon the one which had generated the most enthusiasm, the most warm-up. Very carefully, Mr. Goetz anticipated some of the possible difficulties which might cause his pupils to become bogged down and frustrated. He recognized that people can be overwhelmed by tension if they do not have enough structure for a task to help them decide what to do.

CONDITIONS FOR CREATIVE GROWTH

In the account of Mr. Goetz's behavior several important conditions for creative growth can be identified. Mr. Goetz provided his pupils with models of creative behavior so that they could become familiar with the creative process and its value and so that they might recognize the value of their own ideas. He also recognized the warm-up value of enjoyment, choosing materials which would be interesting, stimulating, and exciting. He set up conditions of progressive warm-up and selected for further exploration the area which had generated the most enthusiasm. He structured the activity so that his pupils would have a chance to learn on their own. Furthermore, he was pleased that they worked on their own and rewarded them for this kind of behavior. He not only gave them opportunities for using their imagination, he gave purposefulness to the activity. Youngsters are going to be uneasy unless they have some kind of guide to appropriateness, and this uneasiness may mount to a point at which it becomes incapacitating. Therefore, Mr. Goetz helped them to develop criteria for evaluating their ideas. He thus recognized that there is a need to suspend evaluation temporarily, but that evaluation and decision-making are necessary accompaniments following the idea-getting stage. There must be guides to behavior or some degree of structure, no matter how much freedom is permitted and encouraged.

Making Your Own Summary

To make this chapter really meaningful, skim through it again and see how many principles you can identify in Mr. Knapp's teaching, as described in the following episode, concerning his creative processes and the conditions that he created for growth among his pupils.

WEEKLY REPORTING TO PARENTS

As the term drew rapidly to a close, Mr. Knapp became more and more concerned about how well prepared his pupils were for junior high school. Each spring, he experienced qualms about how his pupils would fare in a departmentalized situation where they would have several teachers with varying expectations instead of only one teacher-guide. Mr. Knapp mulled over several ideas which might make the transition to junior high school a pleasant experience for his pupils, and then he decided to start a program of intensive evaluation of their academic and social progress.

Mr. Knapp's first step was to notify the parents of his pupils what was in the offing. He hoped that his letter would insure cooperation in his campaign to prepare his pupils adequately for the seventh grade.

Dear ————:

Because the last quarter of the sixth year of elementary school is so important in preparing a pupil for junior high school, I plan to send home weekly reports of your child's academic and social progress, along with examples of his classroom work.

In order that you have a better understanding of the work to be undertaken during the next few weeks, you will be provided with schedules of the assignments which will be given to your child every two weeks. There may be changes in the scheduling, as there frequently are, but the deadlines are to be taken seriously.

Please do not hesitate to call me or write to me, if you have any questions about our work at school. I want you to have as complete and as clear a picture as possible of your child's abilities and achievements before he leaves elementary school.

Sincerely,

HORACE KNAPP

After composing the latter, Mr. Knapp reviewed what had been covered during the year. He made notes of the lessons which had evidently been unsuccessful, and he listed the concepts and skills which had not yet been introduced to the class. By compiling a list of the lessons which he felt should be given his pupils during the remainder of the school year, Mr. Knapp had a good idea of how he should schedule textbook lessons, science and social studies projects, book reports, and the written assignments which were to be completed during the day. He made up a schedule which included the dates that reports were due and the tentative dates for examinations. It also indicated the approximate time when units of study were to be initiated. (Mr. Knapp generally worked out the sequence of the units to be studied without consulting his pupils as to their interest in the units or their familiarity with the subjects which were to be dealt with.) The schedule gave him ample opportunity to introduce and/or to review the skills and understandings which he felt would be most important to his pupils in junior high school. Then he duplicated the schedule, giving two copies to each pupil—one for their own use and one for their parents' reference.

The final phase of Mr. Knapp's campaign involved the means of evaluating the work of his pupils. He decided that his assessment of their progress should be communicated to them as quickly as possible, and so he determined to return written reports and seatwork assignments on the day following their completion (like many another teacher, he had not always been prompt in grading and returning papers). In addition, Mr. Knapp made up a report form which he intended to have his pupils take home with them every Friday afternoon. They were to be returned, signed by a parent, on Monday morning. Since a reporting period had just been completed, the weekly reports would come regularly throughout the fourth quarter and would not conflict with the regular report card. Mr. Knapp reasoned that the weekly reports could be summarized easily and then recorded on the authorized report card at the end of the year. On page 119 is a copy of Mr. Knapp's report form.

How do you think Mr. Knapp's program was received by the parents? Do you think he was exerting himself unnecessarily in devising and carrying out his evaluation program? Would you expect his program to pay enough dividends to make all his efforts worthwhile?

What are the weakest points of the program? What are the strongest points? Should Mr. Knapp have asked his pupils to tell him what parts of the curriculum had been confusing to them or what information and training they believed they needed?

Since a pupil constantly refers to his own standards as well as to the standards of his peers, his family, and his community, was Mr. Knapp wise in emphasizing so greatly the teacher's evaluation of the pupil's performances?

Pupil's name_____

Week of _____

Work Accomplished

Daily assignments completed_____   Quality of work_____
                                         (Two   pieces   of   typical   work
                                         are   enclosed   in   this   folder) *

Oral reports completed_____   Quality of work_____

Written reports completed_____   Quality of work_____

Evaluation of Academic Progress

Arithmetic   Reading
    Average score this quarter____%   Average score this quarter____%
         Gain or loss   ____%   Gain or loss   ____%
    Average score this week____%   Average score this week____%
Language   Spelling
    Average score this quarter____%   Average score this quarter____%
         Gain or loss   ____%   Gain or loss   ____%
    Average score this week____%   Average score this week____%
Science   Social Studies
    Average score this quarter____%   Average score this quarter____%
         Gain or loss   ____%   Gain or loss   ____%
    Average score this week____%   Average score this week____%

Other_____

Social and Personal Growth

Interest and Participation_____

Accepts Responsibility   _____

Courtesy to Others   _____

Sportsmanship   _____

Other Comments   _____

_____ _____
_____
_____
_____

* Enclosed are_____
_____

_____
Signature of parent

REFERENCES

Cunnington, B. F. and E. P. Torrance. *Sounds and Images*. Boston: Ginn & Co., 1965.

Freedman, R. *Teenagers Who Made History*. New York: Holiday House, 1961.

Hebeisen, A. A. "The Performance of a Group of Schizophrenic Patients on a Test of Creative Thinking." Master's research paper, University of Minnesota, Minneapolis, 1959.

Maltzman, I. "On the Training of Originality." *Psychological Review*, 1960, **67**, 229–242.

Torrance, E. P. *Rewarding Creative Behavior*. Englewood Cliffs, N.J.: Prentice-Hall, Inc., 1965.

CHAPTER 6   BECOMING

AWARE:

KNOWING CHILDREN

Banker
Of dreams,
Holding promises with
Interest payable in joy:
Teacher.

The Problem

We have observed repeatedly that those teachers who teach most creatively and whose pupils learn most creatively seem to know the children they teach almost intuitively. How does a teacher acquire the skills of knowing intimately the children he teaches? Try to imagine yourself with the problems of the first-year teacher described below.

Suppose that you are a first-year teacher and that you have just finished your second week of teaching thirty fourth-grade children in a suburban school. Although you enjoy your job thus far and your fellow teachers have been especially helpful, you are bewildered by the great diversity of personalities and needs represented by the children in your classroom. Collectively they are a fascinating group, but you are having trouble nearly every day with your instructional program. None of your carefully written lesson plans has worked as you had anticipated, even though you have made adjustments in both the manner in which the lessons have been introduced and in their content. The principal and your colleagues have offered valuable suggestions, but their advice is not specific enough—and besides, no one can really help you make those moment-to-moment decisions. Although you are not disconsolate, you realize that you must know more about your pupils' backgrounds, abilities, interests, and interpersonal relationships before you can do an effective job of teaching.

FILLING IN THE PICTURE

Your school was constructed three years ago in a rapidly growing suburban area outside a city of several hundred thousand people. There are three other fourth-grade teachers in your building; all of them have taught at least two years. Cumulative record folders for the pupils are kept locked in the office; teachers have access to the folders at any time, but they have to ask the office secretary for a key to the files in order to examine the folders. The school neighborhood contains a fairly good cross section of people in the upper-lower and middle classes. Many of the families have recently moved into the area. The school itself has modern equipment in the classrooms, and the teachers have access to a large variety of instructional aids in a materials center located in the school. In addition, a psychologist employed by the school district visits your building on Tuesdays, and a reading specialist comes on Mondays and Thursdays.

What can you do to obtain pertinent information about your pupils which will help you to provide more meaningful learning experiences for them?

Would it help to involve your pupils more in planning the units of study?

Suggested Solutions

MISS CAROTHERS' SOLUTIONS

Every teacher has his own ways of relating to children. By the same token, every teacher has characteristic ways of learning about his pupils, paying more attention to some data than to others. The methods used by Miss Carothers, a young teacher with an ability to master details, may be of interest to you but they may also be incompatible with your values or your personality.

One of Miss Carothers' strongest convictions concerned the importance of a teacher's knowing as much about his pupils as possible. Therefore, she tried to get as much information about her fifth-grade pupils as she could. In contrast with most of the other teachers in her urban school, she had many extracurricular contacts with her pupils. She came to school early in the morning and left late in the afternoon, and she made certain that her pupils knew they were welcome to come into the room and work or chat during these off-hours. She organized a science club which met every other Thursday. At the beginning of the school year Miss Carothers had her pupils construct time lines which featured the most important events of their lives; and at the same time she gave them questionnaires such as the one which follows:

QUESTIONNAIRE #1

Name _____ Birthdate _____

Address _____

When you have some free time, do you like to read? _____

If so, what kinds of reading material do you like to read? _____

_____

Do you like to write letters to friends or relatives? _____

_____

Why or why not? _____

Do you like to daydream sometimes? _____

Do you like to invent things? _____ What kinds of things do you

like to invent? _____

Do you like to repair things (such as broken toys, bicycles, dolls,
games, etc.)? _____ What kinds of things do you like to repair? ____

_____

Do you dislike carrying out routine tasks (such as washing or drying
dishes, moving trash or garbage, walking the dog, baby-sitting on
the weekends for your parents, etc.)? _____ What are the tasks you

like the most? _____

_____

Do you like to make up stories and write them down? _____

Do you enjoy working more by yourself or with other people? _____

_____

Why? _____

What kinds of activities give you the most satisfaction? _____

_____

Do you ever disagree with your parents? _____ Do you *tell* them
that you disagree with them? _____ Why or why not? _____

_____

Would you like to become a good student?_____

What could you do to become a better student?_____

_____

Would you like to express yourself more freely in class?_____

Why?_____

At home?_____ Why?_____

In December and April she asked her pupils to complete sentences such as "I wish I could_____" and "My mother always_____." From time to time she employed other techniques such as having the children react to pictures and stories. One of her favorite devices was to ask her pupils to keep a diary for a week. (The diaries were not graded or corrected.) In addition, Miss Carothers gave her pupils exercises which provided her with still more information about their social and emotional problems. Here is an example of one of the more subtle exercises.

YOU, THE MAGICIAN

Sometimes, when things aren't going the way we'd like them to go, it seems to us that it would be mighty handy if we could change the world a little. In this exercise you'll be given an opportunity to imagine that you can change things the way you'd like to have them be. If you had magic powers, what things would you change?

1. What would taste better if it were sweeter?_____
2. What would be more satisfying if it were nearer?_____
3. What would be more valuable if it could float?_____
4. What would be nicer if it were smaller?_____
5. What would last longer if it were elastic?_____
6. What would be more fun if it were faster?_____
7. What would be more refreshing if it were green?_____
8. What would be more useful if it were lighter?_____
9. What would be more pleasant if it were silent?_____
10. What would be more interesting if it were shorter?_____

Most teachers think it is a good idea to get away from their pupils occasionally during the day, especially at noon. They are afraid that too much contact with their pupils will be unhealthy or at least reduce their effectiveness. These teachers are also afraid that they will grow stale as a result of being with their pupils too much; they fear their enthusiasm for children will wane. Miss Carothers evidently was not troubled by these fears. *Do you think she has burned herself out by now? Or is the way a teacher relates to his class determined to a large extent by his personality, by his needs, abilities, experiences, and values?*

Miss Carothers also consulted her pupils' cumulative record folders before the school year began and whenever a problem arose with a child. Some teachers feel that if they read the comments of previous teachers in the cumulative record folder they will be prejudiced in some way with regard to the child's capacities or adjustment to school. Instead, they wait for two weeks or so before looking into the folders. *Do you think they are correct in their reasoning? What kinds of information should a teacher have about his pupils before school begins in the fall?*

MRS. HOWARD'S SOLUTIONS

Let's Pretend

Teachers of the primary grades often play "let's pretend" games with their pupils in order to obtain information about them. Mrs. Howard, a second-grade teacher observed during the second week of school, started her session in this way: "Why don't we make believe that we're green—green all over? Imagine that all of us are completely green. Let's think hard about it. . . . If you are green all over, what are you?"

The responses in some cases were predictable: the children imagined themselves to be frogs, caterpillars, and leaves. Other responses were more unexpected: crawdad, aphid, moon monster, chameleon, and rabbit. Mrs. Howard, a veteran who is admired for her sensitivity and for her ability to get children to express themselves, encouraged her pupils to act out their roles. The frogs hopped, one after another, each performance springier than the one before. A few croaked. The leaves fluttered in the wind. Moon monsters menaced. And all the while Mrs. Howard picked up the clues.

The elfish little girl who was new to the school did not want to be a green rabbit; she wanted to be a *white* rabbit.

A moon monster had difficulty in switching back to his role of pupil; he seemed to prefer moon-monstering to anything else.

The third frog hopped audaciously and used his arms in a most froglike manner. He came back to his seat noticeably flushed.

Mrs. Howard felt she knew her pupils a little better after the activity had ended. (It lasted nearly an hour!) Some of the clues, at the time, were just isolated bits of information; but she believed that later on they would take on more meaning.

Does a teacher have to be particularly sensitive and skillful in order to use a technique such as the one just described?

Why do you suppose the little girl wanted to be a white rabbit? If you had been Mrs. Howard, would you have been disturbed by her not wanting to be green?

AN EXERCISE IN SENSING

Mrs. Howard had played another game with some of the children in her neighborhood. It was a variation of the old close-your-eyes guessing game:

"Close your eyes! Hold out your hands. Now guess what is in your hands."

During the summer she had experimented with the objects to be placed in the children's hands. She wanted to use objects which were interesting with regard to shape, texture, and design. The ones she decided to use with her pupils were a $3'' \times 5''$ piece of corrugated foam rubber used as carpet padding; a long, thin, jagged piece of shale rock; a clear glass telephone pole insulator; and a plastic dish brush with a wedge for scraping and a broken handle. In addition to asking the children a series of questions about the identity and usefulness of the object, Mrs. Howard carefully noted their expressions and the ways in which they handled the object.

One of the first children to play the game was Nancy, a pert seven-and-a-half-year-old.

MRS. HOWARD: Nancy, have you ever had someone say to you, "Close your eyes, open your hands, and guess what I put in your hands?"

NANCY: Yes. It was fun, too.

MRS. HOWARD: I'm going to ask you to do that, but I'm going to ask you to do even more than guess. Do you suppose you could tell us how the object feels? . . . What do you suppose it is made of? How many ways could it be used? . . . And tell any other things that you think of as you explore it. Keep your eyes closed as long as you want to keep describing your feelings and thinking. Are you ready? (Mrs. Howard puts a brush into Nancy's hands.)

NANCY: Ooooh! It is so prickly! I don't like it. . . . (She begins to rub it on her wrist.) I think it is a brush, but it is so funny. I don't know what this is, but I think it had a handle here. . . . (Considerable manipulation.)

MRS. HOWARD: Why do you think it is a brush?

NANCY: Because we had one that felt like this at home. . . . It had a long handle, though. . . . Maybe this one was broken, 'cause it feels so rough. Our brush had long bristles, and I think this does too. Can I open my eyes now? . . . I was right! (Big grin.)

MRS. HOWARD: Yes, you are right! You have an excellent memory.

NANCY: May I do another one? That was fun, even if I didn't like the feel.

MRS. HOWARD: Why didn't you like the feel?

NANCY: It made me feel goose-pimply all over. I want to do another one.

MRS. HOWARD: Okay. Close your eyes! (She puts a piece of carpet padding into Nancy's hands. Nancy explores the object without saying a word. She wrinkles her nose, cocks her head, twists and pulls the material, and has a very skeptical look on her face.)

NANCY: Well, it sure is soft and nice. I like to feel this. (Nancy puts it up her face, smells it, then rubs it on her nose.) Ooooh, that was funny! It smells like a rubber band. (She stretches, pulls, and tries to snap it.) It sure moves funny.

MRS. HOWARD: Have you ever felt anything like this before?

NANCY: (With a slight grin) Mmmmmmm, no, I don't think so. . . . Oh, yes, I know . . . it's kinda like foam.

MRS. HOWARD: How do you think you could use this material?

NANCY: I have to think what we have at home. . . . (She rubs her fingers over the bumps and rows.) I don't know what those funny things on it are. . . . It's rough back here on this side. . . . Ooooh, I know . . . I could use it for a dishcloth.

MRS. HOWARD: Could you use it for anything else?

NANCY: Yes! I'd make it into a pillow for my doll 'cause it's so soft. . . . I know I have felt this before, but I have to think.

MRS. HOWARD: Is it hard to think with your eyes closed?

NANCY: Yes, but it is fun. I like this . . . sometimes Mom puts something like that into a pillow. (Nancy rubs it some more, and smells it again.) I want to look now. . . . Oh, isn't that funny? (She rubs it, twists it, smells it, and goes through almost all the same manipulations that she had with her eyes closed.) I don't think I ever saw this before, but I know I have felt foam before. It wasn't bumpty . . . it was smooth and soft.

MRS. HOWARD: Now that you have seen it, how many things could you do with it?

NANCY: I know what—I could cut it, and make it into a rug. . . . My mother could use it for a hot pad. . . . I want to make some shapes out of it. . . . Mother could put a flower vase on it. . . . If it were big, Daddy could put it on the floor of the car. . . . Do I get to do another one? (Mrs. Howard gives the insulator to Nancy. She explores it, responds to the questions, and then opens her eyes.)

NANCY: I thought it would be blue—and it was shaped like a tree! I could put it on top of something like a jar, for a lid. It's kinda like the top on a coffee pot. Why, it has a nice sound. (Nancy taps it on the edge of the table. She snaps her finger against it, and it rings like a glass.) It's kinda like a globe, too. You could spin it like a top.

What kinds of information were made available to Mrs. Howard by Nancy?

Recent studies have indicated that the sense of sight dominates the other senses most of the time. *What are the advantages of using an exercise such as this "What's in your hands?" game over one involving the sense of sight?*

Linda, a five-year-old, also enjoyed the game.

LINDA: (After the introduction) Well, I'm ready. Why don't you do something? Put something into my hands. Ooooh! It tickles. (Linda laughs heartily. She begins to twist, turn, and pat the brush; she rubs the bristles, puts it to her nose, puts the bristles up to her ear, while talking constantly as she manipulates it.) I know what it is. . . . It's a brush. We have one that we got from a Lux bottle! But where is the handle? It should be here. . . . I think this is what you scrape the dishes with. Can I look now? (She laughs delightedly.) But I thought it was going to be *red*. Maybe even have a red and white stripe here. It's just like the one at home. Is there anything else? This is so much fun. Hurry up! I'm all ready . . . oooh, it feels like a washcloth, but it's got fringes on the edge. (Linda puts the back side to her face.) I don't like it for a washcloth—it's too rough. It's fun to roll up. May I look now?

MRS. HOWARD: Does it look like you thought it was going to?

LINDA: Nope. (She rolls it up and looks through it with one eye.)

MRS. HOWARD: How many ways could you use it?

LINDA: (She throws it down on the floor.) Isn't that a cute little rug? (She steps on it.) It just fits my foot, but I can't get my other foot on it. . . . Those things fool you, in the hand. I didn't realize that it was for a carpet. . . . Those things really trick me. Let me do another one!

How typical is Linda of a five-year-old in her verbal abilities? In her reasoning powers? In her desire to explore the unknown?

What differences can you find between Linda and Nancy which might be significant in helping them both learn?

Mrs. Howard found Bill, an eight-and-a-half-year-old and soon to be a fourth-grader, a lively subject also. She presented him with the carpet padding.

BILL: Feels like it's corrugated . . . sort of rubber. (He grits his teeth, tosses it from hand to hand, pulls, stretches, snaps, smells, wiggles his nose, and laughs.) It smells like it was real old, maybe rusty. I think it's been used because something rubs off. It would make a good cushion for my army toys.

MRS. HOWARD: Have you ever felt anything like this before?

BILL: Yes. I think it's kinda like foam rubber. I know I have felt it, but I can't figure out all those bumps and lines. . . . I like to go over those bumps; it's kinda like a roller coaster.

MRS. HOWARD: Could you put it with any other materials and make something out of it?

BILL: I could cut a ring for a jar . . . make a sling shot. I'm sure it's some kind of rubber. . . . Yep, it even tastes like rubber! I could wind it up for a model plane—you know, to make it go. I'd have to cut it in strips, but I'm worrying about those bumps. (After opening his eyes.) Yes, I knew it would make a good pad to put my army men on. It kinda looks like rocks. . . . I thought it would be brown. . . . I've got it! Do you put it under a carpet? . . . I thought so! This is fun. Let's do some more! I didn't know it was so much fun to feel and to think. . . . It's sure hard to tell what you are feeling, though.

Which of Bill's reactions did you find especially interesting?

Notice the types of questions Mrs. Howard asked Bill, Nancy, and Linda. *Are there other questioning strategies you would employ during the course of this game to obtain information about pupils' backgrounds, their mental functioning, or their values and attitudes?*

Gail, who was to enter the eighth grade in the fall, was given the insulator.

GAIL: Egads! What on earth is that? It is so heavy but so nice and smooth . . . it's almost silky. Does anything open up? (She taps, twists, pokes it.) Ohhh, it rocks. Why did it do that? Oh, I know . . . I think it's a vase. It has a funny step—what is this doohinkus? . . . Oh, what fun! It feels so weird! Oh, my gosh, it is completely different from anything I ever felt in all my life! I think it is light blue color. It feels like light blue, and maybe it has some white on the edge . . . No . . . it is so smooth, it must be a glass vase. How could I keep it from slipping . . . I think I would like to put some rubber on it; then it wouldn't roll so. I wonder if something screwed into this hole . . . it has curlicues. (Gail laughs and laughs.) Isn't that silly? It's so hard to describe. I've got an idea: it could be an egg cup . . . a bookend . . . a paper holder . . . put jewelry in it . . . drink out of it. (She goes on with more ideas.) What a challenge to my imagination!

When and where might this technique be used? Do you think Mrs. Howard decided to play this game with second-graders in the fall? Why or why not?

Judging from his remarks, what sort of boy do you think David, an eleven-year-old, is?

DAVID: (Holding the insulator to his ear.) Maybe it's a ball . . . I said it was china, but now I'm not so sure. Maybe it is pottery. I didn't know it would be so much fun to feel and to think, and then to describe it. You can learn lots of things this way. I'm going to make a game out of this idea when I go to Silver Creek Camp. Bet the kids would get a bang out of it. (With the rock.) Is it obsidian? No, it's not smooth like obsidian. It's an unusual shape—elongated and thin. It could be a rock, but it isn't heavy. It could be pumice stone, but it isn't light, and I can't feel any holes in it. It smells so funny . . . kinda like a rock smells, but how can I describe how a rock smells? . . . musty . . . old . . . kinda like it had been used.

During the game, Mrs. Howard noted that David's facial expressions were very drawn and tense. He wrinkled his forehead and raised an eyebrow. He was very slow and deliberate in his responses. *Do her observations surprise you?*

Would you play this game with one child in front of your class? Why or why not?

Mrs. Howard discussed this technique of getting information about children with several other teachers. One of the teachers suggested that the child might make up problem-solving situations in connection with the game. *What do you suppose she had in mind?* Another teacher thought that the child should be asked to make a choice concerning the objects he had been exploring: which of them would the child most want to have with him if he were alone on a desert island? *What additional information could be gained from asking the child to make such a choice?*

Gathering Information About Children

LEARNING ABOUT CHILDREN BY OBSERVING THEM

If it is true that without perception learning is not possible, the perceptually sensitive teacher is the one who knows most about his pupils. To be effective, a teacher must be keenly aware of what is going on around him.

An *observer, according to the late Viktor Lowenfeld (1957), is one who can penetrate the detailed relationships which form a total impression.* In the context of the classroom, this would mean that, in order to observe, a teacher should not only see so that he can recognize things, but he should penetrate into the detailed visual relationships of what he sees. Similarly, a teacher should not merely hear, but he should listen to the sounds of the classroom and attempt to understand their characteristics and relationships.

WHAT SHOULD A TEACHER PAY SPECIAL ATTENTION TO?

Since there is such a great amount of data available to the teacher, what should he attend to particularly? Mary Jo Johannis, a resource teacher [1] composed this list of clues to watch for when observing children:

Does he have any close friends; if so, who are they?

Does he participate in class discussions? Is he able to disagree with others? Does he defend his ideas?

How does he respond when you call on him in class?

How does he manage during study periods? Is he able to learn on his own?

Does he work persistently at tasks which are assigned? Is he willing to attempt difficult tasks?

What is his attitude about unassigned tasks? Does he spontaneously undertake new learning experiences?

Does he stare vacantly at a spot on a page? What happens afterwards when he does this?

Does he finish his work early or late? When he finishes quickly, is his work original and adequately elaborated?

Does he check over his work? Is he able to find and correct some of his own errors?

Does he ask for help unnecessarily? Is he able to consult others, when needed?

Is he usually optimistic or pessimistic? Or, is he realistic in his expectations?

Does he interfere with others? Is he easily distracted by others?

[1] In this instance, a teacher who assists other teachers with their instructional programs and who provides "enrichment experiences" for academically able children.

How does he react to disappointment? Does he rise to the occasion and exert increased energy?

How does he react to praise? Does it produce greater conformity or greater elaboration?

Does he tend to be withdrawn? Under what conditions does he withdraw? Does withdrawal contribute to his creativity?

Is he usually quiet, or is he always in motion? Or is he quiet or active as effectiveness requires?

Is he active on the playground?

Does he engage in organized sports?

Which items on the list above might have been enthusiastically endorsed by Lowenfeld, if any? Would he have applauded them all equally?

LEARNING ABOUT CHILDREN BY MEANS OF DIRECT INQUIRY

Teachers, especially at the beginning of the school year, ask their pupils many questions about themselves. Miss Carothers' questionnaire is rather typical of the kind of device which is used to obtain information in written form quickly. Such questionnaires and opinionnaires work best for teachers of pupils whose handwriting is legible and who can express themselves adequately in writing (it is difficult to devise a good questionnaire for primary grade children).

When it comes to understanding a child, however, nothing surpasses listening to him. Effective teachers somehow find the time to talk with their pupils before the school day begins or after it is over. Informal conferences between teachers and children are generally the most revealing (and often the most important) sources of information about a child.

Another source of information, one which some teachers depend upon to a great extent and which others ignore completely, is that provided by fellow teachers. Probably the greatest value in listening to another teacher discuss a pupil is that the pupil can be seen through another person's eyes. It is extremely difficult to be objective about other human beings, and often getting someone else's impression helps a teacher to get a better understanding of the child as a person.

Perhaps the views of the child which the teacher most wants to learn about are those of the parents. (Parents generally agree about their children, but they also see them from different vantage points; so the teacher is eager to talk with both parents about the child.) In asking questions of a parent about his child, the teacher can gain five kinds of information: (1) he can get an idea of the child's role at home; (2) he can get an indication of how the parent regards the child as a person, as a pupil, as a member of the family, and as a member of the community; (3) during the interview with the parent he may get some glimpses of how the pupil regards his parents; (4) he will probably get some clues as to how the pupil regards him (the teacher); and (5) he should get several indications about how the parent regards the teacher, the school, and education in general.

Finally, the teacher can gain valuable information about his pupils by talking with various members of the community about them. Youth leaders, city and county employees, church members (ministers, teachers of religion, and others), merchants, and play-ground directors all have perspectives which differ, necessarily, from the teacher's. It seems reasonable to assume that a teacher who makes use of several of these sources of information is not likely to see his pupils narrowly.

Parents and community resources should be consulted because some children present quite a different picture of themselves in the rest of their world than they do at school. Just how a teacher goes about consulting community figures will depend upon the nature of the community and the relationships the teacher has established within the community network.

RECORDING INFORMATION

There are many obvious benefits in recording the information that teachers acquire about children, and we might examine some of the ways in which such information is obtained and kept. *Are there unfortunate effects which result from recording data about children?*

Cumulative Record Files. Schools try hard to keep up-to-date records of all the children they enroll. To justify time which teachers, secretaries, school psychologists, specialists, and others devote to maintaining cumulative record files, they should be (1) readily accessible to authorized persons;[2] (2) readable; and (3) pertinent to the special abilities of pupils as well as their physical, academic, and socio-emotional development.

Anecdotal Records. Probably the most difficult job involved in keeping a file of information about a pupil is that of recording anecdotes about him which might be included in his folder. Because of the many demands that are made upon them, most teachers only enter the required information concerning health data, attendance, and testing in the cumulative record folders, supplementing this information with brief statements about their pupils at the end of the year. However, teachers who are concerned about the socio-emotional progress of particular children often record significant incidents of their behavior on a day-to-day basis for a week or a month or even longer. These case studies can provide teachers with important insights about their own personalities and crucial elements in the teaching-learning process, as well as about the children being studied.

Many writers recommend that teachers regularly record anecdotes about all of their pupils. Whenever the teacher finds this procedure possible, the material yielded can be invaluable in understanding his pupils. The accumulation of anecdotes which have been reported by several persons, when interpreted with other data, can be synthesized and used in making decisions about individual children and about the class collectively.

GUIDELINES FOR RECORDING ANECDOTAL DATA

Questions about what kinds of incidents to report and how to report them often plague beginning teachers when they start out to record incidents of their pupils' behavior. Here are a few simple guidelines which might be useful to teachers who are bothered by these questions:

1. The language of the report should be objective.
2. The language of the report should be informal.
3. The incidents selected for reporting can be chosen for two

---

[2] Cumulative record folders should be kept in the teacher's room or in some place where he can get to them easily. Some school districts take a number of precautions to see that the records are never seen by pupils, but these measures should not prevent a teacher from having easy access to the files.

reasons: either they are typical of a recurrent type of behavior, or they are atypical and thus significant as a deviation in behavior. The teacher's judgment as to whether an incident is normal or not should be plainly indicated in the report.

4. Incidents that give glimpses of heretofore unnoticed potentialities as well as those that give warnings of things going wrong in mental and personality development should be included.

5. The report should be made as soon as is reasonably possible following the incident.

6. The actual incident should be clearly distinguished, in the report, from the observer's interpretation of it and his feelings about it.

How does the following anecdotal report rate with regard to each of the six guidelines which have been given? The report was written by a student teacher.

REPORT OF AN INCIDENT IN A FIFTH-GRADE CLASSROOM

As the teacher was reading to the class, there came from the back of the room muffled giggles and whispering. Five pupils (two girls and three boys) were busily engaged in their own sort of giggle-fest. The pupils seated immediately in front of them did not seem to notice their noises or the fidgeting, as they continued to listen attentively to the story being read.

Suddenly the teacher looked up, stopped reading and called one of the three boys to the front of the room and told him to stand next to her desk where he remained facing the class for about fifteen minutes, until the story was finished. The boy blushed, but promptly took his position beside the teacher.

As he approached the desk, those who were involved in the commotion looked a bit puzzled, embarrassed, and quieted down immediately. The rest of the class turned, looked to the back of the room, at each other, at the teacher, and then again at the boy. As they turned their heads forward, their expressions varied all the way from general scorn and puzzlement to pleasure and sympathy. Some shifted uneasily in their seats as if they were embarrassed for the boy and for themselves. Only once did the boy look directly at the teacher.

At first the victim smiled, tried to hold his lips together, and shifted from one foot to the other, with a great deal of poise and self-control. At last he found a place·upon which to fix his gaze (out the window). Later he turned slightly toward the teacher and tried very hard to listen to the story. (It should be noted that as soon as the boy took his place the class settled down and commenced listening once again.)

When the teacher finished reading the story, she asked the boy why he found it so necessary to make such a commotion. He did not answer but continued to look out the window—his face showed no emotion whatsoever. The teacher continued to question him in a quiet manner. He glanced at the class, and offered a genuine apology. She smiled at him, saying it must be one of his bad days, and hugged him as she sent him back to his desk. He smiled and looked very much relieved and walked quickly to his desk. The teacher then directed the class to take out their books and begin working on their arithmetic assignment.

The Personal Time Line Technique. The personal time line, another of Miss Carothers' methods of learning about her pupils, can yield important information about young people. Many teachers introduce their pupils to time lines in connection with social studies units, and so the activity is often quite familiar to many children. For those children who have not constructed time lines, the directions are simple: the line can either be vertical or horizontal; marks are made along the line at regular intervals to indicate time elapsed from the start of the time segment to be considered to the end (in this case, the birth of the child until the present); and the most important events are indicated by a mark and the naming of the event at the appropriate point on the line. Since the pupil is asked to give only the most significant events of his life, the teacher is able to gain insights about the child's problems and his values which he might otherwise not receive.

Here are some of the events which were listed by one boy:

Birth.
Birth of my brother.
Entered school.
Brother threw milk bottle at me. Hit me in head. Only time he
    got best of me.
Got sick for Christmas. Couldn't be in program.

Missed school for six weeks. In hospital for two weeks. Missed
Christmas program.

Nurses gave me a button to call them—only boy in the ward
with one. Because I was so good.

Moved from country school to town school.

Missed first class party because I was sick.

With teachers whom they trust, children are surprisingly willing to name the critical events in their social, physical, intellectual,
and spiritual development; and so teachers using methods such as
this one must be especially careful not to pass along information
which was not meant to go beyond them.

*Which of the items above might have been considered confi-
dential by the boy?*

*What do you suppose the boy was like? Was he aggressive or
submissive? Can you tell anything about his values from the events
he listed on his time line?*

LEARNING ABOUT CHILDREN THROUGH INDIRECT INQUIRY

Without appearing to be "nosey," teachers can obtain reliable
data about their pupils by asking them to engage in activities which
give opportunities to reveal attitudes about themselves, their
schools, teachers and other adults, their peers, and the members of
their families. In a sense, all of a child's actions in and out of the
classroom are significant, when we try to understand why he behaves as he does. Unfortunately, teachers do not have time to make
complete anecdotal records for each of their pupils, and perhaps it
is just as well. To record all of the information that might be acquired about one pupil would be a full-time job for any teacher.
Accordingly, teachers are forced to adopt simple techniques that enable them to obtain information about their pupils quickly. They
also have to store a great deal of information in their memories.

*Information Can Be Acquired by Giving Children Incomplete
Sentences.* Many teachers have been successful in gaining important
insights about how their pupils feel by having them finish incomplete sentences such as these:

I like school best when we_____.
I get angry when _____.
School would be better if _____.
It's fun to _____.
I would like to be more like_____.
I wish my father (brother, sister, mother) would_____.
I wish I could learn _____.
We have too many_____.
If only we (I) could _____.
My mother (father, sister, brother) always_____.
I wish I could spend more time with_____.

When a child's responses to incomplete sentences are retained in his cumulative record folder, interesting comparisons can be made if the same or similar forms are administered in successive years. Some of a child's problems, though utterly real to him, are transitory. Others persist. If the teacher can identify the persistent problems in a child's life, he can more intelligently respond to the child's classroom behavior.

Divergent Thinking Activities. Children are not asked to think for themselves very often. This fact has become evident when we have administered tests of creative thinking to children in schools. They frequently are at a loss to know what to do when we tell them, "Try to think of something that no one else in the class would think of." The experience is disturbing to many; these youngsters plead with us, "What should I do?" and "What do you want me to do?"

When children are permitted to search for different solutions to problems, teachers everywhere make the same two observations. First, they have seen their pupils in a different light; children whom they had considered to be poor achievers have demonstrated talents which their teachers had not suspected. More importantly, pupils who have found that they are capable of producing worthwhile ideas have begun to see themselves differently; their self-concepts have undergone healthy transformations.

Second, it has been noted also that when young people are asked to engage in divergent-thinking activities, some erstwhile stellar pupils usually fail to shine. Among any group of high-achieving pupils there are likely to be some youngsters who are able to obtain outstanding grades because they have learned to attend very carefully to what their teacher wants. These young people study their *teachers* more than they study their subjects. When creative-thinking exercises are administered to groups of children who have generally been preoccupied with finding the "right" answer or the correct way to perform a task, teachers often discover that children they had assumed to be resourceful actually lack imagination and initiative.

Personification Techniques for Learning About Children. Teachers in the primary grades have been able to gain valuable insights about their pupils by asking them to think of themselves as animals. They ask questions such as these:

Would you rather be a *butterfly* or a *squirrel?*
Why?
Even in the winter?
How about the summer?
In the spring?
If you were a squirrel—or a butterfly—what would you like to do most of all?
If you were on the moon, would you rather be a butterfly or a squirrel?
Why?

In analyzing their responses, teachers look to see if their pupils take into consideration such factors as beauty, longevity, mobility, intelligence, danger, and companionship. A child may reveal a good deal about his values and the way he thinks in telling why he would prefer to be a butterfly or a squirrel (a cricket or a bee, a peacock or a whale, a wolf or a tortoise).

Almost all of the divergent thinking exercises contained in our Ideabooks (Myers and Torrance, 1964, 1965ab, 1968) as well as many of the activities suggested in the teacher's guides for the Imagi/Craft materials by Cunnington and a team working under the direction of Torrance (Cunnington and Torrance, 1965) should be useful in helping teachers become aware of their pupils' creative potentialities. Tests of the creative-thinking abilities (Torrance, 1966) can also be useful in helping teachers become aware of potentialities that might otherwise go unnoticed.

Identification with Sex Roles Through Pictures. Elementary teachers have long used photographs, paintings, drawings, and sketches in the classroom quite effectively and for a great variety of purposes; pictures have also been utilized extensively by psychologists in trying to understand children. Without attempting to play psychologist, a teacher can also employ photographs and drawings in his attempts to better understand his pupils. Pictures of boys and girls who are approximately the same age as the members of the class can be shown to the children, and then the youngsters can be asked to guess what the children in the pictures are like, to give suitable names to the children in the pictures, and finally to respond to some rather specific questions concerning the tastes and personalities of the children depicted:

> Which one of the children would be very kind to pigeons and
>   squirrels?
> Which one might love to read books?
> Which one might be fond of spiders and toads?
> Which one might take candy when the man at the store is not
>   looking?
> Which one of them would enjoy scaring people?
> Which one would you like to have as your special friend?
> Why?

When two of the pictures are of girls and one of a boy, the teacher can learn how the girls in the class feel about the roles which their families and society have assigned to them. It may prove disturbing to some young ladies to find that they are not supposed to be interested in creatures such as toads and spiders. On the other hand, some boys may be upset by the idea that boys are not supposed to love books but are primary suspects in petty larceny cases. Enlightening discussions can result from the use of pictures in this way.

Learning About Children by Asking Them to Investigate a Concept. Mr. Martin, a sixth-grade teacher who is fond of designing his own curricular materials, often introduces key concepts by administering exercises that he believes will give his pupils a good understanding of the significance of the concepts. Shortly after his class had begun a unit of study dealing with conservation of natural resources, Mr. Martin gave them this exercise about the idea of preservation.

HOLD IT!

We preserve things in many different ways. In order to keep fish fresh, we use ice. By bronzing them, many people keep the baby shoes of their children in the same condition that they were when the shoes were outgrown. When we want to preserve something nowadays, we may encase it in plastic. In this exercise, you will be asked to think of how a variety of things might be preserved—that is, how they might be kept, maintained, retained, or sustained.

How would you preserve:
1. raspberries?
2. the flavor of mint?
3. the fragrance of roses?
4. the excitement of a holiday?
5. dignity?
6. honesty?
7. a friendship?

Which of the items above would you most like to preserve or have preserved for you?
Why?
Would it really be the same if you tried to keep it just as it is? Explain.
Is there anything that actually never changes?
Why or why not?
What is the difference between conserving something and preserving it?

Mr. Martin discovered that by administering this exercise he could gain information about his students that could not be obtained by either observation or direct inquiry.

Mr. Martin used a similar technique, dealing with the concept of promise or expectation, at the beginning of the school year in order to acquire information about the members of his new class. His students gave revealing replies when asked what "promises" the following events held for them:

the rumble of thunder;
the smell of oil;
the sound of a teacher clearing his throat;
the scratching of a dog;
the hissing of steam;
the ringing of a bell;

a baby beginning to cry;
the sputtering of a motor;
and the ringing of a telephone.

Mr. Martin purposely selected items such as *motor, steam,* and *oil* that would have different meanings for his students, depending upon their backgrounds and interests. By including common events of the household such as the ringing of a telephone and a baby crying, he hoped to obtain clues as to how his students perceived their roles at home. In addition, he wanted to know if all of the events that he listed really were common experiences to his students.

Value of Awareness

The history of invention, scientific discovery, art, music, and literature—all tell us that a keen sense of awareness is the thing that triggers almost every truly creative act. There are many people who feel that inventors, scientific discoverers, and other creative people are just lucky and happen by chance to stumble upon their great ideas. They would say the same thing about the success of the teachers whose experiences are described in Chapter 2. However, a careful examination of great moments of discovery will show that, although chance may have had a role, there was also a strong sense of awareness of the problem and possible solutions. Thus, when chance solutions occurred, these creative people were able to recognize them and follow through with appropriate action to test, elaborate, and communicate the solution. The same must have been true of the teacher of John the vandal, described in Chapter 2. If this teacher had not been aware of John's mechanical genius, his great talent for organizing other boys, and the like, do you think she would have influenced the student council to appoint a boy with such a "bad" reputation as chairman of an important and responsible committee?

In working with children who live in poverty or who differ in race from the teacher, there is a great danger that teachers will be blinded to potentialities because of the low expectations they have of such children. Miss Norris, a third-grade teacher, was about ready to quit teaching. Willie Mae, an unusually tall and vivacious black girl from a disadvantaged home, was unquestionably the leader of a group that drove Miss Norris almost distracted every day. One day Miss Norris related her problem to Mrs. Mann, another third-grade teacher who had assisted Torrance in a three-week creativity workshop in which Willie Mae had been enrolled the previous summer. Mrs. Mann remarked, "I don't know whether it would work for you, but I can tell you one thing that Dr. Torrance did that seemed to help with Willie Mae. He gave her a lot of responsibility and she lived up to it. She had a great deal of influence on the other children and, things went better." Miss Norris doubted that this would work and said that she had never given Willie Mae any responsibility because she didn't trust her. Nevertheless, she began giving Willie Mae some responsibilities such as leading certain activities, carrying messages to another class, returning books borrowed by the teacher to the library, getting additional books from the library for general use and the like. She also began finding unexpected potentialities in Willie Mae. She was an excellent organizer and group leader. She was also a good problem solver and could produce many artful and imaginative ideas. Once again, teaching became possible in Miss Norris' classroom.

Making Your Own Summary

Why don't you examine each of the incidents quoted in Chapter 2 and see whether awareness of problems and potentialities is likely to have been the thing that triggered the teacher's discovery of a way of releasing the child's potentialities?

Actually, there is much theoretical and research evidence to support the idea that awareness is important in all human relations. Harry Stack Sullivan's (1953) entire theory of personality is built around the idea that most of man's troubles in interpersonal effectiveness occur when he behaves toward others as though they have abilities, motivations, interests, and attitudes that they do not in fact have. Thus, knowing others—being aware of their abilities, motivations, interests, and attitudes—is basic to effectiveness in all interpersonal relations and certainly in teaching. Some leadership studies (Havron and McGrath, 1961) have shown that one of the characteristics of effective leaders is the breadth and depth of their knowledge of their men. We suspect strongly that this characteristic would differentiate truly effective teachers from their less effective colleagues.

For an informal check on this idea, you might try to think of the teacher in your own life who influenced you most and the one who influenced you least or who exerted a negative influence upon you. How well do you think each of these teachers knew you?

Another check would be to pick out two teachers of your own acquaintance—one that you regard as having a very healthy, positive effect on students and one that either has little or no effect on children's behavior or who has a very negative effect upon them. Find out in an informal way how much each teacher knows about his pupils. In conducting tests and exercises in creative thinking, we have observed that teachers who have reputations for teaching effectively in creative ways and in facilitating creative growth seem to have very intimate and detailed knowledge of their pupils. They seem to see much meaning in the responses that their pupils make both to the tests and to the exercises. Other teachers seem to be aware of no meaning whatsoever in such productions.

Although we are not suggesting that teachers play at being clinical psychologists, you might like to examine a wonderful illustration of the kinds of understanding that an imaginative and disciplined psychologist can obtain from tests, and from play and work situations like those described in this chapter. You will find such an illustration in Lois B. Murphy's book, *The Widening World of Childhood* (1962). Dr. Murphy used techniques similar to those described herein to find out how children learn to cope with stress and change. We believe, moreover, that any teacher with a desire to know his pupils and a little imagination can achieve something quite similar to what Dr. Murphy has achieved, at least insofar as his own pupils are concerned.

Teachers who want to understand the world of their pupils and to be fully aware of their pupils' potentialities, interests, and motivations need not limit their efforts to standardized tests and observations. There are two other sources of useful information that most teachers seem to neglect. One is the abilities, particularly the creative abilities, reflected in socially disapproved kinds of behavior. Teachers are usually so obsessed with the need to punish disapproved behavior that they rarely use it to glimpse heretofore unnoticed possibilities, glimpses that might serve as the key to freeing that child to achieve his potentialities. Many teachers will argue that it is immoral not to punish a child for undesirable behavior. We believe, however, that it is more immoral to fail to become aware of and develop children's potentialities, or to fail to correct the defects of one's teaching, than to fail to punish children. This does not mean that the teacher must condone disapproved behavior, coddle spoiled children, or the like. It does mean that he must not be so blinded by the disapproved behavior that he is unable to become aware of potentialities, which with intelligent and loving guidance and direction might blossom into outstanding positive achievement.

Another area neglected by many teachers is the learning that takes place outside of the classroom. There are teachers who seem to assume that information and skills learned outside of class are somehow not learned quite legally and thus cannot be credited. Even though a teacher might not want to give credit for this kind of learning, he should at least be aware of it and acknowledge it. The use of checklists of self-initiated learning activities might be useful. A good time to use such a checklist is immediately after the summer or Christmas vacation to find out what learning experiences pupils have had during these vacations. You may be quite surprised about what you learn. In fact we believe that once you really begin to know your pupils, you will find that they are exciting and fascinating with rich possibilities that you had never dreamed of and that you will have an outpouring of ideas for creative ways of teaching them.

REFERENCES

Cunnington, B. F. and E. P. Torrance. *Imagi/Craft Series*. Boston: Ginn & Co., 1965.

Havron, M. D. and J. E. McGrath. "The Contribution of the Leader to the Effectiveness of Small Military Groups." In L. Petrullo and B. M. Bass (eds.). *Leadership and Interpersonal Behavior*. New York: Holt, Rinehart & Winston, 1961. Pp. 167–178.

Lowenfeld, V. *Creative and Mental Growth* (3rd ed.). New York: The Macmillan Company, 1957.

Murphy, L. B. *The Widening World of Childhood*. New York: Basic Books, 1962.

Myers, R. E. and E. P. Torrance. *Invitations to Thinking and Doing*. Boston: Ginn & Co., 1964.

Myers, R. E. and E. P. Torrance. *Can You Imagine?* Boston: Ginn & Co., 1965a.

Myers, R. E. and E. P. Torrance. *Invitations to Speaking and Writing Creatively*. Boston: Ginn & Co., 1965b.

Myers, R. E. and E. P. Torrance. *Stretch*. Minneapolis: Perceptive Publishing Co., 1968.

Sullivan, H. S. *The Interpersonal Theory of Psychiatry*. New York: W. W. Norton & Company, 1953.

Torrance, E. P. *Torrance Tests of Creative Thinking: Norms-Technical Manual* (research ed.). Princeton, N.J.: Personnel Press, 1966.

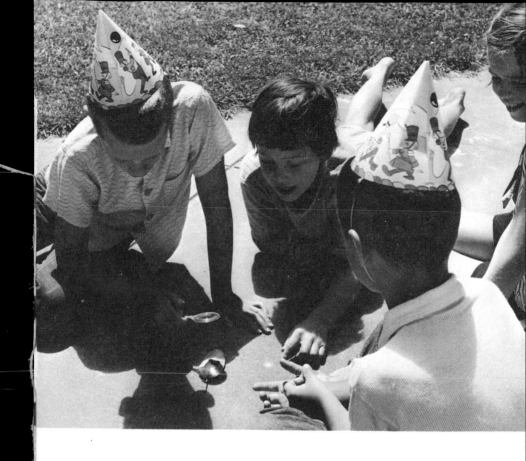

CHAPTER 7 QUESTIONING

FOR INFORMATION

Contact,
Reaching, touching,
Minds sharing mysteries,
Pleasures, puzzles, sorrows, nonsense,
Talking.

The Problem

Miss Marston discovered early in her career that "what works in the classroom today may not work tomorrow." Consequently, when she realized one day that the lessons in the reading workbook which she had been using to help develop the critical thinking faculties of her fifth-grade pupils were no longer effective, she decided to adopt a different technique.

First, Miss Marston concluded that she had dominated the discussions which always followed the filling-out of workbook exercises. Accordingly, she determined to have different members of the class act as moderators of the discussions; and she made a mental note that she should make certain that children who needed the experience of leading a discussion would have an opportunity to do so.

In addition to staying out of the picture as much as possible, Miss Marston decided that she would encourage her pupils to make up their own rules for conducting discussions. The children seemed to her to be quite ready to assume such responsibilities.

Finally, she thought that asking the children to jot down questions about the reading assignment and related matters as they were reading would provide plenty of good material for discussion. There were several pupils with keen minds in her class who had been bored with the workbook and would probably come up with some challenging questions.

Is it possible that Miss Marston was overestimating the abilities of her pupils? Are ten-year-olds capable of conducting discussions? Can they set up the rules for discussing serious subjects? Can they ask worthwhile questions?

What was really Miss Marston's problem? Do you suppose the workbook questions were really responsive to the interests, needs, and thinking of the children in Miss Marston's classroom?

Importance of Asking Good Questions

In the last chapter, we tried to show how different kinds of assignments or questions could be presented to facilitate creative thinking and learning in reading. In this and the next two chapters attention will be given more systematically to the art of questioning and the use of questions in creative learning and teaching.

Since much of a teacher's time is devoted to questions, it is important that teachers ask questions that will determine whether children have really acquired the information and concepts being taught and that will cause them to analyze statements, to put ideas together, to formulate hypotheses and plans, and to grow in awareness. As any parent knows who has tried to get information from a child about his experiences at school, it is not easy to formulate questions to obtain the kind of information he is seeking. Artful question-making is not common among parents. Furthermore, it seems to be almost as unusual among teachers. Consequently, teachers sometimes think that their pupils know something when they do not have the slightest idea as to what it is all about.

The effective teacher may be quite conscious of the techniques he uses in questioning his pupils, or he may be almost unaware of his strategies for eliciting responses. Some teachers, apparently without striving to do so, seem to ask questions in ways that result in things happening intellectually to children. Others work hard to compose questions they hope will be effective.

Although most of the types of questions that will be discussed in these chapters are useful in both oral and written form, the emphasis will be upon methods of questioning particularly suitable for discussions, conferences, or interviews. There will be no attempt to present a comprehensive analysis of test questions; nevertheless, it should be pointed out examinations and quizzes could better serve their function as vehicles for learning if they more frequently incorporated questions calling for redefinition, evaluation, synthesis, and divergent thinking. Many teachers will find helpful guidance in Sanders' *Classroom Questions: What Kinds?* (1966).

Frequently, an adult may be fooled into thinking that children know much more than they do because they are able to use terms superficially. If one begins questioning such children, however, he will soon discover that they do not know what they are saying. This chapter will deal with this kind of question, which might be called the "knowledge-acquisition" question. The next chapter, Chapter 8, will focus on questions designed specifically to bring into play the higher mental processes, and Chapter 9 will deal with that really uncommon kind of classroom question, the provocative one that causes children to think of information and ideas in new ways.

First, let us take an overview of the different types of questions.

Ten Types of Questions

Since the distinctions between some of the classifications of questioning may be unclear, it might be helpful if we take a concept presented in a fifth-grade science textbook and show how it can be used in ten types of questions:

1. *Fill-in.* The faster a fluid such as air or water moves, the_____pressure it exerts.

2. *Retention.* What is the name of the principle which can be stated: "the faster a fluid such as air or water moves, the less pressure it exerts"?

3. *Multiple-choice.* Which of these principles is illustrated by a window curtain's blowing out of an open window on a windy day? (a) Bernoulli's Effect, (b) Newton's First Law of Motion, (c) Corioli's Effect, or (d) Newton's Third Law of Motion.

4. *Analysis.* Does Bernoulli's principle have anything to do with the movement of an airplane? Why or why not?

5. *Synthesis.* If you stepped into a shower stall and turned on the water full-force, and the shower curtain blew in and hit you, what principle might be illustrated by this chain of events?

6. *Convergent thinking.* These three incidents are examples of what principle? (a) A window curtain blows out of an open window on a windy day. (b) Larry steps into a shower stall and turns on the water full-force, and the shower curtain blows in and hits him. (c) Henry places a folded strip of paper below his mouth and blows hard across the top of the paper; the strip of paper rises so that it is perpendicular to his lip.

7. *Open-ended.* What kinds of everyday events can be explained by Bernoulli's principle?

8. *Evaluation.* Do you think that a window curtain blowing out of an open window on a windy day is adequately explained by Bernoulli's principle? Why is it adequate or inadequate?

9. *True-false.* The faster a fluid such as air or water moves, the less pressure it exerts. Is that right?

10. *Provocative.* How might you use Bernoulli's principle to make life more enjoyable or interesting?

There undoubtedly are many other types of questions, but we chose these ten because they are related rather directly to the major thinking operations as defined by Guilford (1967). A number of other models might have been used (Bloom, 1956; Sanders, 1966), but we believe that Guilford's is the most useful in creative learning and teaching.

It should be added that some questions may involve several kinds of thinking. An evaluation question, for example, might require the pupil to remember, to analyze, to recognize, and to produce ideas, as well as to judge. The so-called higher forms of thinking contain elements of the lower forms, but it is also true that a question which calls principally for the recall of information may involve the pupil in discovering relationships; in analyzing a fact, concept, or generalization; and in thinking of other examples. So when a question is identified as a "retention question" or an "evaluation question," it is so labeled because the dominant thinking ability is retention, evaluation, or some other designation that psychologists have assigned to an aspect of mental functioning.

Questioning for Remembering

THE FILL-IN QUESTION

Most of the questions asked in classrooms by teachers are of the single-answer variety: one answer, the one in the teacher's mind or in the textbook, is the correct one. All too frequently in a class discussion the young pupil learns that his role is similar to that of the embattled college student who is being fed completion questions in an examination. All too common is the paradigm which follows:

TEACHER: Mary had a little [pause] . . .
FIRST CHILD: Lamb.
TEACHER: whose fleece was [pause] . . .
SECOND CHILD: White.
TEACHER: As snow.

There are some rather sophisticated versions of this type of monologue-with-responses; but, like the more rudimentary forms, they are still variations of a very familiar questioning technique. This technique is really a game designed to give the teacher a feeling that his pupils are following along, like Mary's lamb, wherever he chooses to go. By hesitating and then waiting for the correct response, he assures himself that his pupils are listening and understanding the presentation. In some classrooms, however, we wonder how much learning actually takes place when the pupils know the script so well that they can plug in the right word or phrase whenever the teacher pauses in his monologue. Let's consider an example of this type of questioning by Mr. Condor.

Mr. Condor was discussing with his class the traits of the Snowy Owl that distinguish it from other owls, and one of his pupils remembered that it ate poultry. Mr. Condor went on to ask additional questions about the feeding habits of the bird.

MR. CONDOR: What do we refer to—or what word do we use to describe the things that this owl feeds upon? There is one word we should know—this was called the owl's [pause] . . . Norman?
NORMAN: Uhh.
MR. CONDOR: The owl's [pause] . . .
NORMAN: Oh, I don't remember.
MR. CONDOR: Laura?
LAURA: Prey.
MR. CONDOR: Prey. The owl's prey! Right!

THE RETENTION QUESTION

The retention question, another device for testing the pupil's memory, was frequently employed by Mr. Pritchett when he was observed teaching language arts to a class of sixth-grade pupils. He was in the midst of an extended lesson whose theme was a linguistic definition of language. Recorded below is a transcription of the beginning of one of the periods devoted to analyzing the definition.

MR. PRITCHETT: You're looking bright-eyed and bushy-tailed! All of you. [Pause] Ken, stand up! [Pause] John, stand up! Sit down, both of you. [Long pause] Any questions? [Long pause] Bev?

BEVERLY: Why did you ask them to stand up?

MR. PRITCHETT: Do I have to have a reason? [The class buzzes. A pupil murmurs, "I guess so."] Why should I have a reason, uh? Why should I have a reason for telling them to stand up? I'm bigger than you are! [Laughter] When I say, "Stand up," you stand up! Ay?

PHYLLIS: What would you do if you asked them to stand up and they didn't stand up?

MR. PRITCHETT: Ahh, that's an unfair question. [Laughter] I'd probably go down and hit them. Something like that. [Laughter] Does anyone know what kind of an action that is that I just used there by doing that? What's the word for what I did? [Pause] Randy?

RANDY: An order?

MR. PRITCHETT: Ah, all right. What *kind*—what kind of an order? Ken?

KEN: Command.

MR. PRITCHETT: No, what *kind*? What *kind*? What kind of an order was that? What kind of a performance was that I just put on? What kind of a performance was that?

KEN: A communication?

MR. PRITCHETT: Well, it was a communication. What kind of communication? [Pause]

HARRY: A speech.

MR. PRITCHETT: All right, but I'm thinking of something else. All right. It was an *arbitrary* thing, wasn't it?

Did you guess that the word Mr. Pritchett was looking for was "arbitrary"? At the end of the episode we finally learned that he was pushing hard for a single word, a key concept in the definition of language that he had been examining with his sixth-graders. When teachers' questions are analyzed, it is surprising how often they are observed to be asking for one word. If a pupil has the magic word, the lesson moves on. If not, the machinery of instruction is stuck, in the manner of a broken record. (Did you notice how frequently in these transcriptions the teachers repeated a question, often using identical wording?) There is a close parallel between questioning sessions such as those conducted by Mr. Pritchett and Mr. Condor and teaching-machine programs. In each situation a pupil must make the desired response before the lesson can continue. However, in the questioning session just one pupil is speaking for from twenty to forty-five others. The teacher goes ahead when the acceptable response is delivered by a pupil, and he has no way of knowing if the rest of his class is actually with him. After two or three questions have eluded a pupil, it is very easy for him to let the others slip by—especially if there are several classmates upon whom the teacher can depend to carry forth the discussion.

To keep more pupils' attention during questioning, there are a few pointers that an experienced teacher keeps in mind. For instance, if you preface your question with the name of the child you wish to call upon, that may be a signal for the rest of the class to stop thinking. "We're safe, for the time being," they may say to themselves. A better practice is to call on the child at the end of the question. It is a good policy to act as if everyone is interested but no one is being grilled. Without being too intense, you can behave as if the question were both intrinsically interesting and challenging. If the teacher is genuinely interested in finding out what the child knows or thinks, this occurs almost automatically.

LIMITATIONS OF MEMORY QUESTIONING

Although the two methods of questioning just discussed are valuable for helping pupils to review information and to evaluate how well they have remembered facts and concepts, there are at least three major difficulties with using memory questions predominantly. First, and most important, when the answers called for are the type that require the pupil simply to recall a word or phrase, no further learning is implied in the questioning-answering process. The goal for the pupil is to fill in the gaps of the presentation, much as he would fill in the missing pieces of a picture puzzle. If it is entirely clear from the presentation what is wanted—as in the case of a puzzle when the picture is nearly completed—there is no challenge to the pupil's thinking abilities. Producing the proper response is simply a matter of knowing the picture—and too often this means knowing the superficial aspects of the subject-matter picture.

The second great difficulty with relying heavily upon memory questions is that they are interpreted by pupils as a system of punishments and rewards. The interpretation of a question-answer situation is a personal matter for each individual. To be called upon by a teacher can be a reward for one child and a punishment for another. The teacher may or may not interpret the situation in the same way that the pupil does. Consciously or unconsciously a teacher doles out rewards and punishments all day long, and the question-answer game is one of the most frequent situations in which this system is practiced. Inappropriate responses are often construed as mistakes and are thus punishable both in the mind of the teacher and in the mind of the learner. Either the child has the teacher's answer and is rewarded, or he does not and is punished. If you remember the responses given by Mr. Pritchett's pupils to his questions concerning the arbitrary nature of language, you can see that a thoughtful and appropriate answer might be an occasion for frustration and confusion (or, in some classrooms, shame) if it is not the answer the teacher is seeking.

If you look carefully at these questioning techniques, another obvious difficulty becomes apparent: since the teacher approves or disapproves of the responses of his pupils according to his private script, the intellectual progress of the pupils is seemingly limited to the accuracy and completeness of the teacher's information. (We say "seemingly limited" because children can make inferences, just as they can form misconceptions, during any presentation; and they may very well link together the bits of information presented and formulate generalizations without being encouraged to do so by the teacher.) The problem of the teacher's correctness bothers many observers, especially now that more and more classrooms are open to fellow teachers, supervisors, parents, newspaper and magazine reporters, and television cameras. When the teacher is incorrect with regard to a fact, concept, or generalization, the critics fear that the pupils will be blighted by the error. Teachers should strive to give accurate information, but we should be more upset by a teacher's disinclination or inability to help his pupils to acquire and use the tools of learning.

ANALYZING QUESTIONING METHODS THAT EMPHASIZE MEMORY

Most variations of memory questioning can be represented schematically in these two ways:

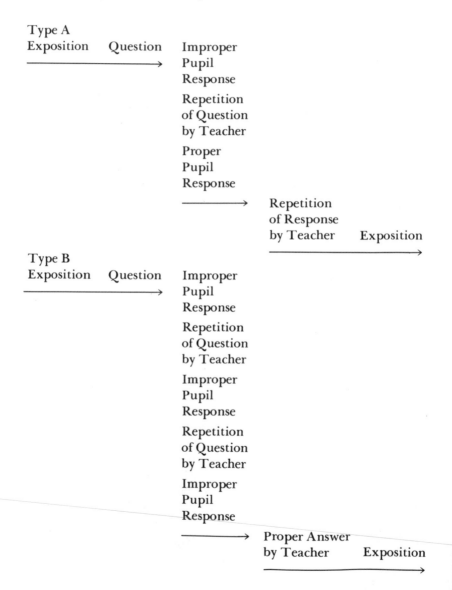

Type A
Exposition   Question   Improper
                            Pupil
                            Response

                            Repetition
                            of Question
                            by Teacher

                            Proper
                            Pupil
                            Response

                                              Repetition
                                              of Response
                                              by Teacher   Exposition

Type B
Exposition   Question   Improper
                            Pupil
                            Response

                            Repetition
                            of Question
                            by Teacher

                            Improper
                            Pupil
                            Response

                            Repetition
                            of Question
                            by Teacher

                            Improper
                            Pupil
                            Response

                                              Proper Answer
                                              by Teacher   Exposition

The arrows represent the *movement* of the lesson toward an instructional goal. The movement of the lesson does not continue until the proper response is plugged into the discourse. Usually, the lesson does not go ahead until the teacher has repeated the correct response, if one is forthcoming from the class. The urge to make certain that the entire class has heard the proper response is very strong in the great majority of teachers who use the technique. Pupils provide little enrichment of the lesson with the insertion of either proper or improper responses. Since the correct response is the one in the teacher's mind (or in the textbook), the pupils are simply filling in words and not adding anything to the presentation. Notice also that there is considerable opportunity for rejection in these two paradigms. For the pupils who respond to the teacher's questions, there is always the risk of being *wrong*. When there is only one proper answer and that answer is to be found in the teacher's mind (refer again to the dialogue between Mr. Pritchett and his pupils), it is almost impossible for pupils to make a contribution. It is easy to imagine how frustrating the exclusive use of this kind of questioning is to the disadvantaged, lower-class child or the child from a background vastly different from that of the teacher.

USING THE MEMORY QUESTIONING METHOD RESPONSIVELY

We might suggest a third way in which memory questions can be employed to accomplish identical instructional objectives:

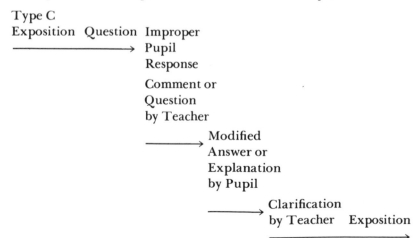

This way of handling the responses of pupils is termed "responsive" because the teacher creates the kind of environment in which children feel safe enough to respond to the teacher, and to each other naturally and imaginatively. The teacher in turn responds to the children in a manner that is marked by the absence of censure and the presence of interest in their ideas. The teacher responds to the ideas of his pupils by suggesting relevant ideas and materials, by clarifying concepts that are unclear in the minds of his pupils, and by acting as an interested sounding board. His most outstanding characteristics are his capacity to listen and to imagine what pupils are experiencing.

Handling interaction in a responsive manner takes more time; however, the pupils have more opportunity to contribute to the discussion, and answers that are not exactly the ones the teacher is looking for are treated as intelligent responses.

MEMORY QUESTIONING AND INCREASING UNDERSTANDING

An example of the teaching of facts for the purpose of acquiring information and not deliberately for the purpose of increasing understanding is this set of seven review questions that Miss Gable gave to her nine-year-old pupils after they had been reading in their geography book.

GEOGRAPHY

Fill in the blanks. Spell all words correctly.
1. The sun and its nine planets are called the_____.
2. Summer, fall, winter, and spring are called the four_____.
3. The places we live in and our surroundings are our_____.
4. North, south, east, and west are called the four_____.
5. The earth spins like a wheel on an imaginary line called the_____.
6. The earth and the other planets go around or_____around the sun.
7. The earth spins or_____on its axis.

As fill-in questions, these sentences emphasize the pupil's ability to recall discrete facts. The facts, of course, are related, but there was no attempt on Miss Gable's part to show how they are related. After the children had finished scoring each other's quiz, there had been no discussion, for example, of the relationship of the earth's position in the solar system to the seasons. Miss Gable had simply told the children that they would have another quiz on Monday (Friday was the day for tests in the school) and that they would have to be able to spell correctly any words that were misspelled on the quiz. If one of the pupils had asked her, as boys and girls sometimes do, why the earth began spinning in the first place, it is unlikely that the question would have been explored by the class with Miss Gable's guidance.

What kinds of questions might be asked to help children see relationships between the facts that are called for in the seven questions? Which facts should be linked especially? What styles of questioning would you use?

Questions That Ask the Pupil to Recognize Information

THE MULTIPLE-CHOICE QUESTION

Of all the types of questions known to teachers, undoubtedly the one used most frequently is the multiple-choice question, especially in written tests. Perhaps this is because of its extensive use in colleges and universities, where classes are large. The great virtue of the multiple-choice question is that it lends itself to rapid scoring. More and more the scoring in high schools, colleges, and universities is being done electronically. Therefore, it is likely that the multiple-choice question will continue to be the most popular kind of question on the educational scene.

However, it is used far less frequently in oral questioning. For instance, in conducting his discussion of language, Mr. Pritchett did not say:

"My behavior, just then, was an example of which one of these charactertistics of language: convention, arbitrariness, abstraction, or symbolism?"

Many times teachers offer alternative answers to their questions, but the questioning strategy is more along this line:

MISS WYATT (holding up a red ball): What is the color of this ball, children? Is it red or blue or yellow? Yes, Mary?
MARY: Green.

MISS WYATT: No, it's not green, is it? Who knows what the color of this ball is? Susan, do you know?

SUSAN: I think it's red.

MISS WYATT: Yes, that's right, Susan. It's *red*.

SCHEMATIC REPRESENTATION OF MULTIPLE-CHOICE QUESTIONING

Most multiple-choice questioning resembles the paradigm for memory questioning. The difference between the two types resides mainly in the form of the question itself. In answering the fill-in question or the retention question, the pupil must produce from his memory a word, phrase, or piece of connected discourse. He had the advantage in the multiple-choice question of being presented with the proper response (along with less acceptable answers).

Exposition	Question	Improper Response from Pupil A		
———————→		Rejection of Answer and/or Repetition of Question by Teacher		
		Proper Response from Pupil B		
		———————→	Repetition of Proper Response by Teacher	Exposition ———————→

SENSITIVE HANDLING OF MULTIPLE-CHOICE QUESTIONING

There is another way of handling incorrect or inappropriate responses to the multiple-choice question in an oral discussion that is usually not available to the teacher in a testing situation. If we take the example of Miss Wyatt's lesson dealing with color, the interaction might go something like this:

MISS WYATT: What is the color of this ball, children? Is it red or blue or yellow? Do you know, Mary?

MARY: Green.

MISS WYATT: Oh, does that look green to you, Mary? Do you remember what color grass is?

MARY: Yes. It is green.

MISS WYATT: Is the ball the same color as the grass?

MARY: No . . . I don't think so. Could that be red?

MISS WYATT: Yes, it's red.

This style of questioning can be diagrammed in this way:

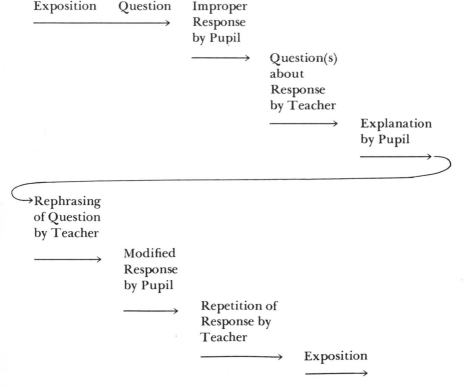

In this paradigm the arrow indicating the movement of the lesson is placed under the pupil's explanation because this indeed may be a contribution not only to his understanding but to the understanding of the other pupils as well. The teacher may or may not repeat the question or the modified response of the pupil.

ADVANTAGES OF THE MULTIPLE-CHOICE QUESTION

As has been pointed out, the multiple-choice question is probably the most popular type of question for teachers and examiners who must evaluate a large number of papers. When the size of a class in elementary school approaches forty (and, unfortunately, too many approach or surpass that number), a teacher may employ the multiple-choice question to measure abilities such as the pupil's ability to interpret, to discriminate, to analyze, to solve problems, and to make inferences. Carefully constructed multiple-choice questions can measure those abilities, thus cutting down on the time the teacher has to devote to correcting examinations. As a matter of fact, any competent person—a teacher's aide, a spouse, a son, or a daughter—can score a multiple-choice test with a properly composed key, thus reducing further the chore of grading the tests and freeing the teacher to spend more time interpreting the reactions of his pupils and consulting with them about misconceptions and gaps of knowledge. Although an analysis of errors made on this type of test does not usually yield much insight concerning pupils' thinking, it does provide extremely useful information. An analysis of the errors pupils make can give a basis for refocussing instruction to produce more thoughtful behavior.

DISADVANTAGES OF THE MULTIPLE-CHOICE QUESTION

MULTIPLE-CHOICE QUIZ

Circle the group of words which is closest in meaning to the word on the left.

1. hoax

                  farm implement   new detergent   trick or joke

2. perpendicular

                      stretched out   exactly upright   parallel

3. emigrate
   removable grill large statue to leave a place or a country
4. integration
   green salad second step in division act of making whole
5. hyphen
   punctuation mark respiratory organ ductless gland
6. infer
   gaseous light to guess to conclude through reasoning
7. cease
   oceans to stop flock of geese
8. chronological
   a strip encircling cars silly or absurd pertaining to time
9. sever
   to cut or separate underground sanitation double-stitching
10. interjection
    a street crossing a part of speech close competition

The pupils who took this quiz were subjected to two kinds of interference problems in trying to choose the correct responses. In the case of a word such as "infer," they had to determine whether this kind of mental activity was closer to concluding through reasoning or to guessing. However, in popular usage, the term "inferring" is often used for "guessing." The teacher consistently put another obstacle in the way of the pupils' understanding by giving as an alternate response a word or phrase that resembled the word to be defined: "oceans" (for "cease") "underground sanitation" (for "sever") "street crossing" (for "interjection") "farm implement" (for "hoax") "removable grill" (for "emigrate") and "second step in division" (for "integration"). The resemblance in some cases was in the sound of the vocabulary word (the fondness of this teacher for puns may have been appreciated by those of his pupils with similar senses of humor), and in other cases the resemblance was in meaning. Alternative responses such as "street crossing" (for "interjection") and "oceans" (for "cease") are called distractors. Their ability to lure pupils into selecting them is supposed to help the teacher discriminate between those youngsters who have understood or who have paid attention and those who have not understood or who have been inattentive. The distractors that contain elements of the correct response, however, often are the choice of conscientious pupils who become confused.

There are nine versions of the multiple-choice question (Thorndike & Hagen, 1961), and the one given above is reputed to be one of the hardest to construct. The multiple-choice question may be a true question in form followed by several possible answers, or it may be an incomplete sentence (called a "stem"), which is followed by several correct or incorrect statements having to do with the problem, graph, or diagram. In addition to the form of the question, there can be three ways for the pupil to make his choice: by selecting the *correct* alternative, by selecting the *incorrect* alternative, or by choosing the *best* of the alternatives. The simple question with a choice of one of our alternatives to be designated as correct is recommended to teachers who are just beginning to construct multiple-choice questions for examinations.

Like the true-false question, the multiple-choice question permits the pupil to guess when he does not really have any information concerning the subject the teacher is presenting. If the teacher asks the question orally, there is an opportunity for him to find out if the pupil has some understanding of the topic; but if the question is given in writing, the uninformed pupil is sometimes as likely to choose the correct response as the pupil is who has become confused by competing alternatives. For this reason, the multiple-choice question is not favored when the teacher has the time to evaluate a pupil's deep understanding of the topic and its relationships to allied topics. In recent years, the multiple-choice examination has been rather vigorously and widely attacked (Hoffman, 1962; Black, 1963) as a device for evaluating educational achievement, awarding scholarships, and the like. A major criticism is that this type of examination discriminates against the creative mind, which grasps relationships that others miss. This, however, is outside the concern of this chapter.

THE MATCHING QUESTION

Rarely is a matching question given orally, but it is a popular device in written examinations for determining whether the pupil has an acquaintanceship with facts, concepts, and generalizations. Once in a great while a teacher might offer an oral question like this one: "We've been studying about three interesting trees this week—the oak, the maple, and the fir. Which of these trees do we call 'deciduous,' which do we call 'evergreen,' and which might be called either 'evergreen' or 'deciduous'?"

However, the exercise which follows is more typical of an occasion when a teacher uses the matching question:

MATCHING-QUESTION EXERCISE

Can you find the right word below to go with the ten definitions? Put the *letter* which is next to the word in the blank space to the left of the correct definition.

Example:____c___ the sun and nine planets

1._____lines going around the earth

2._____the weather conditions

3._____a treeless plain near the North Pole

4._____a large body of salt water

5._____land surrounded by water

6._____a large body of land such as North America

7._____a mountain that spurts lava

8._____imaginary line going around the earth dividing it in half

9._____half of the earth

10._____north, south, east, west

a. hemisphere
b. volcano
c. solar system
d. equator
e. island
f. continent
g. climate
h. ocean
i. tundra
j. region
k. latitude
l. directions

A few hours after nine-year-old Ted had finished this exercise, on which he had received a perfect score, he was asked: "What is a hemisphere?" He was unable to answer. There may have been several reasons for his inability to produce an answer to a question which he apparently could have answered earlier in the day. First, he may have been able to match all of the pairs in the exercise except one or two, and so by the process of elimination he was able to reason that a hemisphere was more like "half of the earth" than "a treeless plain near the North Pole." There is some value in being able to narrow down possible answers or solutions by eliminating improbable ones and then deciding which answer fits best. Unquestionably, however, this process was not the objective Ted's teacher was shooting for—she wanted him to remember the definitions that had been presented in class. Generally speaking, teachers want their pupils to remember facts, definitions, names, and concepts when they use matching questions.

Second, Ted may also have been momentarily confused by the straightforward question and then was unable to recall the definition for a hemisphere. Later on, when he had time to do some rummaging in his memory bank, he did remember it. What does this imply about the exercise and the reinforcement of concepts? It might be that, like the multiple-choice question, the matching question has built into it some provisions for misunderstanding and confusion. The items may become confused in the child's mind when he reviews them. Simply looking at an array of phrases and words that are not clearly understood is a frightening experience for the child who is not quick to store information in verbal form.

A third reason for Ted's drawing a blank with regard to the meaning of hemisphere suggests itself if we consider the motivational aspects of the situations in which he found himself that day. Although he forgot the definition sooner than is usual, Ted's purpose in remembering the definition of hemisphere (if indeed he did learn it) was to get a high score on the examination. In being motivated by what is called external evaluation (that is, by forces outside himself and not for any intrinsic interest in the subject), Ted is certainly not alone. Life to young people seems to be a game in which they learn to do the "right" things at the "right" times in order to acquire the "right" labels—it is a complicated system of rewards and punishments, in which grades are one of the most obvious symbols of success or failure. Ted may simply have forgotten the information because he had learned it only for the test.

The advantage of using the matching question, from the teacher's point of view, is that it allows him to pinpoint those facts, concepts, and generalizations he especially wishes his pupils to remember. When the matching question is composed with care, it is effective in reinforcing concepts and underscoring relationships. However, the teacher must see that it serves the educational objectives that he had in mind in presenting the material. For example, was the intention of Ted's teacher, when she composed the exercise above, to give her pupils a beginning vocabulary of geographical terms or to relate such concepts as lines of latitude and the equator to the phenomenon of tundra? When presenting the matching question—or any other evaluative device—to children, the teacher should ask himself whether his pupils have had the opportunity to obtain the knowledge necessary to perform the task.

From the pupil's viewpoint, the matching question can be fun to answer—in the same way that putting the pieces of a puzzle together is entertaining. There is a fascination in trying to decide which item goes with which and a satisfaction in apparently getting all of the items to match up.

Making Your Own Summary

You might integrate the ideas presented in this chapter by interviewing some child about a concept that he has learned recently. Try to apply as many ideas as you can from this chapter in order to find out whether he really understands the concept or how mature a concept he has acquired.

Record your interview with a tape recorder, have a friend record it in writing, or write it out yourself.

Then review this chapter. Which paradigm or paradigms did your questioning fit? Were you responsive to the answers the child gave? Did you find out whether he really understands the concept or has just remembered some words that mean little to him? Did you find out whether or not he can use the concept as a tool in his thinking?

If you are not satisfied with your success, you might like to try again and see how much progress you made. Mastery of the art of questioning takes practice and continued learning from errors.

REFERENCES

Black, H. *They Shall Not Pass*. New York. William Morrow & Company, 1963.

Bloom, B. S. (ed.). *Taxonomy of Educational Objectives. Handbook I: Cognitive Domain*. New York: David McKay Company, 1956.

Guilford, J. P. *The Nature of Human Intelligence.* New York: McGraw-Hill Book Company, 1967.

Hoffman, B. *The Tyranny of Testing.* New York: Crowell-Collier Press, 1962.

Sanders, N. M. *Classroom Questions: What Kinds?* New York: Harper & Row, 1966.

Thorndike, R. L. and E. Hagen. *Measurement and Evaluation in Psychology and Education.* New York: John Wiley & Sons, Inc., 1961.

CHAPTER 8

QUESTIONING
FOR THINKING

Learning
Minds a-working
Reading, thinking, writing,
Being Curie, Hannibal, Glenn—
It's fun!

The Problem

Mr. McCardle's sixth-grade class was much too docile for his taste. They seemed to be nonthinkers. Mr. McCardle, however, had always depended upon a fair amount of controversy being stirred up during discussions in his classroom, believing that controversy properly guided promotes a higher level of thinking than almost any other strategy. In two months of teaching this class, the only contention among his pupils occurred on the playground. Mr. McCardle's principal concern was that some of his pupils were not involved enough in the subjects which the class was studying to understand their basic structure. In addition, he was one of those teachers who delighted in keeping his pupils mentally on their toes.

One Friday afternoon, after a discussion about democratic ideals had sputtered and then died out, Mr. McCardle sat alone in his room and decided that either he must come up with an idea which would put some fire into the discussions or else change his style of teaching (a style which was considered by most of his former pupils to be quite effective). Then an idea came to him. He knew that the physical-education director for the district had been working hard with his pupils in preparation for the "Junior Olympics" to be held the following week. Therefore, when the children returned from their physical education period on Monday, Mr. McCardle planned to depreciate casually the value of practicing for the various events. (Ordinarily he instructed his own pupils in physical education, but on this occasion a few days had been set aside at the beginning of the week for the physical-education director to help them prepare for the track meet.) Mr. McCardle imagined that by making an offhand remark about what a waste of time practice was for them that he could involve most of his pupils in a lively debate:

"What did you do today? Oh, did he have you passing the baton again? I thought you fellows did that last week. You know, practice does not make perfect."

While Mr. McCardle actually believed in practicing a skill

properly, he armed himself that weekend with arguments about the futility of practicing one's mistakes and the exaggeration inherent in the maxim. He was confident that he would liven things up on Monday.

Do you think Mr. McCardle's pupils took the "bait"? Might it have been more intelligent for him to have changed his style of teaching? Do you think he was picking the wrong topics for questions or that his questions simply did not involve his pupils in thinking?

Thinking, a Reward for Learning

Bruner (1959) and others have pointed out that one of the most important rewards of learning is to be able to use the knowledge acquired in thinking. Bridging the gap between learning and thinking, however, requires expensive energy and usually has to be set in motion by questions that go beyond what has been learned. Psychologists have identified both a number of different kinds of thinking and the kinds of questions that usually bring into play each of these kinds of thinking. In this chapter, we will identify some important kinds of thinking, describing appropriate questions for eliciting each type of thinking, and giving examples of the use of such questions in creative learning and teaching.

Questions Requiring Analytical Thinking

THE INTERPRETATION QUESTION

Many teachers are fond of giving their students statements to analyze, especially in curricular areas such as literature, social studies, mathematics, and science. Classes have been known to spend a week or more interpreting a short passage from a novel, a stanza from a poem, or a theorem. Elementary school teachers probably employ this type of question even more frequently, if not so earnestly, by asking children to interpret words, sentences, and paragraphs. The interpretation question is undoubtedly a useful technique in helping children comprehend written materials. It can be used to help young people see relationships and implications in any kind of idea. For instance, Mrs. Roberts asked her class of eleven- and twelve-year-olds this question:

"Recently a newspaper editor said, 'Conspicuous consumption by Americans overseas is never understood.' What did he mean?"

Beverly, one of her rather shy pupils, offered this interpretation:

"The statement could mean that people of other countries have to use their various commodities sparingly and can't understand why the people of the United States actually 'throw away' a great part of their tremendous commodities they don't need."

Further discussion by the class brought out several of the reasons why Americans are able to consume conspicuously and also the socioeconomic rationale for doing so.

We have been interested in the reactions of people of all ages to highly unconventional interpretive questions such as "Is Alabama inside?" and "Where is the Fourth of July (or the Fifth of May, in Mexico)?" Two sets of this type of question have been published for children in the Ideabooks, *Can You Imagine?* (Myers and Torrance, 1965) and *For Those Who Wonder* (Myers and Torrance, 1966). Most adults find it very difficult to play with these questions. They can only interpret the questions literally. Young children have less trouble answering the questions, partly because the syntax of some of the questions is in their style, but many of them also experience frustration and anger when presented with "Is a month a mile?" and "When is the sky?" The worth of this type of question lies mainly in causing young people to see relationships that are not obvious. The questions invite the respondent to fill in connections and then to explore the reasonableness of certain relationships. Even with children of seven and eight years, a teacher should not try to force imaginative answers from all of his pupils.

Whereas Mrs. Roberts' questions were used in conjunction with her course in social studies, each of our questions is presented out of context. Accordingly, pedagogically there is less justification for "When is the sky?" than "Why don't foreigners understand conspicuous consumption by Americans?" Generally, thinking exercises should be tied directly to the curriculum.

THE COMPARISON QUESTION

The comparison question is an excellent device for helping children gain insights as they compare objects, persons, processes, events, and institutions. Here are a number of examples of comparison questions:

What are the most important differences between college football and high school football?

Which major league baseball team has the best pitching staff? Why? (These comparison questions might also be listed under evaluation questions that call for analysis.)

Is it more difficult to be a child today than when your parents were young? Why or why not?

Why are more potatoes grown in Idaho than in the neighboring state of Washington?

Which country has had the greatest economic growth during its history—Haiti or the Dominican Republic? Why has it been greater?

THE COMPARISON QUESTION

Among other questions that require analytical thinking on the part of the pupil is the one that calls for analyzing a process or a series of events. In answering this type of question, the pupil often must assign significance to different elements or events. Examples are:

How and when did the United States begin to exercise its newfound power as the major economic and military nation of the West?

What were the three major phases of the Revolutionary War?

How does a refrigerator work?

SCHEMATIC REPRESENTATION OF ANALYTICAL QUESTIONING

The paradigm for analytical questioning is only a rough approximation of how most elementary school teachers use it. There are many variations, and they occur mainly in the manner in which the teacher calls for the pupil to develop his ideas and to support them. You will note that the lesson continues to move along when this type of question is used, thus insuring fewer points at which the questioning-answering process can get "hung up." Lulls in the action (in the language of television sportscasters), when questions are answered incorrectly or when the teacher must repeat his question (or thinks he must), are partially responsible for bright pupils losing interest in many discussions.

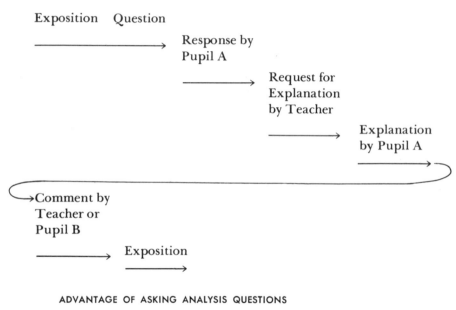

Exposition   Question

⟶   Response by
Pupil A

⟶   Request for
Explanation
by Teacher

⟶   Explanation
by Pupil A

⟶

⟶Comment by
Teacher or
Pupil B

⟶   Exposition
⟶

ADVANTAGE OF ASKING ANALYSIS QUESTIONS

When pupils are adequately informed, the lesson tends to move along at a productive pace with analytical questions. This type of question encourages orderly thinking because it requires the pupil to break down statements, processes, organizations, and events into their essential elements. Moreover, in answering most analytical questions, the pupil must be able to give reasons for his answers, and this gets him into the habit of being less reckless and more logical in his thinking. He learns to penetrate the issues and to look for the basis upon which statements are made and acts are performed.

DISADVANTAGES OF ASKING ANALYSIS QUESTIONS

Questions that require analysis are perplexing to pupils who do not have sufficient background of experience or information with which to break down the subject matter into its component parts. Without knowing anything about the mechanical parts of a refrigerator, a pupil is lost and worse when he tries to answer the question about how a refrigerator works. (It is usually wise, then, for a teacher to make certain that his pupils are well-informed concerning the subject before he gives them very many analytical questions.) Although the analytical question is an effective tool for provoking thought and promoting understanding, too many analytical questions become tedious and can spoil a child's enjoyment of almost anything, including the reading of stories.

Questions Requiring Synthesis

When an individual combines parts, elements, and ideas so as to bring into being something that was not clearly seen before, he is synthesizing. Teachers seldom ask children to review the facts they have gathered and to formulate hypotheses concerning the ways in which the facts are related; but they would be at a loss if they could not engage their pupils in writing reports, letters, and stories and in making pictures, murals, collages, dioramas, mosaics, papier-mâché and clay figures. Formulating hypotheses is a very important step in the scientific method of solving problems, and children nowadays are introduced to the scientific method very early in their educational careers. After they learn about the scientific method, pupils should be encouraged to put their knowledge to use and make hypotheses about phenomena that they read about, discuss, and observe. This is an example of what is often done to help pupils synthesize information:

MR. MANN: We've learned that there has been considerable strife in the Congo, and now the Belgians have all left that country. There has been trouble between Kenyatta and his followers and the colonial government of Kenya—the British have had their problems too. Just recently we've received reports of violence in Rhodesia. What can you say about these happenings? Are they connected in any way?

MARILYN: Well, one thing you can say is that the people of these countries are all inspired by a feeling of wanting to be independent—a kind of nationalism. It's not quite the same feeling that we had during the Revolution, though, because these people have been in Africa much longer than the Europeans who have been governing them.

There can be very little doubt that Marilyn received a nod of approval or a high grade in Mr. Mann's gradebook for her response.

TWO PARADIGMS FOR EMPLOYING THE SYNTHESIS QUESTION

On page 180 are two models for using questions that lead to synthesizing information. They represent two opposing teaching methodologies.

You can see that the second type of questioning involves the pupils more in the synthesizing process and that it is also more time-consuming. *Which method have you encountered most frequently?*

What do you think about the way Mike handled this synthesis question?

Putting Things Together

Suppose you are given these three things: a crayon, a paper bag, and a safety pin. Then you are told that you must give back one of the three things. Which one would you give back? Why? What could you do with the other two things? Could you use them together? How? Write your answers and ideas on the lines at the right and below.

I'd give back the crayon back and cut 2 round circles in the bottom of the bag. Then I'd put a baby in the bag and take the pin and pin it hard enough on the bag so that the bag would not fall of the baby and use it as a baby dipper.

Figure 4. Mike's Response to "Putting Things Together." Exercise from R. E. Myers and E. P. Torrance, *Can You Imagine?* (Boston: Ginn & Co., 1965), pp. 36–37.

What if you are given a comb, a paper napkin, and a nail? Which of the three would you give back, if you had to give one back? Why? What could you do with the two things which you still have left? Could you use them together? How? Write your answers and ideas on the lines below.

I'd give back the comb and take the napkin and wipe the rust off the nail.

Figure 4a. Continuation of Mike's Response to "Putting Things Together."

ADVANTAGES OF QUESTIONING FOR SYNTHESIS

A hallmark of the highly effective teacher is that he creates a climate in which pupils can explore and discover. He facilitates the kind of learning that is rich with generalizations and insights. The question that asks for synthesis of information, then, is one of his favorite methods of facilitating learning and thinking. Because it comes after pupils have had certain experiences or have gathered facts that are somehow related, the synthesis question cannot be used continually. However, teachers vary in the frequency and manner in which they use this kind of question. At one end of the continuum, they set up activities such as the "What's in the Box?" game. (Pupils make a wild guess about the identity of the object in a box, then eliminate most of their guesses by experimenting— shaking the box, smelling it, hefting it, etc.—and finally come up with a "best" guess.) On the other end of the continuum, they may try to provide their pupils with a learning atmosphere (employing materials, discussions, and activities) in which children are encouraged to generalize and hypothesize and then test their ideas. The synthesis question can be used in any area of the curriculum and with all kinds of children.

TYPE A
Exposition:
First Fact
Second Fact
Third Fact   Question

$\longrightarrow$ Pupil's Generalization or Hypothesis

$\longrightarrow$ Clarification   Exposition
by Teacher
$\longrightarrow$

TYPE B

| Exposition (Introduction) | Question | Response by Pupil A (First Fact) |

$\longrightarrow$

$\longrightarrow$ Comment by Teacher
and Invitation to
Class to Provide
More Information
$\longrightarrow$

$\longrightarrow$ Response by
Pupil B
(Second Fact)

$\longrightarrow$ Comment by Teacher
and Invitation to
Class to Provide
More Information

$\longrightarrow$ Comment by Teacher
and Invitation to
Class to Generalize

$\longrightarrow$ Response by
Pupil D
(Generaliz-
ation)
$\longrightarrow$

DISADVANTAGES OF SYNTHESIS QUESTIONING

If the teacher follows the model represented by the Type A paradigm given above, he will experience less difficulty in obtaining responses to his synthesis questions. Having set up the information for the pupils to put together in some form (as Mr. Mann did in asking for generalizations about events in Africa), the teacher need only wait for his pupils to make the connections and arrive at a generalization or hypothesis. The disadvantage of this method is that it limits the responses of the youngsters to select the significant facts for their examination. On the other hand, if the teacher chooses to follow the Type B model, which represents an inductive approach, pupils may never arrive at a generalization at all because they are inept at seeing which facts are significant and related. The resolution of this problem is really a matter of determining which teaching style—the expository mode or the hypothetical mode, in Bruner's (1960) terminology—is most congenial to your personality and abilities, and of course those of your pupils as well.

THE CONVERGENT THINKING QUESTION

In convergent thinking the individual puts together information in such a way so as to arrive at a correct, best, or conventional answer or solution. Mr. York, an Englishman who emigrated to Canada after World War II, depends greatly upon questions requiring convergent thinking to encourage his pupils to think with him as he leads them along fascinating and challenging intellectual paths.

The following excerpt is from a lesson which was designed to point out to a sixth-grade class the many English cognates of Latin numbers.

MR. YORK: What language did the Romans speak?

ROBERT: Latin.

MR. YORK: They spoke Latin. What language did the people who lived in Great Britain (at the time of the Roman invasion) speak? [Long pause] Well, they were savages, of course, but they did more than grunt. What did they use? Geraldine.

GERALDINE: English?

MR. YORK: English? No, they didn't speak English in those days. Notice I very carefully said Britain and not England because Britain didn't become England until, ooh, about a thousand years ago. They had a language which you still find around there, changed a little bit. They call it—I call it "Kel-tic" [Celtic]. If you want to pronounce it "Sel-tic," I won't argue with you. I call it "Kel-tic." The Irish have gone back to their old Celtic language. And, uh, the Welsh. Well, we generally call it "Welsh," but they have a name for it—they call it "Kimra." What do the Scots have?

GARY: "Gaelic?"

MR. YORK: "Gaelic." Well done. [Pause] Well, these languages came somehow from a different place from Latin. I'm not quite sure how. But English has a great deal of Latin in it. It's kinda fun sometimes to find out just which words came from Latin and what they mean because of what the Latin words meant. Let's try the numbers. Latin numbers. [Mr. York writes "unus" on the chalkboard.] Number one. [Pause] "Unus." That's a nice easy one, isn't it? Is it ringing any bells? Well, I'm going to write the other nine down while you're thinking about them, and then when I've done that, you can tell me if you can think of an English word that came from each of these. [He writes the other Latin numbers, in a column, beneath "unus" on the chalkboard.] All right, number one. "Unus." Tell me an English word we have that comes from "unus."

CARL: "Un." "Un." [Pause] "Un?" It stands for "one."

MR. YORK: No, I want an *English* word. [Pause] Something horrible is happening to the armed forces in Canada right now. At least I think it's terrible. What is it? They're all being joined together, aren't they? Instead of having a navy, an army, and air force, we're going to have just *one* service. What's the name for it? Geraldine?

GERALDINE: "Unit?"

MR. YORK: It will be a unit when it is finished, yes, but there is a verb which means "the making of one."

GEORGE: "Think" is what they call it. They call it "Think."

PETER: The initials.

GEORGE: They call it "T.H.I.N.K."—that's the initials of something.

MR. YORK: Ah. I haven't heard about that. They're being *united*—that's another one. "Unify" is the word that means "the making of one." All right, what about "duo"? [Pause] Two people over there, side by side, one of them should have it, ay, Carl?

CARL: It should be something like two.

MR. YORK: "Duo." Because this means "working in two ways," doesn't it? What's the word for choir, with only two people in it? Betsy?

BETSY: A "duet"!

MR. YORK: A "duet"! Eh, I'm going to give you another with this one [Mr. York writes "bis" on the chalkboard] because most of our words don't come from the Latin word "two"; they come from the Latin word "twice"—and that's "bis." Now, do you know any words that have a beginning something like that which means "two"? [Pause] How did you get to school this morning, George?

GEORGE: Pardon?

MR. YORK: How did you get to school?

GEORGE: On my bike.

MR. YORK: Good for you! Can anybody think of an English word where we have this "bis" meaning "two"? Real tough, isn't it? Colleen?

COLLEEN: Bicycle.

MR. YORK: "Bicycle"! What do you call a bicycle with only one wheel? [Pause] Phillip?

PHILLIP: "Unicycle."

MR. YORK: A "*uni*cycle"! With three wheels? [Pause]

PHILLIP: "Tricycle."

MR. YORK: A "*tri*cycle"! And that "tri" comes from this "tres."

This rather lengthy excerpt from Mr. York's lesson was chosen because it reveals the manner in which he typically involves his pupils with a topic. Notice that he employs the retention question often to keep his pupils thinking with him.

THE REDEFINITION QUESTION

Among the most challenging questions a teacher can ask are those that require the pupil to redefine an object, animal, person, or event. The redefinition question calls for the pupil to see something in a new light, to perceive functions and characteristics that are not obvious or usual. The mental process involved in responding to redefinition questions usually requires synthesis and what we have defined as creative thinking.

If your class is studying how time is reckoned, here are some questions which require the pupil to redefine the functions and uses of ordinary clocks:

"What is a clock besides an instrument for keeping time?" (This question might encourage the pupil to see a watch as a piece of jewelry, thus sharpening his perception of the article as a badge of prestige, or a means of influencing others.)

"What is a clock when it has stopped running?" (Perhaps this might seem a philosophical question to some pupils. Others could be stuck with only the notion that a clock which is not working is a useless mechanism. It is interesting to note how pupils react to questions such as this one.)

In addition, the teacher of a primary class might want to engage her pupils in some "riddling" in order to deepen and broaden their understanding of the traffic light. Here are three possible riddles that she might use:

"Why is a clock like the sun?" (Man's first clock was the sun, and most of the people on earth still use it principally for reckoning time.)

"Why is a clock like a teacher?" (Once it's wound up, it doesn't stop for a long time.)

"Why is a clock like *you?*" (It needs power to make it go—power from a spring, electricity, magnetism, the movement of a wrist, etc.—just as a child needs power—which he gets from eating food, motivation, etc.—to make him go.)

After they have solved a few riddles, the children can be encouraged to devise their own. Frequently they can invent very clever riddles, but the main advantage in their making up their own riddles is that they will then be searching for relationships, thus increasing their understanding of the topic.

REDEFINITION QUESTIONS IN THE CURRICULUM

Being able to redefine objects (organisms, institutions, processes) to solve problems has many obvious, practical everyday advantages. This type of question can increase the pupil's ability to learn facts, concepts, and principles. Therefore, it might be helpful at this point to give an example of the use of the redefinition question in conjunction with the regular curriculum.

Take, for example, at the primary level, a group of children studying traffic safety, with their teacher stressing the purpose of the traffic light. The teacher might pose these questions to encourage the youngsters to increase their knowledge of the makeup and function of a traffic light:

"Does the traffic light take the place of anyone?" (Yes, a policeman who would direct traffic at the intersection. In some cities, of course, the traffic light and the policeman are used alternately.)

"How does the traffic light resemble a clock?" (It is regulated by a timing device, and has a cycle—red-yellow-green-yellow-red-yellow-green, etc.—as the clock has- 1-2-3-4-5-6-7-8-9-10-11-12-1-2-3, etc.).

"What is a traffic light besides a signal to tell people to stop and to go?" (It is a fixture—something that people who go by every day see, in the same way that a tree or lamp post is seen by people who pass by. It is a "friend" that you can depend upon to help you get across the street safely. It is a giant flashlight that has bright, attractive colors, often shielded by hatlike things which project over the lens. It is something that birds can perch upon, but rarely do.)

Because the pupil looks at whatever he is redefining from a different perspective, he should see "new" relationships between the object being redefined and other objects, organisms, institutions, and processes. For the pupil, these discoveries can be routine observations or they can be genuine insights. When the insight has special meaning for the pupil, it invests formal learning with an excitement that is invaluable in promoting self-initiated learning.

PARADIGM FOR CONVERGENT-THINKING QUESTIONING

The scheme for convergent-thinking questioning can be represented in this way:

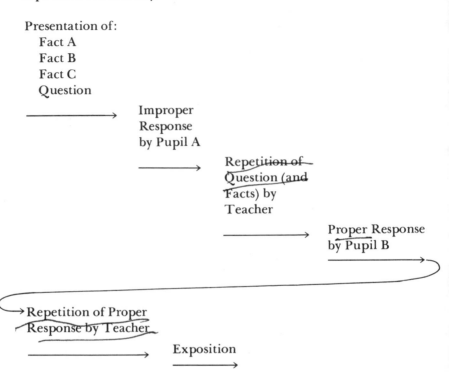

Presentation of:
    Fact A
    Fact B
    Fact C
    Question

⟶   Improper
Response
by Pupil A

    ⟶   Repetition of
Question (and
Facts) by
Teacher

    ⟶   Proper Response
by Pupil B

Repetition of Proper
Response by Teacher

⟶   Exposition
⟶

The ideal paradigm for many teachers, of course, would be one in which there was no incorrect response. For the sake of having a rough approximation of a "typical" interaction, we are including one improper response; obviously, there may be none or a great many. (This is true of the other paradigms in this chapter as well.)

What guesses would you make about a teacher with a class whose improper responses were extremely rare?

HANDLING THE CONVERGENT-THINKING QUESTIONING RESPONSIVELY

In the episode above when Mr. York gets a response (the acronym "T.H.I.N.K.") that he had not anticipated and does not know how to evaluate, he wisely accepts it and goes ahead with his questioning. Had he not been so intent upon getting the proper response he might have invited the pupil to explore the subject further. By encouraging pupils to explain their responses, a teacher can let them know that he values their contributions. This way of conducting the convergent-thinking questioning is represented by the paradigm:

Presentation of
    Fact A
    Fact B
    Fact C
    Question

⟶   Improper Response
    by Pupil A

    Request for More
    Information by Teacher

    Additional Information
    by Pupil A (or Pupil B)

    (Comment by Pupil B)

    (Comment by Teacher)

    Repetition of
    Question by Teacher

        ⟶   Acceptable
        Response
        by Pupil A
        or Pupil B   Exposition
        ⟶

The teacher may or may not wish to add his comments to the remarks of his pupils before he resumes his pursuit of the answer to his original question. Permitting the digression may take the discus-

I feel secure with right answer
2 classification

sion far afield, but the digression could be more instructive than coming up with the answer to the teacher's question.

HOW MIGHT INFORMATION QUESTIONS BE USED?

Information questions serve many useful purposes. When the teacher is able to pose questions that can be answered by facts, most young people feel secure—whether or not they can supply the desired information. They feel secure because they know all they have to do to be "good" or "bright" or cooperative is to produce the correct answer on cue. This feeling is often notably absent when open-ended questions are asked. It is comforting for pupils to be able to say "quadruped" when someone asks them to give a name for a four-legged animal. "Quadruped" and "four-legged animal" go together—they fit—and pupils know that there is some kind of congruence or consonance involved in pairing them. They feel secure because they are able to link the two expressions. This feeling is legitimate in spite of the probability that the information (that is, the fact that a four-legged animal is a *quadruped*) will be utterly useless to all but a very small percentage of the pupils who learn the definition.

Another popular way of determining whether pupils have acquired information is to ask them to classify phenomena. Classifying (shown in the immediately preceding example) is a very valuable intellectual skill that man has developed during his evolution, and it has enabled him to control or bring order into his environment to an extent that would not have been possible if he had not had this ability. This type of convergent thinking is especially worthwhile for pupils when used in conjunction with analyzing, synthesizing, hypothesizing, and evaluating activities. Nevertheless, whether he works with "slow learners" or with "academically able pupils," the goal of the creative teacher with regard to the teaching of facts is to help the pupil see how the fact makes sense in a larger context.

Whenever possible, the creative teacher arranges a situation in which the pupil will have opportunities to cope with questions such as these: (1) What is the genesis of the fact? (2) Is it likely to be considered a fact indefinitely, or will our interpretation of it change? (3) Is it reasonable in the light of other known facts?

The Open-Ended Question

The term "open-ended question," as it is used here, refers to any question that invites a great diversity of responses or divergent thinking. Open-ended questioning involves the pupil in thinking of possibles and going off into different directions to find an answer, instead of striving for one "correct" or "accepted" answer. The pupil responds in terms of his own experiences whatever these may be.

Perhaps because they are usually close to their pupils psychologically and physically, the teachers of five-, six-, and seven-year-old children often are very successful in conducting sessions in which open-ended questions free the children to express themselves. This excerpt from a session of "Just Suppose" with Mrs. Fortson and her kindergarten class is representative of the kind of interaction that can result when open-ended questions are used.

Mrs. Fortson's introduction or warm-up included these remarks:

"These pictures are called 'Just Suppose,' so let's have fun with them, and we will all just suppose and see what things we can come up with. See what your ideas are and what good supposers you are. Now I'm going to read what they say and you look at it, and then you can raise your hand and we'll start 'Just Supposing.' "

The lesson proper began:

MRS. FORTSON: Now, you all see it. (She holds up a picture of a prehistoric scene.)

CLASS: Ah . . . a dinosaur . . . unhhh . . . grrrr!

MRS. FORTSON: Everybody will have a chance to "Just Suppose," but I'm going to read what is on the back [of the picture] to start your thinking. Look hard as I read it: "Just suppose when you went to see a prehistoric exhibit at the museum that it came alive" . . . all the stuffed animals came alive and you would be in that time—in the time of the dinosaurs long ago—"and you would know more than anyone, what would you do and what would happen?" Bobby?

BOBBY: You'd be eaten up!

MRS. FORTSON: Uh, Betty?

BETTY: You'd get squashed because the dinosaur would step on you.

MRS. FORTSON: You think you would get *squashed* because the dinoasur would step on us? Uh, what do you think would happen, Maria?

MARIA: He would eat you up.

MRS. FORTSON: You think he'd eat you up. Janie?

JANIE: You could get a ride on it.

MRS. FORTSON: You could get a ride on it. How would you manage that?

JANIE: You could hop on its . . . (Several voices interrupt.)

MRS. FORTSON: Wait just a minute. She said you could get a ride on it.

JANIE: You could get on his back before he could start to walk, and then when he started to walk you'd be on his back, and then he would just keep on giving you a ride.

MRS. FORTSON: You don't think he would see you there on his back? Why not?

JANIE: Because you're so small and he's so big.

MRS. FORTSON: Oh, my goodness! You think that the prehistoric animal would be *so* big and you'd be *so* small, he wouldn't even know you were there—and give you a free ride? Let's have some other ideas. Paul?

The children went on for another ten minutes imagining that with a father and brother the dinosaur could be lassoed and trained, that someone would faint, that a "free jumping ride" would be had if they could "climb up his tail and slide down him," and that the dinosaur could be escaped by blasting off in a rocket and going to the moon. They were mostly rather harsh with the dinosaur, however, taking a knife and chopping it, tripping it, chopping off its legs and then having it for dinner, killing it with a slingshot, chopping down a tree and having it land on the dinosaur, fighting the dinosaur with rocks and making it lose its teeth, and getting a poison snake to attack it. Why do you think the children expressed so much fear in their reactions to the picture and question? The children responded eagerly throughout the discussion; in fact, it was difficult for Mrs. Fortson to finish the first question and go on to the next one.

PARADIGM FOR OPEN-ENDED QUESTIONING

There are a great many kinds of open-ended questions. We shall deal with only a few in this chapter to represent the enormous variety of this mode of questioning. Thus, the paradigm is only representative of teacher-class interaction generally.

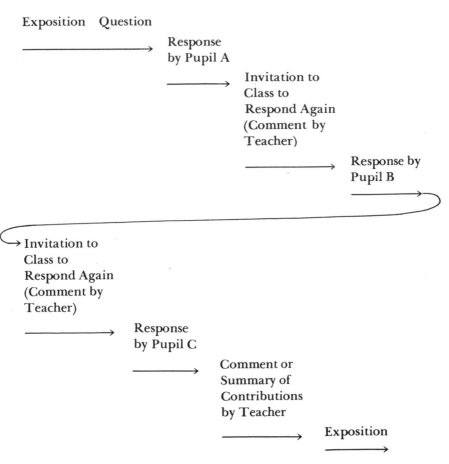

Exposition   Question

⟶   Response by Pupil A

⟶   Invitation to Class to Respond Again (Comment by Teacher)

⟶   Response by Pupil B

Invitation to Class to Respond Again (Comment by Teacher)

⟶   Response by Pupil C

⟶   Comment or Summary of Contributions by Teacher

⟶   Exposition

The teacher may or may not wish to comment upon the various contributions by his pupils. Often it is wise not to comment because you find yourself in the position of having to make some kind of evaluative remark. Summing up at the end of the pupils' responses is often helpful in clarifying what has been said. It also leads the way naturally into a short contribution that you can make without "hogging the show" or "stealing the thunder" of your pupils.

Although the paradigm for the open-ended question is apparently simple to follow, it really takes considerable skill to use effectively. There is a tremendous difference in the manner in which teachers receive their pupils' responses, ranging from no comment at all to rejection ("Now why did you say a thing like that, Billy?") and enthusiastic endorsement ("What a wonderful idea!"). The responsive teacher, however, is not usually an effusive one. He shows his acceptance in many ways other than by praising. For example, his manner can communicate very effectively that he is happy to receive the contributions of his pupils. On the other hand, if he should single out what is good in one child's idea, he is placed in a position where he feels he should say something positive about every child's response. As is often pointed out, premature evaluation of divergent productions is inhibiting, especially to those individuals who are timid about revealing something about themselves (for creative thinking more than any other kind tells a great deal about the individual).

The accepting-respecting attitude necessary to encourage divergent thinking is hard to describe because it varies from teacher to teacher. Even though Mrs. Fortson has the kind of manner which inspires young children to respond, it is impossible to capture very much of it by reproducing what she said in asking her pupils to "Just Suppose." The fascinating and frustrating part of trying to discover just what makes a teacher the kind of person who inspires children to be truly excited about expressing their ideas is that teacher behavior cannot really be reduced to an analysis of either verbal or nonverbal elements. Many intangibles operate to make teachers effective, ineffectual, or harmful. The teacher who never smiles can be just as stimulating as the one who smiles continually. (If he smiles all the time, smiling may have only limited effect on the children.) Observers discover this when they see a teacher who does all the "right things." That is, the teacher asks interesting questions, is pleasant, supports or praises his pupils when they are deserving, assists them in evaluating their own work, presents stimu-

Must Open ended

lating materials, and has a good understanding of the educational objectives he is trying to achieve.

All of these "right" behaviors on the teacher's part are most persuasive in rating the teacher as being outstanding—until the observers attend to the reactions of his pupils. In the case of some ineffective teachers, it may be simply a matter of really not valuing the children as individuals, a feeling that is communicated somehow to them. It could also be that the teacher is only going through the motions in the approved fashion, and the children are not fooled—he doesn't really care much for children. Whatever is operating, the pupils are not excited about learning and thinking —and this is unnatural for children. We are only certain of one thing: when a teacher doesn't accept and respect children, very little of what he does will be effective in helping them grow intellectually, socially, and morally.

ADVANTAGES OF THE OPEN-ENDED QUESTIONING

If you will refer back to the paradigm for open-ended questioning you can see that pupils' responses are not rejected by the teacher. Ordinarily he accepts all reasonable responses. The teacher may not receive a particular response enthusiastically, but when he engages in open-ended questioning he is calling for a variety of answers and he accepts all offerings.

In the case of some questions, such as "What do you think of when you see these lines?" or "What do these wiggly lines make you

Figure 5. "What do you think of when you see these lines?"

think of?" the responses will be on the same level. That is, one child may see this incomplete figure as a fish about to jump for a worm in rough water and another may see it as a man, a snake, and a cane. (The first child has synthesized the lines into an integrated picture, while the second child has seen the lines as representing separate and unrelated objects. When asked if the man were going to pick up the cane and hit the snake, the child said: "No, he's not going to do that." There was no intent on his part to have the objects relate to one another.) Each response is equally valid and each is worthwhile in that it represents the way the child perceives the lines. Accordingly, the element of competition is mostly removed from this learning situation, and there is no need for the teacher to correct or assign grades.

In actual practice, of course, a pupil's response may have more or less of some quality the teacher values; but the teacher should withhold his judgments until later when all of his pupils have had a chance to explore the question and their reactions to it fully. Many teachers have a good deal of trouble restraining themselves from making positive, supportive comments during the early stages of questioning, and there are some investigators of the creative-thinking process who endorse this way of accepting pupils' ideas especially if verbal approval is consonant with the teacher's personality and pedagogical style. In carrying out an activity such as the one with incomplete figures, however, there is usually no excuse for evaluating the pupils' products at any time. The great virtue of open-ended questions is that the pupil's responses are regarded by him and his teacher as being worthwhile in themselves.

One of the most gratifying results of open-ended questioning is that pupils discover that they have worthwhile ideas. Open-ended questions that feature original thinking can do a great deal for a child's self-concept, and they can also help the teacher. Simply employing this method of questioning can add zest to a drab program. One veteran teacher said that her entire educational philosophy had changed after she had administered a series of exercises consisting of tasks similar to the one above with the incomplete figure. Her seven-year-olds had really opened up and had become very enthusiastic about school. Their productions were acknowledged by other pupils and teachers to be vivid and highly original. The teacher expressed her reactions to the experience in this way:

"I'm just terribly excited about what my children are doing. It's the most important thing that has happened to me in all of my teaching! At the same time, I'm saddened when I think of all the children I've kept locked up for thirty years."

Questions that call for divergent thinking enable those pupils who have not shone when memory and convergent-thinking questions were asked to demonstrate that they can think too. In fact, one of the most persistent findings by teachers themselves when they have utilized open-ended questions and activities that feature divergent thinking is that a new set of luminaries begins to sparkle. The children who are the stars when activities call for recognizing, remembering, and repeating are quite often undistinguished in responding to open-ended questions. "What do *you* want me to do?" or "What am I *supposed* to do?" they ask.

This turn of events can be quite unsettling to a teacher who is pretty well convinced as to who his "best" pupils are and who thinks he knows what the intellectual capabilities of his pupils are. After the initial surprise, the teacher begins to see merit in the re-

Boats and Things

Think of a boat—any kind of boat. If you would like to, draw a picture of your boat.

What can your boat do? My boat can do many things, here is what it can do. It can drive on roads, fly in the air, swim in the water, land on Jupiter, and transport people and animals.

When you think about your boat, what other thing do you think about? Why don't you draw a picture of it and write about it right here?

Once my boat made a trip to Mars and we met funny man. I bougt a coloring book from Mars and then I went back to earth.

Figure 6. Mike's Response to "Boats and Things" Exercise from R. E. Myers and E. P. Torrance, *Can You Imagine?* (Boston: Ginn & Co., 1965), pp. 12–13.

Now, think of your boat and the other thing which goes with it, and also think of an old hat. Color the old hat at the right or draw one that you like better.

What might happen when there is a boat, a _____ (the thing you think of when you think of a boat), and an old hat? Draw a picture showing what happens, and then tell about it.

My hat is Orion 8 a flying saucer from Vandyke Barraks.

Figure 6a. Continuation of Mike's Response to "Boats and Things."

sponses of formerly obscure pupils. What is more, he begins to appreciate better how their minds work and that their ideas can be not only original but valuable. What teacher could fail to see something in the responses of Mike to these questions?

The findings of these teachers are confirmed by research and by the observations of perceptive people everywhere. Some children are very good at recalling events, facts, symbols, and discourse from their "memory banks." Other children are particularly good at solving problems that have conventional or correct answers. They efficiently process information and arrive at accurate or satisfactory answers and solutions very quickly. Others are excellent at recognizing and identifying names, objects, symbols, processes, verbal expressions, etc. Still others, who may not excel at remembering, recognizing, or problem solving, are unsurpassed at combining ideas and elements into new forms. They are the original thinkers. There are also those children we call "creative" who are not so good at producing new forms but who are highly skillful at elaborating upon the ideas of others or giving them a new twist. Yet we act as if the child who excels in one of these areas should be very good in all of them, and as if the young person who is not good in the skills rewarded most in classrooms should be good in nothing.

One of the particular strengths of open-ended questions is that they prompt the pupil to learn more about the subject under discussion because he must be able to support his responses. Moreover, when the pupil is serious about exploring hypothetical questions that relate to his life and to the curriculum, he becomes interested in facts, relationships among facts, and theories that he otherwise would not have considered. Even when he does not try to answer the hypothetical question orally, this kind of question tends to make the pupil more aware of relationships among facts than he would have been had he just read about them in books.

Taba and Elkins (1966) cite the use of open-ended questions as an especially appropriate teaching strategy for use with disadvantaged children. Each child can respond at his own level and in this way the teacher can help him build upon what he already knows. Open-ended questions are admirably suited to pre-primary children with a wide range of ability and experience. Each child can be involved at his own level and can contribute to the group's experience.

DISADVANTAGES OF OPEN-ENDED QUESTIONING

With immature pupils, the open-ended question may encourage silliness. Unless the teacher sets the stage properly by pointing out the benefits of exploring freely into the question, some youngsters do not see much value in producing responses that are not "right" or "wrong." When asked questions that can be answered with conventional or authorized responses, they know how to play the game; but when invited to produce original or unusual responses, they react by becoming wild or silly.

The open-ended question upsets some children. To be presented with a situation in which any reasonable response is legitimate disturbs some serious-minded children. They feel uneasy because there are no hard-and-fast rules, no sharp distinctions between good and poor responses, and no specific directions as to how to produce the "right" kind of response.

A transition period might precede the serious use of open-ended questioning if you have been giving only questions that have just one answer. For young children, questions such as "Why is a shoe like a boat?" permit a variety of responses, but point to several which are obvious and so will be considered "correct" by pupils who are uneasy in situations that are not rigidly defined. These

youngsters, if encouraged to go ahead with other less popular answers, will gradually feel freer to do so.

Questions Calling for Evaluation

JUDGMENTS ABOUT THE VALIDITY OF STATEMENTS

A familiar type of question for challenging the reasoning powers of high school and college students is one which goes something
like this: "What about it—would you accept that statement?" This
question forces the student to analyze the elements of the statement
and to see whether they work together logically and whether they
can be supported by other evidence. He must then make a decision
as to whether the statement is logical or illogical (reasonable or
silly; straightforward or misleading; sensible or impractical). Nearly
everyone seems to agree that giving young people practice in making judgments is excellent preparation for the decision-making they
are already doing and will do as adults.

Teachers of children throughout the elementary school years
should require pupils to examine critically statements made by authors; fellow pupils; newspaper, magazine, and television reporters;
and, yes, teachers. The best way to encourage critical thinking is to
give children the skills for making decisions about the validity of
statements and arguments. They need criteria by which to judge
whether statements and arguments are internally consistent, correct,
suitable, acceptable, moral, or valuable. These tools can be acquired
incidentally during the course of discussions and investigations (and
this is the most desirable and effective way if you are alert enough
to see the openings and raise questions about the correctness and
appropriateness of what people say and do). Or they can be learned
by more formal means through exercises of this sort:

IS IT *Reasonable* OR *Silly?*

This is an exercise to help you develop the ability to determine
the reasonableness of statements. It is particularly important that
you learn to distinguish statements that are reasonable from those
that are illogical or invalid.

Read the sentences below and decide whether or not they make sense. If you believe that a sentence is reasonable, write an *R* in the space to the left of the sentence. If you believe that it is silly, write an *S* to the left of the sentence.

_____1. Bobby turned on the light so that he could hear the radio better.
_____2. His strength gone, Timmy was unable to pull open the huge stone door.
_____3. Blinded by the terrible dust storm, Mrs. Nelson crouched behind a rock and waited until she heard her husband's call.
_____4. After Mr. Jennings lost his voice, he was forced to shout his directions through a megaphone.

When you construct your own exercises you should be cautious about peremptorily labeling a pupil's response correct or incorrect. Especially in exercises such as the one above, it pays for both the teacher and class to allow all the arguments a pupil can advance before a decision is made as to whether the reasoning of the respondent is valid. For instance, with regard to the first statement above, it is conceivable that a pupil might believe the statement to be "reasonable" when the teacher has deliberately attempted to construct an illogical statement. The pupil would be right, of course. Bobby might be a two-year-old who hasn't made the right connections between the various appliances and their switches in his home. Or he might be an inmate of a mental institution. What is more, peculiarly enough, radios have been known to do such things when other electrical gadgets are turned on or off. The pupil could back up his opinion with arguments such as these, and he would probably be more correct than the teacher.

QUESTIONS ENCOURAGING SENSITIVITY TO PROBLEMS

Teachers should ask questions that require their pupils to be aware of the needs of others, of deficiencies in institutions and processes, and of improvements in materials and organizations. To illustrate this type of questioning, we can use a section from the exercise that accompanies *All-Around American: The Ben Franklin Story* (Cunnington, et al., 1965). The narrator of the recorded dramatization lays the foundation for the exercise by asking this question: "What do you suppose it was that made Ben Franklin so able to make all those wonderful contributions to his fellow man?" He then points out that Franklin had a great talent for invention, a genuine understanding of science, and, significantly, an awareness of the needs and problems of others. The narrator then proceeds with the business of the exercise:

"I'll bet that all of you, if you had the opportunity, would feel mighty proud to make a contribution or two for your fellow Americans, as Franklin did. But what kind of contribution? To what walk of life would you make your contribution? Where would your contribution fit best?

"To find the answers, suppose you do what Franklin himself did. Look around you. Perhaps the three most familiar places you'd look would be your community, your school, and your home. Is there anything about your home town, your school building, your classroom, or your own home that your friends, your acquaintances, or even your parents find annoying—anything which they feel presents a problem, and could stand improvement? Something you believe might be changed for the better? Perhaps they'll tell you that there aren't enough lakes near their homes, or enough skating rinks to skate on. . . . Maybe the streets in their neighborhoods aren't properly lighted, or aren't wide enough for the traffic load they must carry. . . . Perhaps they feel that the halls in school are too noisy. . . . Maybe the playground isn't as well equipped as they'd like it to be, or perhaps their classrooms aren't arranged quite the way they think they should be. . . . Maybe you'd like to invent something which would help them to more quickly and easily cut the grass or clean off the walks around their homes, for example, or assist them to do their homework with a minimum of effort and a maximum of perfection.

"Although the things I've just mentioned are quite different from one another, they have one thing in common: they all come under the heading of problems—problems which your friends have probably noticed at one time or another, problems which have really gotten 'under their skin.' Chances are, you'll be able to add some problems of your own to this list.

"As a matter of fact, why not make up, right now, a list of all the things which have presented problems to you and your friends lately? . . ."

Do you think that the narrator provided the pupils with too many cues? After asking questions, teachers sometimes make the mistake of offering leads or cues in order to encourage responses from their pupils. You might not realize that you are guiding the responses of your pupils as much as you actually do. One excellent way to determine if you are providing your pupils with more cues than they need is to make a tape recording of yourself conducting a discussion. You can also learn whether you are cutting off responses before your pupils are finished and whether you are calling upon the same pupils to come through with the answers you are searching for.

PARADIGM FOR USING EVALUATION QUESTIONS

The two essential matters in evaluation questioning are (1) to have your pupils give reasons for their decisions and (2) to get more than one expression of opinion from the class, especially when you are leading a discussion that allows for more than one plausible judgment.

Exposition
———————→

Question Asking
for Judgment or
Decision
———————————→

Response and
Explanation
from Pupil A
———————————→

Comment and
Repetition of
Question by
Teacher
—————————————→

→ Response and
Explanation
from Pupil B
———————→

(Summary by Teacher)
———————————————→

Exposition
———————→

PARADIGM FOR EMPLOYING EVALUATION QUESTIONING RESPONSIVELY

In handling the evaluation questioning method responsively, the teacher makes certain that his pupils have the criteria for judging clearly in mind before he calls for them to make a decision. He also does a great deal to help provide the accepting atmosphere necessary if constructive thinking is to occur.

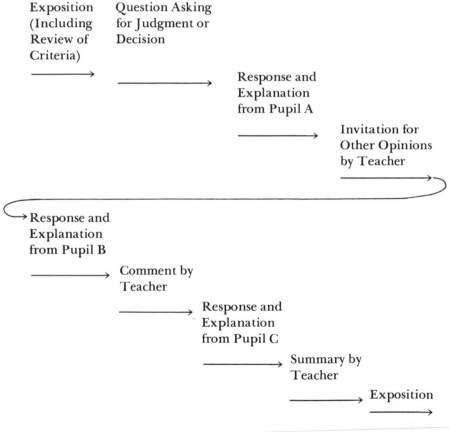

The teacher may or may not choose to summarize the contributions of pupils before going ahead with the lesson. In many cases, the lesson will take a different direction as a result of the discussion. Notice that it is not necessary for the teacher to comment after pupils have responded. In a responsive environment there may be a succession of comments by pupils without intervening remarks by the teacher. The teacher's role is often one of regulating the flow of ideas. The paradigm might also indicate that, instead of the teacher's summarizing the contributions of his pupils or rephrasing their generalizations, a pupil could perform this important function.

ADVANTAGES OF EVALUATION QUESTIONS

Inasmuch as evaluation or decision-making is the heart of rational behavior, it is hard to overdo this kind of questioning. The evaluation stage of the creative-thinking process changes what may be fancy to possibility and frequently reality. Accordingly, it is a very necessary part of all the creative arts and sciences. The evaluation question should provide pupils with practice in making decisions about all kinds of matters both in and out of school.

DISADVANTAGES OF EVALUATION QUESTIONS

Generally, in order to employ the evaluation question effectively, a teacher must prepare his pupils by helping them learn to set up criteria for problems and questions. It takes a good deal of practice before children know how to set up criteria by which persons, events, organizations, processes, objects, and products can be judged. Therefore, if the teacher has not laid the groundwork by introducing activities in which his pupils can acquire this skill, it is unlikely that the evaluation questions he poses will be really effective.

The True-False Question

In form, the true-false question is an evaluation type of question, requiring the pupil to make a decision about the correctness of a statement. In practice, it has more the character of the memory question or its first cousin, the multiple-choice question. In some cases the pupil recognizes the statement in the form presented as something he has seen before. In other cases he may search his memory about certain facts or principles to see if the statement rings true. Sometimes in order to determine its validity he must be concerned as to how the elements of the statement fit together. However, when delivered orally it is usually a device to trap the unwary and inattentive ("Fairbanks *is* the capital of Alaska, isn't it, Fred?").

ADVANTAGES OF THE TRUE-FALSE QUESTION

Since it has aspects of most of the other types of questions, the true-false question also has their virtues and faults. It is usually short, and thus may appeal both to the test-maker and to the examinee. Many more true-false items can be handled during an hour, for instance, than either multiple-choice or short-answer questions. According to some authorities, true-false items are best adapted to easy and accurate measurement of the student's knowledge of specific facts.

DISADVANTAGES OF THE TRUE-FALSE QUESTION

As a test item, however, the true-false question is not well loved by students, especially when the statement incorporates trick words or ambiguous phrases. When the pupil has a good imagination and can see many possibilities and relationships, he often becomes confused because he sees both truth and falsity in the statement. The pupil may well see an implication in the statement that the teacher or test-maker had not seen. He may actually be penalized because of his thinking powers. The true-false question does little in the way of helping the pupil organize the information he has into coherent and meaningful patterns.

Why Bother about Strategies of Questioning?

It is impossible to know to what extent the effective teacher is guided in his behavior by deliberate strategies. Although he may consciously try to lead his pupils to discover certain facts and then to form generalizations, much of what he does and how he reacts to pupils cannot be planned. A creative teacher, by definition, is intuitive and spontaneously flexible, and so we might expect that his success is attributable in part to those aspects of his behavior that arise spontaneously and that derive principally from what he is as a human being.

The power of the teacher's personality is undeniably important in bringing about pupil growth in the acquisition of knowledge, skills, and understandings and in the development of positive attitudes toward learning and thinking. The relationships between a teacher and his class are based upon a number of factors, many of which are quite subtle and not discernible to an observer.

Accordingly, you have a right to ask: "Why bother about questioning methodology if a teacher either has the 'magic' or hasn't?" The answer is a declaration of faith, one shared by anyone who hopes to help education in the United States become more humane. We are convinced that positive, gratifying teaching experiences can affect attitudes, which in turn will affect behavior. In other words, experiences in the classroom that are satisfying for both pupils and teachers can significantly change the behavior of the pupils so that they learn to enjoy learning and thinking in school.

Not only do pupils need continuous reinforcement and reassurance, so do their teachers. The teacher needs to feel that he is genuinely helping most of his pupils, that he is succeeding. Probably one of the best ways he can earn this feeling of satisfaction is to incorporate a variety of methods and materials into his program. The research evidence attests to the principle that providing a variety of activities and materials serves to insure success for more pupils than any other provision a teacher can make. The suggestions in this chapter are offered in the hope that they will enlarge your view of questioning and perhaps add to your stock of teaching alternatives.

Making Your Own Summary

This chapter contains many ideas for developing the kinds of questioning skills necessary for creative learning and teaching. Few teachers possess all of these skills and teachers can improve those they have acquired by deliberate practice and evaluation. We suggest, therefore, that you select one type of questioning that you would like to improve and work on that. If you are not now actively teaching, find some child or young person and engage him in an interview about something of interest to him. Try to apply the ideas in this chapter that concern the type of questioning you have selected. Record your interview by whatever means are available and then analyze the results.

How closely did your interviewing follow the paradigm given for the type of questioning you used? In what ways could you have made the interview more productive? What do you think was accomplished through your little experiment?

REFERENCES

Bruner, J. S. "Learning and Thinking." *Harvard Educational Review*, 1959, **29**, 184–192.

Bruner, J. S. *The Process of Education.* Cambridge, Mass.: Harvard University Press, 1960.

Cunnington, B. F., E. P. Torrance, R. E. Myers, P. Buckland, and R. Peterson. *All-Around American: The Ben Franklin Story.* Boston: Ginn & Co., 1965.

Myers, R. E. and E. P. Torrance. *Can You Imagine?* Boston: Ginn & Co., 1965.

Myers, R. E. and E. P. Torrance. *For Those Who Wonder.* Boston: Ginn & Co., 1966.

Taba, H. and D. Elkins. *Teaching Strategies for the Culturally Disadvantaged.* Chicago: Rand McNally, 1966.

CHAPTER 9 ASKING

PROVOCATIVE QUESTIONS

Classroom,
Ideas bloom,
Growing, creating, extending
The mind to endless limits of the
Universe.

207

The Problem

Mr. Darrow was considered by his fellow teachers as an unusually gifted—and peculiar—man. He had been a professional musician before becoming a teacher, and his principal hobby was designing and building furniture. Perhaps it was because he did not enter the teaching profession in the ordinary way that Mr. Darrow had a "different" approach to his job. He played his guitar and sang with his sixth-grade pupils almost every day, for instance. Mr. Darrow also believed in having his pupils find things out for themselves. He wanted them to think about the issues that were confronting their parents and others. He also wanted them to know what was going on inside and outside their community.

As a result of his beliefs about learning and living, Mr. Darrow often discussed both practical and philosophical problems with his pupils. When one of his pupils remarked that he had read that three persons had suffered from food poisoning in a local restaurant, Mr. Darrow challenged his class with: "How much cleaner are the restaurants than the kitchens in your homes?" The children accepted the challenge by going to the city hall to find out about the regulations regarding health and cleanliness for public eating places, drawing up a checklist of conditions necessary for a hygienic kitchen, inspecting the kitchens of all the public eating places in the city, inspecting the kitchens of their homes, and giving the results of their findings in written and oral reports. As a consequence, the principal of Mr. Darrow's school received three telephone calls that were highly critical of the children's investigations and two that were complimentary (all of the negative comments came from parents). The pupils' findings generally indicated that the people who served food to the public were very conscientious and quite aware of their responsibilities.

When several of Mr. Darrow's pupils expressed a keen dislike for the city's law enforcement officers, the majority of the class members joined in with comments about how unfair and prejudiced toward young people the police were.

"Who is more prejudiced—you kids or the police?" Mr. Darrow asked quietly.

"The cops are!" thundered the class.

Mr. Darrow invited his pupils to prove their assertion; and, after two days of discussion, they adopted a plan for determining what prejudices were operating in the community with respect to the attitudes the police and juveniles held for one another. As a consequence, two boys spent two hours a day for a week riding in a squad car. A team of a boy and two girls interviewed teens and sub-teens who had violated the city's laws and had been dealt with by the police. A sergeant and a detective, on separate occasions, spent an entire school day with the class. At the end of the investigation, one of the two boys who had originally brought up the subject of police prejudice toward young people expressed an interest in a career as a probation officer. Mr. Darrow's pupils concluded that there was indeed prejudice on both sides, but they found that there were more unjustified feelings and beliefs by young people concerning police than vice versa. The dangers of stereotyping and rumor-mongering were brought home clearly to the children as a result of their research.

Effective teachers are skilled in predicting the effect of an assignment, a piece of instructional material, or a particular teaching strategy on their pupils. When the creative processes of children are set in motion, however, a teacher can never predict precisely what will occur. This is particularly true when the teacher asks provocative questions—questions that cause children to see things about themselves in new ways, to question the status quo, and to investigate. In their zeal to find out the truth, children may upset school administrators, parents, and community leaders. Thus, the teacher who asks provocative questions takes a considerable risk.

Do you think teachers should take such risks? Why?

How can a teacher continue to ask provocative questions and reduce the danger of repercussions?

Extending the Pupil's Thinking

The preceding chapter dealt with questions that set in motion the higher mental processes and bridge the gap between learning and thinking. In this chapter, we will attempt to push the matter of questioning still further. In creative learning and teaching, it is important that questions encourage children to extend their thinking and to see new relationships, to discover gaps in their knowledge, and to cause them to want to acquire more information or to engage in new activities. We are convinced, therefore, that the teacher who regularly asks questions that require his pupils to struggle with and for ideas is facilitating their education in a way that no one or nothing else can. These are questions which provoke pupils to think about matters that extend beyond the material presented by their teachers or textbooks. They involve the pupil cognitively and emotionally by:

1. Encouraging him to combine that which is given in the question with relevant information already possessed, thus causing him to retrieve, review, and re-evaluate previous learnings.

2. Causing him to become aware of gaps or deficiencies in his store of information, thus encouraging him to seek additional information because he has become aware of the need for new information.

3. Encouraging him to see facts, processes, events, people, institutions, ideas, etc. in new ways (and thus understand them better).

4. Making it more likely that he will look for implications in the ideas inherent in the questions (for example, possible consequences and ramifications).

Probably, however, the most important reason for asking provocative questions is to cause children *to want to learn*.

Learning How to Formulate Thought-Provoking Questions

Torrance has successfully used one of the items in Burkhart's (1963) Object Questions Test in helping his university students to understand the elements that make up provocative questions and to develop skills in asking them. He first asked the students to "think of some provocative questions about 'ice' which should lead to a variety of different answers and arouse interest and curiosity in others concerning ice." Given below are some representative examples of their productions. Note that some of the questions would evoke convergent-thinking responses, even though the students were requested to contrive questions that call for divergent thinking.

Why is some ice cloudy and other clear?
What are the best conditions for preserving ice during hot weather?
Why does one piece of ice cream seem colder than another?
What shape of ice freezes fastest? Slowest?
What shape of ice thaws fastest? Slowest?
How can ice be used as a source of power?
Why must we use water? It's so messy.
Can ice be made in a vacuum?
Why does very cold ice stick to your hand?
Can ice be super-cooled?
Does it give off energy?
Will ice become warmer or colder without melting?
What would happen if ice didn't float?
How could it be used for clothing?
Can ice be used as dynamite?
What would our lives be without ice?
Can creatures live in ice?
Could a ship be made of ice?
What uses can be made of polar ice formations?
How do we use ice in mechanical ways?
What if all the polar ice melted?
How many ways could colored ice be used?

After devising a number of these questions themselves, the students are invited to select the five most provocative questions from a group of fourteen questions dealing with this same subject. These are the questions:

1. At what temperature does ice freeze?
2. If the world should perish, do you think it would be by ice?
3. What colors are found in an ice cube?
4. What do we have ice for?
5. When you look through ice, how do objects appear to you?
6. Is a pond ever solid ice?
7. How much water makes a pound of ice?

8. Where in the oceans is ice a danger?
9. Is ice or water larger in volume (for its weight)?
10. If ice was not naturally occurring, would men have discovered it?
11. How might furniture of ice affect our living patterns?
12. Knowing the physical properties of ice, what would the world look like to a person suspended in ice?
13. Can you imagine how a favorite spot would look through an ice cube?
14. What emotions does ice remind you of?

Try it yourself. Which five do *you* think are the most provocative questions? (See the scoring key at the end of the chapter.) *Can you think of other similar subjects that could be used by you to prompt pupils to stretch their minds?* Apparently there is a definite positive relationship between a person's ability to produce unusual, thought-provoking questions and his ability to distinguish the more provocative questions from the less provocative ones in Burkhart's list. We believe that once a teacher learns the key elements of a provocative question, he will be able to better formulate such questions and will be more likely to employ these questions in teaching. This is a skill that requires deliberate practice, especially because we have had so much practice in asking factual questions that call only for the reproduction of the information contained in the textbook or in the teacher's lectures.

Asking Hypothetical Questions

In the Gifted and Talented Child Program of Omaha, Nebraska, teachers are urged to give their pupils opportunities to engage in activities that have been identified by Bloom in his *Taxonomy of Educational Objectives* (1956) as *translating, interpreting, extrapolating, applying, analyzing,* and *synthesizing.* Extrapolating is defined in the guide that provides the rationale for the project as being able to go beyond the given data to trends and tendencies. These are some of the examples given in the guide to illustrate this cognitive ability:

1. The Communists believe that the individual exists only to serve the state—a useful cog in a machine, a cog easily replaced if it

becomes faulty. How would justice be advanced by anyone who accepted this theory?

2. You are a member of a U.N. conference to decide limits of territorial waters. What factors would you want to consider? What difference would it make if the limits are 3, 30, or 3000 miles?

3. If you were made principal of your school, what changes would you make?

4. If you were a fish, how would you eat, sleep, travel, and communicate?

The "what-would-happen-if" technique of extrapolation recommended in the Omaha Gifted and Talented Child Program has been used successfully by many teachers to encourage their pupils to understand better the nature of an event, process, institution, force, or condition of the present or past. For example, in order to encourage their pupils to discover the far-reaching and penetrating results of the Spanish conquest in the Western hemisphere, teachers have asked questions such as these:

What would have happened if an Englishman, instead of Columbus, had landed on an island in the Lesser Antilles in 1492?

How different would the world be now if Columbus had landed on the coast of Brazil?

In what ways would the course of history have changed if Cortez and his men had been killed by Montezuma?

What would have happened if the Spanish expeditions had not contained men of the Church?

Teachers of younger children have sparked many good thinking-and-doing sessions with questions such as these, designed to ignite imaginations:

What would happen if all the flowers in the world were yellow?

What would happen if all of the television stations went on strike and there were no television programs for a year?

What would happen if all of the shoes in the world were the same size?

What would happen if we had just a half-hour of classwork and the rest of the day were recess?

What would happen if peas tasted like candy?

Asking Provocative Questions to Encourage Thoughtful Listening

The use of provocative questions is invaluable to the teacher who wishes to assist his pupils in acquiring concepts in depth. For example, if the children in a sixth-grade class have undertaken a unit of study dealing with communications, they might well listen to the recording of *Commander of Communication: The Samuel F. B. Morse Story* (Cunnington and Torrance, 1965a). Before listening to the recording, a teacher might introduce his class to the Morse Code; and, once the children are fairly familiar with that system of codifying messages, he could ask if any of them would be interested in trying to devise ways of improving or simplifying the code. After they have listened to the dramatization of the highlights of Morse's career, these questions might be asked to help the pupils understand some of its implications:

Why do you suppose it took Morse so long to perfect his telegraph?

Was the need for a rapid communications system greater during the first part of the nineteenth century than it had been during the latter part of the eighteenth century? Why do you think so?

Do you know of any living person who has been able to attain great eminence in two highly different fields, as did Morse? If not, why do you suppose that men today are rarely able to gain fame in two or more fields?

What kinds of messages were most frequently carried by the telegraph during its early years? Why do you think so?

During the course of the unit the teacher might ask questions such as these to extend his pupils' thinking:

In how many different ways could a *light* be used as a communications device?

In how many different ways could a *bell* be used as a communications device?

In how many different ways could a *whistle* be used as a communications device?

In how many different ways could an *odor* be used as a communications device?

If the teacher of a fifth-grade class were interested in helping his pupils to delve more deeply into their study of the Colonial Period, he might present the Imagi/Craft recording of *All-Around American: The Ben Franklin Story* (Cunnington and Torrance, 1965a), to them. To prepare his pupils for the recording, the teacher could ask them questions such as these:

> Have you ever thought of a new idea which might prove to be of help, either in work or play?
>
> What objects, customs, institutions, or facts would you change if you had the chance?
>
> Which local and national agencies and organizations make your lives more interesting, healthful, and fun? (Franklin instituted not only police, fire, and hospital protection for his fellow Philadelphians, but also originated a circulating library and an academy, which in time became known as the University of Pennsylvania.)
>
> Can you name an important invention of the past ten years? In what ways is it important? How do you think the inventor got the idea? Are there any disadvantages in our having this invention? Can you think of any additional improvements for the invention? How would you go about working them out?

After the children have listened to the recording, the teacher could query them along these lines: *

> If Franklin were alive today, on what "problem areas" of the individual, the community, the nation, and the world would he be working?
>
> What are *two* other ways of saying:
>
> A penny saved is a penny earned.
>
> A rolling stone gathers no moss.
>
> Early to bed and early to rise, makes a man healthy, wealthy, and wise.
>
> A bird in the hand is worth two in the bush.
>
> Lost time is never found again.
>
> An ounce of prevention is worth a pound of cure.
>
> Hunger never saw bad bread.

* Most of these ideas came from Pearl Buckland, the principal author of the teachers' guide for *All-Around American*.

When you're good to others, you're best to yourself.
Great talkers, little doers.
A quarrelsome man has no neighbors.

Did Franklin originate all of the sayings in *Poor Richard's Almanac?*
From what you know of his life, do you think Franklin ever failed at anything? Why do you think so?
Why didn't anyone else think of bifocal spectacles or a lightning rod or a citywide mail delivery service before Franklin did? (Or did someone?)

Asking Provocative Questions to Encourage Thoughtful Reading

Certainly the most common device for encouraging thoughtful reading is the question, but rarely does a teacher's question suggest to a pupil that he should go beyond what is found on the printed page of his required reading. For example, the questions below are typical of those asked by teachers when they attempt to help their pupils understand the content of a story, poem, or article. Let us imagine that a group of ten-year-old youngsters has been reading about the musical prodigy, Wolfgang Amadeus Mozart, and then are presented with these questions:

Why was Mozart called the "Boy Wonder"?
At what age did Mozart start writing music?
What kinds of music did Mozart write?

You will recognize all of these questions as being the kind that asks the pupil to recall factual information (referred to in the preceding chapter as the retention question).

In contrast, the following kind of question might be asked of the same children after reading about Mozart:

Can we call Mozart a *genius?* What is a genius? Do we have any geniuses in the world today?
Have you ever heard the term *prodigy?* Does it have anything to do with the expression "prodigal son"? Might someone be an athletic prodigy as well as a musical prodigy?
Do you think Mozart's life would have been easier if he had lived

in the twentieth century instead of the eighteenth? Why or why not?

If you imagine that *you* yourself are a musical genius, what have you learned from reading about Mozart's life that might help you avoid some of the troubles that hounded Mozart throughout his lifetime?

Each of the questions in the second set encourages the pupil to see relationships that would never be seen if he were asked only retention questions. Importantly, all of these questions involve the pupil personally in the subject matter, and they should provoke him into finding more information as he becomes aware of the incompleteness of his knowledge.

You may have noticed that both sets of questions were to be presented to a pupil or to a group of pupils *after* reading the material about Mozart. In some ways it is more important to ask thought-provoking questions *before* children plunge into the reading in order that they be in a proper mood and so that they may be alert to certain elements in the material. In addition, appropriate questions can heighten anticipation and increase enjoyment when they are asked before a reading assignment is begun. *What would be a good set of questions to ask before a group of nine- or ten-year-olds start reading a book about Wolfgang Mozart?*

Questions to Encourage Individuals to See New Relationships

In developing a collection of exercises or activities to encourage primary-grade children to extend their imaginations (*Can You Imagine?*, 1965), we began thinking of posing questions that would make young children pause and reflect. Although the questions selected were designed to puzzle the youngsters, interestingly enough it has turned out that they are far more perplexing to adults. Here are the original five questions:

Why does this?
When was tomorrow?
Who would you think?
Where is never?
When is the sky?

In general, children are able to interpret the questions so that they can produce answers. Many adults, on the other hand, have a great deal of difficulty in seeing how the questions can make any sense at all. Although the exercise was not a favorite of the primary-grade children who initially field-tested the twenty-six exercises which comprise *Can You Imagine?*, it did not seem to be rejected by these children. Subsequently, there have been no complaints from teachers or their pupils about the exercise's causing frustration or irritation. In contrast, approximately half of the members of our graduate and undergraduate courses have evidently experienced some mental anguish when they have been asked to "make sense of five questions that may seem crazy to you." This is the way a veteran male teacher reacted to a set of questions similar to those above.

Is a month a mile? *In relation to time it is correlated as mile is to measurement.*

Do pickles come in the summer? *They come into being as cucumbers, but not pickles until fall or winter after the pickling process.*

Does the sun sound tired today? *I have never thought of the sun in this relation and never expect to do so.*

Is a boy before a woman? *If he's been sent to the office and there's a woman principal.*

Where does the cold go? *It is absorbed by objects or into the air, which may later be warmed up by absorbing heat.*

Not all teachers are so reluctant to be playful, fortunately, as these responses to the same questions demonstrate:

Is a month a mile?

It only seems so when you are making the uphill struggle from one payday to the next.

If you measure all the things you should do in one month, it is more than a mile.

A month can be a mile or it can be an inch, depending on whether it's the month before school is out or during summer vacation.

Some months are many and many a mile, unto a million miles. Many a moment may be a mile—may be a millimeter.

Do pickles come in the summer? *~right~*

In the form of long-lost relatives if you rent a summer place at the beach.

Certainly; when else? Earlier they are dormant and embryonic.

If they're "dillies" they come often, especially at the end of "that course" in summer school.

Depending on the word "pickle"—lots of pickles come in the summer to parents when the children are at home.

Where does the cold go?

When one becomes friendly with another person, the coldness of a stranger dissolves into warmth and friendliness.

Off to find a place where his creative talents will be more welcome and his finished products not be looked "down upon" by a hot sun.

Heat expands, cold contracts, cold contracts into a minute snowball and retreats to the top of a cumulus cloud to wait until the sun gets tired of being so gay.

The typical response to the first question, "Is a month a mile?" is "No, a month is a measure of time, and a mile is a measure of distance." You can see from this small sample of responses from one group of twenty teachers that when questions of this kind are not rejected or treated too literally, the individual can see relationships that would never have been seen with the serious, logical mind's eye he uses in the classroom. "Yes, a month is a mile," as one teacher said, "if you are a snail on a business trip."

Research on Provocative Questions ~Rarely asked~

Studies of classroom behavior, unhappily, indicate that provocative questions are rarely asked at any level of education. One study (Fowlkes, 1962), for example, showed that over 90 percent of the questions asked by junior high school social studies teachers call only for the reproduction of textbook information. When efforts have been made to encourage teachers to ask provocative questions, it has become obvious that not enough teachers possess these skills. Presumably, they stopped practicing them at an early age and find it difficult to ask other than factual questions. As we have said earlier, however, we believe that through deliberate, disciplined efforts all teachers can doubtless improve the quantity and quality of their provocative questions and, with them, the quality of their pupils' learning.

Making Your Own Summary

Mrs. Dowling was puzzled. She was also hurt. The results of an experiment conducted in her school district showed that her pupils had failed to improve their scores in one section of a social studies test battery. The tests had been administered to four fifth-grade classes in two schools before and after a unit dealing with the concept of culture. Her class had improved somewhat more than two of the classes and not as much as the other on the first section featuring questions of recall, but there was actually a slight decrement between the pre-test and post-test scores of her pupils on the part dealing with questions of application, analysis, and synthesis. When the social studies consultant who was conducting the experiment submitted the scores to Mrs. Dowling, it seemed to her that he emphasized the fact that her class ranked last on the application-synthesis section. He also intimated that it was more important than the other part of the test battery. She had never cared much for the young man; and since he had less than half as much teaching experience as she had, she had often wondered out loud why the district had felt it necessary to hire him. Other teachers had agreed with her.

Mrs. Dowling had always prided herself upon doing a particularly effective job of teaching critical thinking, and she thought that social studies was probably one of the strongest areas in her instructional program. She made certain that the material assigned in the textbooks was read by requiring her pupils to write out the answers to the questions at the end of the chapters. Frequently she engaged her pupils in games which had them citing places, persons, events, and dates that had been presented in the texts, films, and filmstrips they had studied. The proof of the effectiveness of her program, she believed, had been the first-place prize one of her brightest pupils had won in the yearly essay contest about Americanism. An officer of the local American Legion Post, the sponsor of the contest, had said that the winning essay was one of the best that had been submitted in many years. Obviously, Mrs. Dowling thought, the results of the tests were spurious. Her pupils always excelled in social studies.

Judging from what is reported above, do you think that Mrs. Dowling was really emphasizing critical thinking in her social studies program? What classroom activities might have involved her pupils more directly in evaluating statements, positions, and events, and in synthesizing ideas? What out-of-class activities might have sharpened their skills in analyzing, synthesizing, and applying ideas? What kinds of questions would you recommend to Mrs. Dowling as being likely to effect growth in critical thinking?

REFERENCES

Bloom, B. S. (ed.). *Taxonomy of Educational Objectives. Handbook I: Cognitive Domain.* New York: David McKay Company, 1956.

Burkhart, R. C. and G. Bernheim. "Object Questions Test Manual." University Park, Pa.: Department of Art Education Research, Pennsylvania State University, 1963. Mimeographed.

Cunnington, B. F. and E. P. Torrance. *Commander of Communication: The Samuel F. B. Morse Story.* Boston: Ginn & Co., 1965a.

Cunnington, B. F. and E. P. Torrance. *All-Around American: The Ben Franklin Story.* Boston: Ginn & Co., 1965b.

Fowlkes, J. G. *The Wisconsin Improvement Program—Teacher Education and Local School Systems.* Madison, Wisconsin: University of Wisconsin, 1962.

Myers, R. E. and E. P. Torrance. *Can You Imagine?* Boston: Ginn & Co., 1965.

Torrance, E. P. and E. Hansen. "The Question-Asking Behavior of Highly Creative and Less Creative Basic Business Teachers Identified by a Paper-and-Pencil Test." *Psychological Reports,* 1965, **17,** 815–818.

SCORING KEY FOR EVALUATIONS OF UNUSUAL QUESTIONS ABOUT ''ICE''

Score the five questions chosen or checked according to the values indicated below.

<u>0</u>   1. At what temperature does ice freeze?

<u>2</u>   2. If the world should perish, do you think it would be by ice?

<u>1</u>   3. What colors are found in an ice cube?

<u>1</u>   4. What do we have ice for?

<u>2</u>   5. When you look through ice, how do objects appear to you?

<u>0</u>   6. Is a pond ever solid ice?

<u>0</u>   7. How much water makes a pound of ice?

<u>0</u>   8. Where in the ocean is ice a danger?

<u>0</u>   9. Is ice or water larger in volume (for its weight)?

<u>4</u>   10. If ice was not naturally occurring would man have discovered it?

<u>4</u>   11. How might furniture of ice affect our living pattern?

<u>4</u>   12. Knowing the physical properties of ice, what would the world look like to a person suspended in ice?

<u>4</u>   13. Can you imagine how a favorite spot would look through an ice cube?

<u>2</u>   14. What emotions does ice remind you of?

CHAPTER 10

TEACHING CHILDREN TO ASK QUESTIONS

Wonder,
Perception's torch,
Enlightening, exciting minds
Striving desperately to know:
Questions.

The Problem

When you first met your third-grade pupils in September you were delighted with their enthusiasm for learning and their apparent eagerness to please. They had appeared to be, of all the groups of children you had taught, the most nearly ideal. Now it is January and you are trying to understand a growing discontent within yourself. The children are in many ways just as responsive to your teaching as they were in the fall. But not one of them has shown any interest in launching a project of his own and carrying through with it until completion. Rarely has one of them asked a question to find out something.

Every time you ask your pupils if they have any questions, they just sit quietly and nervously. Every time you ask them to decide for themselves how an arithmetic problem might be tackled, how a skit could be presented, or which science unit could be presented, all that you get from them are embarrassed expressions and pleas for your assistance. If you provide your pupils with a clearly defined plan, they invariably do quite well. If the instructions are incomplete, however, they just wait to be told what to do. They never ask questions to find out what to do.

You are convinced that your pupils should be given opportunities to develop their skills in asking questions to find out things. *What can you to do develop these skills?*

ADDITIONAL INFORMATION

Your school is located in the suburb of a rapidly growing city. It was built two years ago to accommodate the children living in a new tract of homes that was constructed to meet the demands for housing in the area. The principal of your school is a young man of twenty-eight who was a sixth-grade teacher during his three years in the classroom. His staff is composed almost entirely of young teachers. About one-third of them are men.

Most of the parents of your pupils are employed by two large manufacturing concerns. Approximately one-half of the mothers have full-time jobs. Many of the parents have expressed a genuine concern about the quality of schooling that their children are receiving. They seem to be very eager to cooperate with the school in every way. They are influenced to a certain extent by the policies of the corporations which employ them. Education and self-improvement are stressed by both corporations. The school board is made up of local businessmen and one administrative officer of a minor rank of the larger manufacturing concern.

What kinds of questions might you ask to provoke the children to ask further questions? What kinds of assignments and projects might get them interested in asking questions to find out things? What kinds of classroom procedures might encourage them to ask these kinds of questions?

Pupils Should Also Ask Questions

Although the kinds of questions teachers ask have a great deal to do with the progress pupils make in acquiring information and skills and in developing their thinking abilities, it is important that pupils ask questions too. It would seem that getting children to ask questions is no problem at all. Parents often remark that they are beset with an endless barrage of questions from their children from the time they are able to talk. Interestingly enough, analyses of verbal interaction in classrooms at all academic levels do not confirm the notion that pupils are bombarding their teachers with questions.

Even when urged to ask questions, pupils are often reluctant to do so. Young children will often respond with a statement, rather than a question, when asked to compose an appropriate question concerning some topic. This was the reaction of five-year-old Scott when Mrs. Fortson asked her preschoolers to formulate questions about a Picasso painting.

MRS. FORTSON: Tell me what questions you would ask Mr. Picasso about this picture. What are the things you want to know about when you look at this picture? Scott?

SCOTT: He made it for all the people to see.

Suddenly the rules had been changed—the children were to think of questions rather than answers—and Scott, a highly verbal and aggressive youngster, did not know the proper way of reacting. We have found this kind of behavior typical in every school we have visited. Moreover, in the individual administration of the Ask-and-Guess Test in the primary grades, such behavior continues to be typical. Even when graduate students are asked to teach and learn by asking, similar behaviors are elicited.

What Kinds of Questions Do Pupils Ask?

We know, however, that children do ask many questions in school. If we examine the kinds of questions that they ask, we may obtain some hints about how they can be helped to improve their questioning.

Pupils ask questions that will enable them (1) to obtain permission and to understand procedures; (2) to secure information about how to perform tasks; (3) to acquire facts; and (4) to gain understanding of concepts, generalizations, processes, etc. These are by no means all of the types of questions that children ask in school, but they include the great majority of questions asked by them. A fairly close look at each of these kinds of pupil questions should also reveal some of the forces at work in classrooms which cause pupils to seek answers or to remain silent.

QUESTIONS REGARDING PROCEDURES

Procedural matters bulk large on the list of questions that most teachers process each day. Here are some examples of the various types of questions children ask regarding routine and scheduling. Generally speaking, the questions at the beginning of the list indicate the presence of rules and restrictions, and those toward the end imply increasing freedom to inquire and discover.

May I go to the lavatory?
May I have another piece of paper?
May I go to the library to get another book?
When will we get our papers back?

Are we going to have a movie on the wildlife of Canada?

When can we present our skit?

Are we going to launch our model rocket at 2:00 today?

Who will be the judges for the debate? Are we going to discuss the rules?

Is it all right if we invite Mr. Miller to come and talk about architecture on Thursday?

Although questions of scheduling are uncommon in many classrooms because the teachers have made times, places, and procedures explicit, they are more frequent and more important in the classrooms of teachers who plan activities and units of study with their pupils. There are definite advantages for the teacher who makes all or most of the decisions about the daily activities; and children usually feel quite secure in such situations. On the other hand a question such as "Who will be the judges for the debate?" indicates that the children will probably be more involved in the planning and carrying out of the activity and will gain more from these experiences than the pupils of a teacher who introduces the activity, decides how it will be carried out, and then leads a discussion on the benefits of debating the topic.

QUESTIONS REGARDING TASKS

If the pupil and the teacher are to cooperate in the educational enterprise, questions regarding tasks and directions are necessary. They become less important in cases where pupils plan with their teachers and where pupils often carry out their investigations independently or in small groups. But a certain amount of direction-giving is simply part of the scheme of things in every classroom. Depending upon their ages and the skills of the teacher in defining tasks and giving directions, children generally do most of their questioning in this category. It may or may not be fair to say that the skills of a teacher in defining tasks and goals and in giving instructions are reflected in the number of questions of this type that his pupils ask. The intelligence and family backgrounds of the children have a great deal to do with the frequency with which they ask questions about tasks. Nevertheless, an abundance of questioning and answering about tasks is wasteful of the time and energy of both the teacher and his pupils.

The questions given below are typical of the kinds that elementary teachers receive every day. They are given in an order which approximates a dependence-independence continuum for the pupil.

Should we write on both sides of the paper?

When is this due?

Can you show me how to bisect this line with my compass?

Should I put my giraffe on the table to dry?

I didn't understand what we're supposed to do. Would you tell us again?

Would you explain what you mean by "average" in that problem on our assignment sheet?

How many pages does it have to be?

Why do we have to have a test on that?

Are we supposed to go on reading in the book, or can we do something else?

Could I put my report on Tanzania into a story about a lion, written from the lion's point of view?

Is it all right if I draw a picture about the book I read instead of writing a report on the book-report form?

Do you think we could learn more about the Olympics by having our own "Junior Olympics" at school than by having a committee report on it?

Many of the questions above are representative of the verbal interactions that drive teachers to distraction—or other jobs. Unless a teacher has by chance been assigned a group of highly immature and dependent youngsters, it is likely that by carefully checking on the manner in which he has been assigning tasks for his pupils he can quickly do something to reduce the number of times he repeats directions. There are a few questions that he can ask himself that should enable him to locate trouble-spots in his instructions.

1. Did I have the attention of the entire class when I gave the directions?

2. Did I choose an appropriate time to give the directions? (Was it a time when the children were ready to receive directions?)

3. Do the children understand the reasons for their doing the task?

4. When I give directions, am I using language that they understand? If the directions are spoken, am I speaking so that they can all hear me?

5. Do I prepare the children for tasks by "setting the stage" with remarks which will get them ready for the activities they will be engaging in?

Questions concerning the evaluation of performance are common in some classrooms. Examples are:

Is this all right?
Do you like this?
Should I have used a different word?
I'm going to throw this away (*which is the declarative form of* Don't you think this is pretty good?)
How did I do?
How might I have improved my talk? (my drawing?) (my poem?) (my hitting?)

Since these questions often deal with tasks, they can be included in the category above, although they might easily comprise a separate classification.

QUESTIONS REGARDING INFORMATION

Pupils still consider teachers as prime sources of information. Although television and encyclopedias are also especially popular sources among ten- , eleven- , and twelve-year-old youngsters, and the teacher may not seem quite the omniscient being to children of those ages that he does to younger children, the teacher is regarded still as a marvelous and ready dispenser of information.

Unfortunately, there are two serious difficulties for the teacher if he or she consciously or unconsciously assumes the role of "Mr. Answer Man" or "Mrs. Answer Woman." First of all, there is considerable evidence to prove that providing children with the answers to their questions whenever the teacher is capable of doing so is not conducive to their intellectual development. The children tend to forget the answers almost before they can write them down on their papers. (In fact, we have had some pupils who were not able to remember the answers that long.) Having done very little to acquire the information, the pupils who are supplied quick answers to their questions frequently lose them immediately. Secondly, nowadays the so-called knowledge explosion makes it extremely difficult for a teacher to pose as an authority on very many subjects. Grammar and punctuation, perhaps, but little else. Even the most knowledgeable teachers bow often to the superior knowledge of their pupils in many areas of the curriculum, particularly in science and social studies. Not only is it pedagogically unsound to try to supply pupils with rapid-fire answers to questions requiring factual knowledge, it can be embarrassing. The effective teacher today is not a know-it-all but a co-experiencer.

Here is a list of questions which are representative of the queries teachers receive for information. The questions are arranged, roughly, in an ascending order of autonomy on the part of the pupil.

How do you spell "train" ("picture," "mirage," "vertical," "Philadelphia," etc.)?

Where is the big dictionary?

What do you call this rock?

I can't find "hormone" in our science book—where can I find it?

Where can we go to find out the average amount of rainfall in our area?

What's a "pension"?

Does a flying squirrel fly, or is it just gliding?

Is there really an elephant burial ground?

Did women really wear clothes like that then?

Why do people pay taxes, anyway?

Could the craters on the moon have been caused by meteors striking it?

Which could give me more information about South Atlantic currents, the encyclopedia or the atlas?

Do you think we could find out by phoning Judge Doughty if prisoners are eligible to vote?

I need some help in drawing my plans for my future house. Do you think Mr. Ayers would have time to help me if I phone him?

Questions such as these can lead to fruitful investigations, as most teachers have discovered. If the child really wants to know the answer, he is willing to expend some energy in obtaining it. However, if he is accustomed to getting quick answers that involve little probing on his part, he soon adopts the attitude that there are easy solutions to problems—and when the solutions do not come easily he could figure they are not worth working hard to obtain.

QUESTIONS REGARDING UNDERSTANDING

We might arbitrarily divide into two categories the questions that children ask in order to better understand their world. One category could contain those questions that are related to their academic lives, and the other, those questions that derive from their nonacademic lives. However, it is often not practical to distinguish one type of question from the other, nor is it desirable to do so usually; and we suspect that in the classrooms of the most effective teachers it is impossible to do so. Here is a brief list of typical questions that children ask in order to increase their understanding of an endless variety of topics. Again, the questions are presented in such a way that those which show the most dependence upon the teacher are at the top of the list and the questions which show the greatest autonomy on the part of the pupil are given at the bottom of the list.

What do you mean by "versus" ("oval," "perpendicular," "margin," "texture," etc.).

What does "escalate" ("arterial," "pedestrian," "transient," etc.) mean?

Why do you invert the fraction?

Why do I see color on soap bubbles?

Where does water come from?

Why do people call each other "Mr." and "Mrs."?

Why are there cracks in the cement (concrete)?

Yes, I know it's a gas called carbon dioxide, but why does it burn my hands?

After I take a bite of an apple and leave it somewhere, there is a brown spot where I bit into it. Why is that?

Why do we call our government "democratic" when it has some of the same characteristics as socialistic government?

In many ways the questions that reveal a child's concern for understanding phenomena, processes, institutions, concepts, generalizations, and laws are the most important with which a teacher can deal. The teacher often is less inclined to answer the more complicated or profound questions because time is limited and he does not want to give an offhand or overly simplified answer to the pupil. Nevertheless, questions such as "Where does water come from?" should not be dismissed or ignored. In Chapter 11 an attempt will be made to point out ways in which these questions can be handled.

The Roles of the Teacher

The kinds of questions children ask teachers are indicative of their conception of the roles the teachers are playing in the classroom. For instance, if a class of pupils asks questions mostly concerning permission, they probably consider their teacher a babysitter or a warden. If most of their questions are about the ways in which they are to perform their tasks, children probably see their teacher as a boss or supervisor; some may see him as a drill sergeant. It is likely that many children see their teacher as a repository of information when their questions are mostly of the factual type. If a preponderance of their questions concern the things in their lives they wonder about and want to understand, a group of children probably regards its teacher as a co-experiencer.

How do your pupils regard you? In all likelihood, you take many roles in your classroom. However, it should be revealing to learn a little more about the ways in which your pupils regard you. Why don't you record the nature of the questions that you are asked during two or three different activities? If you do not have a tape recorder, it will be difficult to note the various questions the children ask, but it can be done in a crude fashion by tallying them when you have a free moment. With a tape recorder, you can pick up most of what transpires in a discussion (but not individual conferences, which are equally as important). Here is a form for a tally sheet which might be used to determine the roles you play in three teaching situations.

TALLEY SHEET OF PUPIL QUESTIONS

Type of Question	Period #1 (10–20 minutes)	Period #2 (10–20 minutes)	Period #3 (10–20 minutes)	Totals
Procedure ("May I?" "When?" "Where?" etc.)				
Task ("How?" "How much?" "Should I?" etc.)				
Information ("What?" "When?" "Who?" etc.)				
Understanding ("Why?" "What does this mean?" etc.)				

By looking at the column totals, you can get an idea as to whether the various activities are conducive to pupil questioning. You should also be able to tell if you are reaching some of your teaching objectives. If you examine the four totals, you can get some kind of picture of the roles you are playing. In addition, by finding the total number of questions asked and then determining the percentage of tallies in each category, you can get a good estimate of how your pupils think of you in the classroom. You can decide then if this is the way you want them to think of you.

THE TEACHER WHO IS IN CONTROL

By studying the kinds of questions children ask their teacher, a great deal can be learned about the ways teacher and children regard one another. When the teacher makes all or almost all of the decisions concerning the curriculum, the daily routine, the contents

of the classroom, and the movements that take place in the classroom, the questions he receives are mainly those that have to do
with administration and permission. These are typical of the questions this kind of teacher hears:

> May I go to the cloak room to get my pencil?
> Do we have any more orange construction paper?
> May I go to the library to look up "amphibious reptiles"?
> May I have a band-aid, please?
> Could I have a red pencil to correct these papers with?

Some genuinely wonderful people belong to this category of
teachers, and, we hasten to add, many of them are quite effective in
helping children to accumulate knowledge and to think clearly.
Their classrooms, however, are not the kind that vibrates with
ideas. Since there is generally no reason to assist their pupils in
learning to ask better questions about what they are or are not permitted to do, the teacher who is in control is usually not concerned
with helping children to formulate more productive questions.

As a matter of fact, this teacher may have a classroom in which
children learn that asking questions is a risky business, especially
when the answer is not a matter of procedure or is not readily accessible to the teacher. Questioning can be most dangerous for the
pupil when he persists in getting an answer in the face of teacher's
evasive tactics. The provocative question (see Chapter 9) is almost
always embarrassing to this teacher, and his pupils learn to avoid
expressing their curiosity in such terms.

Even in relatively advantaged schools, about 25 percent of the
children say that they are afraid to ask questions in school (Torrance and Gupta, 1964). In some schools, this percentage rises to 70
percent. In less advantaged schools, we have observed that children
seem to be even more fearful of asking questions than in the advantaged schools where our studies have been conducted.

THE TEACHER WHO PLANS WITH HIS PUPILS

The teacher who plans with his pupils the sequence and content of the subjects to be studied and the activities to be engaged in
is likely to listen to a variety of different kinds of questions during
the day. He may receive a number of a routine nature, questions

about assignments and materials and scheduling and such; and he may also receive some that bring him into a cooperative relationship with his pupils and cause him to help them to search, to compare, and to make judgments. He is likely to be confronted with such diverse questions as these:

Where did the word "okay" come from?
Do you think we could study the wildlife of the wilderness when we start the unit on Canada?
Can Cheryl and I go to the office to get some more tempera paint for the mural?
When are we going to elect a new class president?
How do you spell "mirror"?
Which encyclopedia would be better to use in making my report on transportation in Mexico—*Compton's* or *World Book?*

The teacher who involves his pupils in planning the experiences of the class is usually receptive to questions, and he will also usually have more tally marks in the cells for "Task," "Information," and "Understanding" on the Tally Sheet for Pupil Questions than the teacher who is in control.

THE TEACHER WHO CO-EXPERIENCES WITH HIS PUPILS

A third kind of teacher is the one who learns along with his pupils. He is not a co-learner in the sense that he is on the same intellectual level with his pupils; he is, rather, a co-experiencer who, along with his pupils, seeks information and understanding and is open to new experiences. The teacher who co-experiences with his pupils usually plans with them, but he also facilitates a learning atmosphere in which everyone learns from each other. There is more pupil-to-pupil questioning and answering in his classroom, not because he has abdicated his role as leader and guide (if this were the case he would be very ineffective) but because he has opened the channels of communication and permitted his pupils to try out their ideas in a climate of psychological safety. He is likely to field a great variety of questions, as is the teacher who plans with his pupils, but there are generally fewer of the housekeeping variety and more of the provocative kind. The co-experiencing teacher is likely to have questions such as these put to him:

Inductive approach (handwritten annotation)

Are you going to play chess with us this noon?

Why does the principal do all of the talking in the student council meetings?

What's so important about having good handwriting? Businessmen have secretaries to do their writing, and my big brother types all of his assignments in high school.

Are there as many Democratic papers as Republican papers? I think all three of the papers in this county are Republican, aren't they?

If we weren't fighting the Communists in Vietnam, who would be? Would there be any war?

These three brief characterizations are obviously not meant to be an exhaustive list of teacher types. They are given only to indicate how the teacher's attitude concerning the responsibilities of his pupils in directing their learning can affect the kinds and quantities of questions the children ask. Neither do the sketches constitute three mutually exclusive categories; there is considerable overlapping in the behavior of individual teachers. Many autocratic teachers plan certain activities with their pupils. Conversely, a co-experiencing teacher can be quite autocratic when the occasion demands.

Still another important point to be made concerning the roles of the teacher is that with the advent of the "new math," the "new science," the "new social studies," and the other curricular innovations of the past decade, a shift of emphasis has been made with regard to the elementary teacher's attitude toward information. He no longer is thought of as the receptacle of facts and concepts. Because of the so-called knowledge explosion, he is now considered a *guide* to young people in their search for information and understanding. Accordingly, the elementary teacher is now discovering facts, relationships, abstract concepts, and principles along with his pupils. By virtue of his greater fund of information and his maturity, he is able to guide his pupils in how to use their knowledge wisely. Although he does not use the inductive approach exclusively, the co-experiencing teacher understands how it can be effectively used to help pupils learn how to think critically and creatively. It is the open-minded, experimentally-oriented teacher who is able to handle the "new" methodologies. Unfortunately, perhaps, the teacher who must maintain control at all times is ineffective in the discovery approach to learning and teaching, what Bruner (1960) has called the "hypothetical mode" of teaching. On the other hand, the teacher who is not hemmed in by prejudices and preconceptions and who is willing to admit that his pupils may be more knowledgeable about many things than he is, has had less difficulty in trying to accommodate his teaching to the discovery approach.

This is not to say that the only teacher who is doing a good job of helping children grow intellectually and morally is the teacher who co-experiences. There is much to be said for the highly motivated, humane teacher who is comfortable only when he is in complete command of the classroom. Children frequently benefit greatly from this teacher, especially when he is able to communicate the feeling that he really cares what happens to the children whom he teaches. The "ideal" teacher, in the opinion of a majority of elementary school children, is one who is fair, who is eager to help, who trusts his pupils, and who enjoys being with young people. (See Chapter 13 for the characteristics that are most valued by children.) The style of teaching may be far less important than some crucial personality variables in encouraging children to learn and to think.

Encouraging Pupils to Ask Productive Questions

Although children very often ask excellent questions, they also ask questions which are foolish, unnecessary, poorly expressed, irrelevant, untimely, impolite, and aimless. These questions that do not lead to constructive thinking and doing might be called "unproductive." True education, however, is concerned with asking appropriate questions and getting useful or interesting answers, and so teachers should encourage their pupils to ask questions that will be instrumental in their acquisition of knowledge and understanding. We can call these questions "productive."

Is there any reason to suppose that if the teacher himself asks a large number of questions that the pupils in his classroom will also begin to ask questions? Probably not. It depends upon how the teacher asks his questions and what types of questions he asks. It also depends upon whether he is really interested in answering questions; he may believe that it is up to the pupils to answer *his* questions. To a very large extent, whether pupils ask questions or not is determined by how the children and teacher interpret their roles. If they think that school is a place where adults ask questions and children answer them—and that is the impression that observers receive when they enter classrooms throughout the country—the pupils will not be popping up with many questions.

We know that one of the chief ways in which children learn is by imitating adults. If we reflect that the teacher is one of the most influential models in a child's life, we might suppose that if he asks questions that are pertinent, penetrating, and provocative, his pupils will learn to do likewise. Although there is some evidence that pupils tend to follow their teachers' leads in the kinds of thinking they do (Gallagher and Aschner, 1963), it is improbable that the example of their teachers alone will cause young people to formulate appropriate and productive questions. But there is a good deal that teachers can do to help their pupils learn how to ask good questions. First of all, they can show their pupils that questions are the basic tools for acquiring information which will enable them to develop concepts and to form generalizations. Children can learn that questions are composed for various reasons, that they can be constructed in many ways, and that they can lead to certain kinds of activities and accomplishments.

Teaching Children Why and When to Ask Questions

Pupils can be taught to ask appropriate questions at times when answers will do the most good for them. One of the most important types of question is the one that the individual puts to himself. This type can be crucial to the success of an endeavor, as when the individual asks questions to organize his thinking (e.g., "What don't I know about this?" "What do I want to know?" "What do I want to accomplish?" "What am I doing?"). Teachers can encourage their pupils to ask themselves these questions when they start projects.

Questions which can be put into the form of hypotheses and then tested are extremely important in any kind of investigation. For example, "Why does the bedroom door close when the front door is opened?" can lead to an hypothesis after the individual has gathered more data. Young people should be encouraged to ask questions whenever they are puzzled and want to understand the reasons for events and for physical or social phenomena. The key to helping them ask productive questions of this type is in having them evaluate their own questions to see if the questions are really asking what the pupils want them to ask. "Is that really what you're after?" you might say to a child.

In addition to the need to have things explained, children have the need to try things out. The curiosity which leads to experimentation can be given form and direction when young people express this desire to find out in the form of the question. "What would happen if I did this?" is a common question in the minds of children of all ages, and it is asked in a multitude of contexts. The teacher can help his pupils compose productive questions concerning experimentation by having them carefully define the conditions under which the experiment is to take place. (In some cases the teacher may be able also to help his pupils foresee the consequences of the experiment, as when a six-year-old asks: "What happens when you put toothpaste and hair spray in a basin of water?" The question the child should also ask is: "What will my mother do?")

A common variety of question is the one asked for the purpose of getting a quick reply. It may be an expression of curiosity ("Why did you do that?"), or it may represent a superficial problem ("Where shall I put these crayons that keep rolling off the table?"). Questions that lead to understanding are invaluable in or out of school. Those that can be answered easily by the pupil himself, when he considers the problem for a moment, are a nuisance to teachers. Therefore, many teachers work hard to get their pupils into the habit of sizing up the situation before posing questions that might be handled by the pupil himself. On the other hand, "children want to know when they want to know," and so the legitimate question which has a quick payoff should not be ignored. These are the questions that are asked when the individual wishes to have a concept clarified; an ambiguity resolved; a fact, action, or rule interpreted; a generalization briefly explained or illustrated; or a process analyzed. The teacher can point out how his pupils can ask these questions of appropriate persons at times when the answers will do the greatest good.

Another familiar purpose of questioning is to obtain a better idea of how to behave. That is to say, the answer to this type of question serves as a guide for behavior ("How do you draw a horse?" "Should I write on both sides of the paper?" "Is everyone going to dress up for the Halloween party?" "Why is everyone heading down the hallway?"). When answers to this kind of question are not forthcoming, the individual is often anxious and disoriented. As with the quick-answer question, a teacher's withholding a response is not justified unless the answer is self-evident. Therefore, the teacher's job is to help children differentiate between those questions which are necessary and those which are not.

Questions which narrow down a range of possibilities represent another important conceptual tool; and this kind of question is becoming popular in elementary, junior high, and senior high schools principally as the result of the experimenting and theorizing of Bruner (1960, 1961), Suchman (1966), Fenton (1964), and others. The old Twenty Questions game has been incorporated into the curriculum in various guises and with very satisfactory results in many cases.

Those questions which assist the individual in organizing material into categories or units can also be very fruitful. A question such as "Is this essentially a problem of communication or transportation?" might be useful to a twelve-year-old who is trying to understand the high incidence of disease in a remote rural area. This kind of question is really analyzing (or troubleshooting, when done in certain contexts); and it is recommended that *all* teachers encourage their pupils to utilize this type of question. These are examples of its use in varying situations:

Did I miss in my estimate because of my inaccuracy in measuring or because of the method I used? (Troubleshooting)

What were the major influences upon Woodrow Wilson's attitude toward England before the United States declared war? (Analysis)

Was it the way I mixed the flour and salt that caused the whole thing to crumble? (Troubleshooting)

Why did my speech go over so well this time and not last time? (Analysis)

What were the major factors that caused the passenger pigeon to become extinct? (Analysis)

Teaching Pupils Questioning Strategies

INQUIRY SESSIONS

More and more teachers are finding it profitable for their pupils to develop their problem-solving skills by learning to ask questions yielding information that can lead to solutions. The impetus for this approach has come from psychologists such as Jerome S. Bruner (1961) and J. Richard Suchman (1966) who have tried to put research findings about how human beings learn into procedures or strategies that can be effective in the classroom. Countless teachers have employed the basic principles of this approach for years, and are now pleasantly surprised at how up-to-date and fashionable their teaching has become.

Mr. Mann's use of the "inquiry method," for instance, was a modification and extension of a technique he had used for many years. He believed that by showing his own curiosity about the world to his pupils he would demonstrate that he approved of their inquiring into the phenomena and events that interested them. Therefore, from time to time he would bring to the attention of his class a perplexing experience of his and ask them to help him explain it, trying to choose events and observations that might be challenging to his pupils and also identifiable as belonging to their world. For instance, he would ask his pupils about magnets that had lost their power to attract, roads that had ice only where a creek flowed underneath, and mounds of dirt next to the cracks of sidewalks. (Suchman has called these puzzling happenings "discrepant events," that is, instances when experiences cannot be accommodated into the learner's conceptual framework.)

Mr. Mann also instituted an "I. Club" for the pupils who successfully explained a puzzling event—(It was two weeks before the children decided that they were trying to become members of the "*Inquirers* Club.") Here is an example of Mr. Mann's use of the inquiry approach with ten- and eleven-year-olds.

MR. MANN: Several years ago a Japanese ship left port and headed for the open sea. When it had reached a spot about five hundred miles from the nearest point of land, the captain gave a signal and the crew spilled a half-ton of pearls over the side. What questions can you ask that might help you explain this apparently unreasonable (and true) happening? Ask only questions that can be answered by "yes" or "no." Each of you can keep up his questioning until he decides to "pass" to someone else.

VICKI: Were they crooks who were being chased by the police and wanted to get rid of the evidence—the pearls—so they wouldn't be jailed?

MR. MANN: No.

VICKI: I pass.

HARRY: Was the captain driven crazy by a mysterious drug, and then he forced his crew to throw the pearls overboard?

MR. MANN: No.

HARRY: I pass.

JENNY: Did the Russians break a Japanese code and then follow them in a sub, and then they surfaced and were about to get the pearls, and so the captain told the men to throw the pearls overboard?

MR. MANN: No.

JENNY: I pass.

MARY: Were they doing anything illegal?

MR. MANN: No.

MARY: Uhh . . . I pass.

JEFF: Was the captain following orders from someone?

MR. MANN: Yes.

JEFF: From the Japanese government?

MR. MANN: Yes.

JEFF: Was it the war or defense department?

MR. MANN: No.

JEFF: Was it the part that has to do with trade with other countries?

MR. MANN: Yes. That is, I believe so.

JEFF. Was it because they had *too many* pearls?

MR. MANN: Yes. That's half of it. Can you get the rest?

JEFF: Uhh. Gosh, I don't know.

MR. MANN: Go ahead—try another question.

JEFF: Was it because they wanted to keep the price of pearls high?

MR. MANN: Yes. You're in the I. Club.

This type of question is most successful when the children have a background of information which will enable them to make certain inferences about the event. Some of Mr. Mann's pupils had a little information with which to work, but most were at a loss to understand the strange story. Jeff was one of four or five boys in the class who read widely and who had been rewarded for producing ideas throughout his five years of school.

ANALYZING THE QUESTIONS

When the teacher is interested in having his pupils develop strategies for solving problems, he encourages them to ask questions that, at the outset, will enable them to exclude a large range of possibilities. Vicki, Harry, and Jenny were not following any particular plan in their questioning; they were advancing hypotheses to explain the event at the very beginning of the session, before accumulating a store of information upon which a plausible hypothesis might be based. This kind of questioning is what Bruner calls "potshotting." Mary, on the other hand, asked a question that eliminated further unproductive guessing about how the captain and his crew were breaking the law. Other appropriate questions might have been:

Was the captain following the orders of someone at home in Japan?
Was the *time* when they did this important at all?
Did they do it in secret?

Jeff used Mary's question as a lead in formulating his own questioning strategy. Knowing that there was nothing illegal about the jettisoning of the pearls, Jeff then started a sequence of questions that could lead to the cause of the event. With some encouragement at the end by Mr. Mann, he was able to pinpoint the reason for the peculiar behavior of the Japanese.

Some teachers who employ this technique coach their pupils in locating constraints in the problem that will lead to productive cycles of questions. They show their pupils how they can avoid pursuing lines of inquiry that lead nowhere. When they have had experience with this type of questioning session, pupils learn to gather their evidence in a systematic way, looking for relationships between the facts that they are accumulating. They learn that their ability to store and to organize information is the key to problem solving.

Probably the best discrepant events for inquiry sessions are those which are experienced by the pupils themselves. The curiosities of the pupils will provide an ample supply of puzzling events and observations, and so no teacher should ever run out of subject matter if he wishes to use this approach in helping his pupils to acquire inquiry skills. The pictures in textbooks are also an amazing source of ambiguities and uncertainties for elementary grade children. Most adults seem to assume that children are born with the ability to read pictures even if they cannot read the printed word, but this is far from true. Even simple pictures are filled with mysteries, particularly for disadvantaged children who have grown up without picture books in their homes.

reinforce facts, clarify concept

Are We Overemphasizing Class Discussions?

In view of a rapidly accelerating interest during the past decade in analyzing the verbal interactions of pupils and teachers, it should be noted that the vehicle for almost all of these exchanges is the class discussion. For practical reasons, the class discussion is the most convenient mode of instruction for investigating the verbal behaviors of teachers and pupils; the analyst is usually able to record a number of obvious reactions of pupils to their teachers and vice versa. Unfortunately, elementary teachers whose style is not especially compatible with the class discussion will not benefit so much from either an analysis of what happened during one of their discussions or a close study of the techniques of leading a discussion. Even though discussing problems and materials with an entire class is an exceedingly valuable method of reinforcing facts, clarifying concepts, and fostering insights, there are many teachers who—for reasons of personality, background, and class makeup—seldom employ this technique.

Moreover, it is just as important to note that there are pupils who do not react positively to the class discussion. Some can respond more readily in small groups of three to six. Others express themselves best when exchanging ideas alone with the teacher. These two ways of communicating should not be omitted in any review of the interactions of pupils and teachers. It makes considerable difference to a good proportion of any class whether the dialogue being carried on occurs in a large group, in a small group, or in a pupil-teacher conference.

A study directed by Torrance (Torrance and Freeman, 1968) provides some useful guidance concerning group size and question asking by children. The study involved five-year-old children and examined the effects of groups of 24, 12, 6, and 4 on question-asking behavior. In the test task, groups were required to produce questions concerning Mother Goose prints. It was required that the questions be about things that could not be ascertained by looking at the picture. It was found that children in groups of 4 or 6, compared with children in groups of 24 and 12, asked more different questions, less frequently repeated questions already asked, and asked more "why" questions and discrepant-event questions.

The results concerning repetition of questions are especially impressive. About 48 percent of the output of the 24-child groups were questions that had already been asked. (This is a frequent basis for short attention span, especially in classes of pre-primary children and disadvantaged children.) When group size was reduced to 12, the percentage of repeated questions dropped to 19 percent of the total output. This dropped to about 5 percent when group size was reduced to 6 and did not drop further when group size was reduced to 4. Far greater involvement in the question-asking process was also observed in the groups of 4 and 6.

The findings of this study suggest that many problems of inattention and short attention span possibly could be avoided by the use of small groups. This is in harmony with the suggestion in much group dynamics theory that there is less regressive behavior in small groups than in large ones or in individual situations. It is also in harmony with an observation by Maya Pines (1967) in reviewing the major current revolutionary programs in pre-primary education. She maintains that one of the most important common characteristics of all of the pre-primary programs that have had some success in providing disadvantaged children with the skills they need in school is that the teachers have worked with small groups and individual children and hardly ever with the class as a whole. In addition, Taba and Elkins (1966) have observed among disadvantaged children an inability to work alone and a necessity for teaching strategies that involve work in small groups.

any teachers, especially in urban ghetto and other disadvantaged communities, fail miserably in their attempts to conduct class discussions. The sad truth seems to be that few teachers possess the skills for conducting truly involving and dynamic class discussions. While in our opinion, most teachers can acquire the necessary skills and achieve rewarding results, the acquisition of those skills takes "know-how," practice, feedback of results, and solid hard work. One of the most helpful sources of "knowhow" is Glasser's (1969) *Schools Without Failure.* Glasser developed his methods for use in disadvantaged schools with failure-oriented children and young people, drawing upon his experience in the field of group psychotherapy. He strives for increased involvement, relevance, and thinking, and has taught his methods to school counselors and classroom teachers.

Much that goes on between teachers and pupils is not susceptible to analysis. In our desire to understand cause-and-effect relationships in the teaching-learning process, attempts have been made to quantify this interaction. Such information has been helpful to teachers in gaining insights about their verbal interactions with children, but thus far we do not have very helpful techniques for assessing the nonverbal and often powerful ways that teachers have of facilitating learning.

Interestingly enough, instructional techniques are becoming more depersonalized with the increasing use of closed-circuit and open-circuit television, teaching machines, language laboratories, and data-retrieval equipment. At the same time, teaching is becoming more personalized, as teachers have adjusted to the electronic age and have begun to perform those functions which they alone can perform—in the areas of being sensitive to children's needs, diagnosing learning difficulties and planning programs for their remediation, guiding learning-thinking experiences, supporting pupils emotionally and intellectually, and opening up new vistas for study and appreciation.

Making Your Own Summary

All year long your sixth-grade pupils have "done their work" dutifully, but they have rarely been excited by your instructional program. In order to encourage them to become curious and to investigate things that puzzle them, you have brought a number of objects into the classroom (stuffed animals, gadgets, contour maps, etc.); but your pupils have seemed only slightly curious about them. You decide that before the end of the school year you must get your pupils puzzled or excited about something. *But what can you do?*

Yours is a small-town school which has a tradition of orderliness and sterility. The "virtue" prized most by your principal and nearly all of your fellow teachers is silence. A visitor walking down the halls is invariably impressed by the apparent industry of the children in each classroom. All of the pupils are at their desks reading or writing, and little or no sound emanates from the rooms except when instructions are given or when films are shown. The members of your class represent an average range of intellectual talents and socioeconomic backgrounds. Other than their having experienced five years of dreary seat-warming, you see no reason why they should not respond more enthusiastically to your lessons.

Since this is only your second year of teaching at the school, do you think it is safe to try any "new" techniques? Are there any points to keep in mind when you teach a routine mathematics or social studies lesson that might provoke some thoughtful questions from your pupils? What aspects of your own behavior might be examined if you are serious about wanting to foster curiosity in your pupils?

REFERENCES

Bruner, J. S. *The Process of Education.* Cambridge, Mass.: Harvard University Press, 1960.

Bruner, J. S. "The Act of Discovery." *Harvard Educational Review,* 1961, **31**, 21–32.

Fenton, E. *Teaching the New Social Studies in Secondary Schools: An Inductive Approach.* New York: Holt, Rinehart & Winston, 1966.

Gallagher, J. J. and M. J. Aschner. "A Preliminary Report on Analyses of Classroom Interaction." *Merrill-Palmer Quarterly,* 1963, **9**, 183–194.

Glasser, W. *Schools Without Failure.* New York: Harper & Row, 1969.

Pines, M. *Revolution in Learning.* New York: Harper & Row, 1967.

Suchman, J. R. "Inquiry Workshop: A Model for the Language of Education." *The Instructor,* August/September, 1966, **76(1)**, 33, 92.

Taba, H. and D. Elkins. *Teaching Strategies for the Culturally Disadvantaged.* Chicago: Rand McNally, 1966.

Torrance, E. P. and M. H. Freeman. "Group Size and Question Asking Performance of Pre-Primary Children." Athens, Ga.: Research and Development Center, University of Georgia, 1968.

Torrance, E. P. and R. Gupta. "Development and Evaluation of Recorded Programmed Experiences in Creative Thinking in the Fourth Grade." Minneapolis: Bureau of Educational Research, University of Minnesota, 1964. Mimeographed.

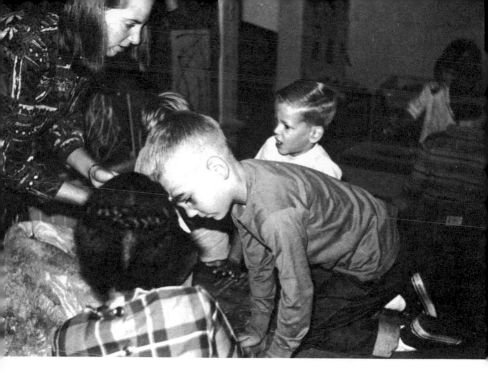

CHAPTER 11

PROVIDING

A RESPONSIVE

ENVIRONMENT

Sharing:
A conspiracy
Acted out in common,
Concern for our discovery
Of life.

The Problem

Mrs. McGuire found her fourth-grade pupils unimaginative in their creative writing. Even their "friendly" letters were very trite in style and content. They had not had much experience in writing creatively at school, but she still felt that the themes they used and even their words were highly imitative. Mrs. McGuire knew that children need models for their writing, and she had expected that they would imitate her and the authors of books they had read. Instead, they tended to mimic each other.

After giving the problem much thought, she decided to try to loosen up their imaginations by having them compose limericks orally. She planned to tell them one or two of her favorite limericks, and then accompany herself on the piano to make sure that they grasped the limerick's rhythm and structure. She hoped that the children would soon get into the spirit of having fun with words and ideas.

How do you suppose Mrs. McGuire's plan would work with the children? Why?

Mrs. McGuire knew that one device might not be enough to get the children thinking along fresh lines, so she planned to follow up the limerick session with a lesson in which her pupils would supply new endings to a story with which they were familiar. Then she thought they might be ready to work in small groups and make up short plays. By asking the class to guess the ending of each play before it was revealed by the players, she hoped that the children would realize that the most enjoyable plays are those which surprise.

Do you think Mrs. McGuire planned her attack intelligently? Might she have been wiser to have found out how the children responded to the first lesson before working out the details of subsequent lessons—or is it a good idea to have a tentative plan for an entire series of lessons to give purpose and direction?

If Mrs. McGuire had reacted to the things that her pupils had been writing, what effect do you think this would have had?

What do you think would happen if she had talked with them about the ideas expressed in their writings? About the picturesqueness, vividness, and flavor of their language? The originality and surprisingness of their plots, settings, and solutions? The humor in their writings?

What Is a Responsive Environment

Before Chapter 10, most of this book was about ways of providing a stimulating environment to facilitate creative behavior. Even in Chapter 10 there was much concern with the kind of stimulation necessary to encourage children to ask questions. The real payoff when children ask questions, however, depends upon the kind of response their questions receive. If their questions are ignored or ridiculed, they will cease to ask questions, or their questions will become very stereotyped and lacking in vitality. If children's questions are respected, they will continue and improve in provocativeness. If a teacher is unable to respect the questions children ask, it is probably unwise to stimulate children to ask questions or to initiate learning activities of any type.

The concept of "feedback," derived from electronics and used frequently in psychology (Lewin, 1947; Bradford, Gibb, and Benne, 1964), is a key one in providing a responsive environment. Hundreds of educational experiments have demonstrated the value of feedback, or information about results, in facilitating various kinds of learning. Social psychologists such as Lewin (1947) have maintained that improved functioning cannot occur without some kind of feedback. This idea suggests that children should be able to ask questions and get responses. Such questions are of two basic kinds: "What information do I need to understand this idea, to acquire this skill, or to solve this problem?" and "How am I doing?" Obviously, such information should help children improve their functioning. It enables them to clarify or identify their goals, determine the path to their goals, and develop strategies of action to achieve their goals.

This does not mean that the response of the teacher to all questions should be the giving of the information requested. It is important that children be encouraged to find sources of information other than their teacher's when they seek information or feedback about their performances.

We believe that the information that children process for themselves will be obtained autonomously when their personalities and abilities *and* the psychological and physical conditions permit independent learning and thinking. However, we also believe that the teacher should guide and assist his pupils in seeking, locating, and evaluating information. Although the teacher does not have the same responsibilities in a responsive environment that he has in a stimulating one, he still has highly essential roles to play. These roles require different skills from those traditionally associated with teaching (such as those of giving information, punishing, praising, and controlling).

It is especially important to have the guidance and support of teachers when children do original thinking. When a young person links together ideas and elements into a production that is new (at least for him), the idea, whether expressed in words or materials, is uniquely his own. It therefore has a relationship to him that another person's idea can never have. Because of this kinship, the child is reluctant to expose his idea to others for fear that it will be attacked (and, of course, this would be a *direct* attack upon him).

The responsive teacher is the indispensable agent in the process of encouraging the child to express his idea, to evaluate it according to criteria that he has set up for himself, and finally to modify or refine it. The teacher can protect the child from unnecessary criticism or censure by creating an accepting classroom atmosphere. He can help the child to devise meaningful and reasonable standards with which to judge his idea or performance. He can guide the child to find models to which he can refer. He can point out the strengths of the idea and lead the child to discover its faults. In short, the responsive teacher can give the child information that he might not obtain from any other source, and the information can be given in the light of the child's own background, abilities, and personality.

The teacher can respond to pupils in numerous ways. In this chapter, four of the most important types of interaction through which teachers respond to pupils will be discussed: (1) reacting to unusual questions, (2) reacting to imaginative and unusual ideas, (3) showing pupils that their ideas have value, and (4) tying in evaluation with causes and consequences. The evidence presented in this chapter comes largely from reports of teachers who participated in a study conducted by the authors (Torrance and Staff, 1964).

What Happens When Teachers Try to Respect Unusual Questions?

In a study involving teachers from thirteen different states and the District of Columbia, we (Torrance and Staff, 1964) asked teachers systematically and consciously to try to apply the following five principles for creating a responsive classroom environment:

1. Be respectful of unusual questions.
2. Be respectful of imaginative and unusual ideas.
3. Show your pupils that their ideas have value.
4. Occasionally have pupils do something "for practice" without the threat of evaluation.
5. Tie in evaluation with causes and consequences.

Many people wondered if the principles which were formulated might be too obvious, but it was apparent to us that the principles were not fully understood by a majority of the teachers we observed. We believed, however, that by deliberately trying to use the principles as guides in their everyday interactions with children, teachers could help their pupils realize their creative potentialities.

The respondents were rather evenly distributed from teachers of kindergarten through the eighth grade. They were told in the questionnaires that we realized that all teachers apply these principles to some extent, and were urged to experiment with more deliberate application of the principles within the limitations of their teaching situations. To avoid the presentation of lengthy tables, most of the results will be presented in narrative form, and only responses given by at least 5 percent of the teachers will be mentioned. Some teachers reported behaviors in two or more categories. For this reason, the responses summarized will rarely, if ever, add up to 100 percent.

In over 75 percent of the 114 respondents' reports, the incident mentioned was identified as occurring in the classroom; in 5 percent, outside the classroom; in 65 percent, during class time; in 19 percent, outside class time; in 56 percent, as relevant to the curriculum; and in 17 percent as not relevant to the curriculum. The teachers identified the questioner as a boy in about 54 percent of the reports; they indicated that the questioner was a girl in 11 percent. The sex of the questioner was not specified in the remainder of the cases.

The teachers reported a variety of reactions to the unusual questions; but, interestingly, the majority of them did not indicate that they had been initially receptive to the questions. The most frequently reported teacher reactions are:

	Percent
Puzzlement	22
Irritation and annoyance	17
Avoidance, making light of question	13
Desire to answer question immediately	13
Surprise or shock	13
Amusement, laughter	11
Admiration, sympathy	7
Interest in finding out	6

The pupils were reported to have reacted more positively than the teachers to the unusual questions asked by their classmates:

	Percent
Interest, acceptance, excitement	46
Amusement, laughter, giggles	39
Puzzlement, curiosity	15
Anxiety, tension	7
Irritation, disgust	6
Surprise, shock	6
Disinterest, scowls	6

In responding to the query on the questionnaire concerning how they had shown respect for the unusual question, the teachers' strategies reflected these typical patterns of interaction between teachers and pupils:

	Percent
Answering the question directly	44
Letting the class answer or discuss the question	22
Helping class answer by discussing.	13
Praising, giving recognition	11
Helping pupil find answer to question	9
Helping class answer question by reading, testing	9
Stopping laughter	7

As we have already indicated, in spite of the indications of displeasure and discomfort on the part of the teachers, the unusual questions seemed to have been received quite well by their pupils. Of the respondents, 37 percent reported that the questioner gained satisfaction as a result of asking the question. Increased interest on the part of the class was reported by 32 percent as the immediate effect. Their pupils developed new insights, reported 15 percent of the respondents, while 7 percent noted a lack of satisfaction and continued undesirable behavior in their pupils.

Although one-third of the teachers reported no long-range effect, continued or increased motivation and improved insight or judgment were each reported by 22 percent of the respondents. Increased respect among their students for the questions of others, continued curiosity regarding the subject of the question, and decreased fear of asking questions among pupils were each noted by 7 percent of the reporting teachers.

It might be interesting to examine a few of the reports in order to obtain some insights into the thinking of a few of the teachers who voluntarily returned the questionnaires.

In the example which follows, a third-grade teacher gave an evasive response to a commonly asked question:

1. *What was the question, who asked it, and what were the general conditions under which it was asked?*
   Concerning my name. My students wanted to know what I was called when I was a little girl. Also, very interested in how old I am. The general conditions were just an ordinary classroom situation when we were becoming acquainted at the beginning of the year.

2. *What was your immediate reaction?*
   I kidded with them—made up a silly name and an outrageous age.
3. *What was the immediate reaction of the class, if observable?*
   Laughed—thought it was funny and it was dropped.
4. *In what way was respect shown for the question?*
   They were curious.
5. *What, if any, were the observable effects (immediate and/or long range)?*
   When report time came, they found out what my first name was and nothing has been said since. It was just curiosity on their part.

Although the question, "How old are you, teacher?" is nearly inescapable for primary teachers, it is not unusual for a teacher to sidestep it.

Several of the reports suggested that one of the best ways of showing respect for the unusual questions of children is to become genuinely interested in exploring the pupil's question. The experience of a fourth-grade teacher who reported this approach is described below.

1. *What was the question?*
   What becomes of men salmon when females go upstream to spawn?
   Who asked it?
   Mark.
   What was the general condition under which the question was asked?
   Social studies class—study of Seattle and the salmon industry.
2. *What was your immediate reaction?*
   I'd like to know, too.
3. *What was the immediate reaction of the class, if observable?*
   Hushed by boldness of question.
4. *How was respect shown for the question?*
   I was interested and admitted this interest. I read the entire life story of the salmon and other supplementary material.
5. *What, if any, were the observable effects (immediate and/or long-range)?*

Immediate effects, intense interest in the life of the salmon. Long-range effects, class, as a whole a shy group, less afraid to ask questions and display interest.

We wondered if there might be any corroboration in the results of this study of the assertion that children lose much of their curiosity by the time they reach the fourth grade, and so a comparison was made of the amount of respect for children's questions manifested by the primary teachers and by the intermediate teachers in their reports. Whereas 43 percent of the intermediate teachers showed definite respect, 72 percent of the primary teachers indicated such respect for the unusual questions reported. Of the intermediate teachers, 40 percent showed a lack of respect for the unusual questions, compared with about 19 percent of the primary teachers. These data would seem to confirm the assertion that primary teachers are more accepting of children's divergent behavior. *It may well be that children are not less curious during their fourth year in school but that their teachers are less acceptant of their pupils' thinking.* On the basis of these and other data, four general inferences seem justified:

1. There were a number of teachers to whom the principles were meaningless. They simply did not understand what the principles represented.
2. Many teachers were unable to accept the principles because they were not admissible to the teachers' value systems.
3. The teachers who were able to accept the principles had value systems which were consonant with the principles.
4. The temperaments or personalities of some teachers do not permit significant alterations to be made in the manner in which they interact with their pupils.

These inferences have considerable significance for pre-service and in-service programs that are concerned with making education in America more humane. To begin with, although teachers serve as examples for children—it is sometimes said that they teach more by example than by exclamation—like other human beings, teachers have defects of character. Some of them are stubborn and some are vain. Many are defensive. Others are self-centered. Yet, to help children grow in socially desirable ways, they must be honest and unselfish. This means that a teacher who attempts to bluff his way through situations in which he finds himself poorly informed or not informed at all will usually lose the respect of his pupils and hence will be ineffective in helping them grow morally and intellectually. This also means that the teacher who peremptorily dismisses questions or refuses to allow his pupils to investigate a point or subject which interests them does not fulfill our expectations with regard to the ways teachers should interact with children.

What Happens When Teachers Try to Respect Imaginative Ideas?

Because the second of the five principles for rewarding creative behavior is broad in scope and application, the teachers reported a wide range of imaginative and unusual ideas by their pupils. In spite of the fact that about one-third of the ideas were naive concepts or dealt with fantasy behavior, the most frequently mentioned teacher reaction was pleasure or approval (34%). These were the other most commonly reported reactions of the teachers: the idea seemed silly, immature, unreasonable, wild, or fantastic (20%); the idea was received with surprise, shock, skepticism, etc. (18%); the idea was received with disapproval, an attempt was made to dissuade the pupil, etc. (18%); compassion, pity, or sympathy was shown for the pupil (9%); the idea was grasped as motivation for a new unit (5%); it was received with amusement or laughter by the teacher (5%).

The most frequent reactions of the children to the imaginative or unusual ideas paralleled their teachers': the idea was received with interest, excitement, or approval (39%); the idea was received with laughter, amusement, giggling, etc. (21%); the children reacted with puzzlement, surprise, doubt, etc. (13%); the children were disapproving, restraining, etc. (9%); it stimulated other ideas (5%).

These were the most commonly mentioned ways by which respect was shown by the teachers and their classes for the imaginative or unusual ideas: discussed, explained, or considered the idea

(39%); the class approved the idea (21%); an experiment was conducted or the idea was tested (14%); some other activity was substituted or the idea was evaded (11%); the idea stimulated another activity (9%). It is quite interesting to note that 11 percent of the teachers' reports offered substitution or evasion of the idea as a demonstration of respect.

The immediate and long-range effects of the incidents seemed to be more beneficial to the pupils who offered the ideas and to their classmates than might be guessed from the initial reactions of the teachers and pupils. The most frequently reported immediate effects were: satisfaction or pleasure (39%); interest or motivation aroused (35%); sustained effort (18%); continued curiosity or questioning (7%). The most commonly mentioned long-range effects were: satisfaction or sustained interest (23%); change in attitude or behavior (23%); new pupil insight (11%); stimulus for other original ideas (9%); execution of experiment at home or discussion at home (5%); dissatisfaction or rejection of idea (5%). As may be inferred from these data, most teachers reported multiple effects.

Pupils want their teachers to be responsive to their needs, easy to talk with, and respectful of their ideas. (See Chapter 13 for the elementary pupil's conception of an "ideal teacher.") Therefore, in attempting to put the five principles into practice, the respondents were trying to be the kind of teacher their pupils most likely wanted them to be. It is difficult, however, for many teachers to be respectful of their pupils. In the case of this sample of teachers, a disturbingly high proportion of the initial reactions to the imaginative or unusual were negative: 20 percent reported the ideas were immature, unreasonable, wild, or fantastic; 18 percent reported they received the ideas with surprise, shock, or skepticism; and 18 percent disapproved of the idea or attempted to dissuade the pupil of its validity.

As in the case of response to unusual questions, a comparison of the respect manifested in the reports for the unusual ideas of their pupils by the intermediate and primary grade teachers was made; and the results of the analysis indicated that, again, the primary teachers were more respectful in their behavior.

What Happens When Teachers Show Children That Their Ideas Have Value?

A responsive classroom is a place where, without being afraid of ridicule or ostracism, pupils can try out their ideas and receive feedback as to whether the ideas are understandable, satisfying, workable, logically organized, or acceptable. The reactions of the teacher and of other pupils will ordinarily be the most significant bits of information accessible to the pupil who expresses an idea. Therefore, it would seem that a responsible teacher is one who both encourages his pupils to express themselves and indicates his respect for their ability to produce ideas. The reporting teachers showed that they valued their pupils' ideas by using the ideas, by permitting the children to try them out, by giving public recognition to the ideas, by approving them, and by other means. The list of ways in which the teachers showed their respect for their pupils' ideas, as shown below, might be a handy reference for the teacher who conscientiously wants to create a classroom climate that encourages creative thinking:

Reaction Reported	Number	Percent
Used or applied idea, material, etc. contributed by pupil	36	58.0
Provided time to implement idea, changed schedule, etc.	21	33.9
Demonstrated idea was true or permitted pupil to do so	14	32.6
Permitted or encouraged further inquiry	13	21.0
Listened or watched with interest	12	19.3
Agreed with, approved, or praised idea	10	16.1
Provided materials or other resources to implement idea	9	14.5
Gave public credit or recognition for authorship of idea	7	11.3
Questioned originator of idea further	5	8.0

Again it will be noted that many teachers reported multiple out-comes.

It might be supposed that such supportive behavior on the part of the teachers would have had salutary effects upon their pupils. Judging from the reports, the children responded very positively to the respect accorded their ideas. An analysis of pupil behaviors is shown below:

Reaction Reported	Number	Percent
Expressed pleasure, smiled, brightened with happiness, etc.	27	43.5
Expressed approval of classmate's idea, perfor-mance, etc.	23	37.1
Followed through with idea, imitated, etc.	20	32.2
Enthusiastic, absorbed activity	18	29.0
Increased acceptance of originator by class-mates	15	24.2
Increased interest in learning, increased par-ticipation	15	24.2
Spread of creative ideas, confidence, in other areas of work	10	16.1

Apparently one of the major difficulties in applying the principle of showing children that their ideas have value is that in the minds of many teachers and adults there is considerable doubt as to the worth of children's ideas—they honestly do not believe that children are capable of producing ideas that have value. If the teacher holds such a belief, whether knowingly or unknowingly, he will not be effective in putting this principle into practice. We can only suggest that people who are unconvinced as to the value of children's ideas keep an open mind and try to assess objectively the novel productions of young people.

One mark of the highly creative person is his self-starting ability. The problem of parents and teachers is to keep it alive. It is hindered, unfortunately, by overly detailed supervision and too much reliance on prescribed curricula.

The reason for evaluating and crediting self-initiated learning and thinking is quite simple. Because grades are important to students, they tend to learn whatever is necessary to obtain the grades they desire. If teachers base grades on memorization of details, students will memorize texts and lectures. If grades are based upon ability to integrate and apply knowledge and produce solutions to problems, they will attempt to do this.

Children are often impatient with themselves when they cannot accomplish a task in the manner that they think they should be able to. Frequently the model that they have given themselves to aspire to is unattainable. Thus, primary-grade teachers often have the problem of convincing a youngster that his production is of genuine worth. He may want his picture to look like a very good likeness of whatever he is drawing when he does not have the skills to make a representational drawing, or he may want very much to fashion his clay in the way that an admired classmate does. Mrs. Strickland, a veteran teacher with boundless energy and enthusiasm, encountering such a problem, handled it in this way:

"Cyndi was a fifth-grade girl, large for her age, a quiet cooperative worker. She never wanted to do any kind of art, would always be late in starting, and would never complete a project.

"This art lesson was a poster of the student's own choice or design, done in the crayon-resist technique. During the class period she came to my desk a couple of times and said she didn't want to finish her picture. I said, 'Cyndi, I want you to finish your picture. I'm sure it will look much different when it is finished.' She felt that all the other students did much better work.

"I told her that no two people did the same kind of work and each person's own idea was important. I said, 'Perhaps you'll come up with an idea that no one else has.' When she had completed her picture she asked me not to let the other students see it. I told her I would like to mat the picture and put it on the wall because I saw something different in her work. She said, 'O.K.' I just put the picture on a dark green background and placed it on the wall with all the others. It was completely different. All the others were designs in very brilliant colors—sort of 'pop art.'

"Later we talked about the technique, colors, design, etc. When we came to Cyndi's picture I waited for comments from the class. Then at the right time I said, 'Cyndi, I like your picture; it reminds me of a Grandma Moses painting.' Then a class member said, 'Yes, it really does.' Cyndi's face lit up immediately. She smiled a big smile. In the past she had thrown all her work in the wastebasket. I told her I thought she should keep this picture but if she decided that she didn't want it that I would like to frame it and hang it in my house. She said, 'I want you to have it if you will do that.'

"The class made many nice comments about her design, color, etc., and said that she had really come up with a different idea. A few days later her mother came to school and told me how pleased Cyndi was—that she was able to do something sort of special."

What Happens When Teachers Try to Relate Evaluation to Causes and Consequences?

In addition to obtaining feedback regarding their verbal behavior and their performance of tasks, children receive considerable information about other aspects of their behavior in the classroom. The teachers in our study adopted a variety of strategies with regard to tying feedback to causes and consequences, but simply comparing one technique with another can be misleading. For instance, you can imagine two teachers explaining the dangers of a certain kind of behavior in completely different ways. One might dwell upon the painful consequences and actually intend to frighten the child so that the behavior would not be repeated. Another might depict the danger in more objective terms, stressing the sequence of steps that could lead to a mishap.

It hardly seems necessary to say that children receive an abundance of feedback regarding their behavior. In this sense, the "old-fashioned" classroom is a very responsive place for children. It is important to say, however, that young people have a great need to obtain feedback that is constructive, that will enable them to modify and improve their behavior. Too much of the feedback children receive is confusing, dishonest, humiliating, destructive, and demoralizing.

The manner in which the teacher who reported the following incident handled a sensitive and common problem demonstrates the teacher's role in a responsive environment with regard to divergent behavior.

1. *What was the nature of the behavior to be evaluated? Who was involved?*
   Pupil showed great reluctance to attempt to learn cursive writing.
2. *What was your personal evaluation of the behavior?*
   Child, though larger and heavier than most children in the class, was immature, and his coordination was not normal. He was left-handed and told me his previous teacher insisted that he use his right hand when writing. He was not enjoying success in his endeavors.
3. *How did you or the class show the relationship of the behavior to cause and / or consequences?*
   I told the child that there were several other left-handed children in the class and pointed them out to him. It was emphasized to all that no attempt would be made to change writing hands. The boy was shown an example of work by one of the left-handed writers and was encouraged. All his early efforts were praised, regardless of the poor quality (how much better he was doing than he had been doing). After confidence was gained, refinements were made. At no time did the class ridicule his early attempts. In fact, more rapid learners offered assistance.
4. *What were the effects, if observable (immediate and / or long-range?*
   Marked improvement in writing, spelling, and reading.

Not only was the teacher supportive of the child's efforts to learn to do cursive writing, the other pupils were very helpful in encouraging the boy's attempts. There is no better teaching situation than this kind; but teachers do not inherit cooperative, accepting classes—they create them.

Group discussion is the most popular method reported by teachers in this study (38%) for showing this relationship. A relatively large number of teachers (22%) also relied upon natural consequences such as injury, pain, and illness to demonstrate the relationship between behavior and causes and consequences. In some cases, the pupils themselves made explicit the relationship. In others, the teacher made the point. Scolding, isolation, class criticism, and other punitive techniques add up to a sizeable proportion of the methods used by respondents.

The following report by a second-grade teacher reflects an attitude that naturally accompanies the role of the teacher as protector. The attitude is especially pronounced in classrooms with younger children because they must heed the teacher's words for their own safety.

1. *What was the nature of the behavior to be evaluated? Who was involved?*

   We discussed safety in the hall. We all decided that we must keep our eyes open at all times and watch where we are going. That morning on the way to snacks a girl walked into a door that was open.

2. *What was your personal evaluation of the behavior?*

   I wondered if I had made myself clear in telling the students to watch where they were going—or if the girl had paid attention in class discussion that morning.

3. *How did you or the class show the relationship of the behavior to cause and / or consequence?*

   The bump that the girl modeled for the next few days was living example of what happened when one person did not watch where she was going.

4. *What were the effects, if observable (immediate and / or long-range)?*

   The bump on the girl's face was very effective.

Few teachers are able to tolerate the kind of aggressive behavior described in the following report by a fourth-grade teacher and at the same time teach what would seem to be a wonderful lesson in respect for individuality.

1. *What was the nature of the behavior to be evaluated? Who was involved?*

   We were talking about boats and this caused quite a disturbance with a few boys, as they own boats, and they began to fight over which motor was the fastest. This actually came to a fist fight.

2. *What was your personal evaluation of the behavior?*

   I was glad that they could respond so as to defend a belief that they had.

3. *How did you or the class show the relationship of the behavior to cause and / or consequence?*

analogy

weed

We talked about all of the cars there are and made a list of the different ones owned by the families in our own room, and we tried to show that everybody has tastes and they differ.

4. *What were the effects, if observable (immediate and/or long-range)?*
   The children listened very carefully and discussed the problem. They seemed to respect individual preferences or tastes and from this they asked the boys to bring pictures and information about their boats.

It is interesting to note that the teacher writing this report mentioned no single thought about punishing the boys. Do you believe that she did, in fact, punish the boys who had the fist fight?

By far the most frequent category of behavior reported by teachers in this study is "improved or changed behavior." Most of the other categories indicate in some way an improved or changed behavior (cessation of offending behavior, improved group functioning, voluntary constructive behavior, more problem-solving behavior, and greater acceptance by peers). Only eight percent reported negative behavior (recurrence of offending behavior, tantrums, etc.).

What Is the Study's Significance?

Even though the values and traits of the teachers who participated in this study could not be determined with any degree of certainty from their reports alone, it was possible to detect an enthusiasm for teaching. As might be expected, those teachers who gave the most detailed reports almost invariably had interpreted the principles correctly. They seemed to enjoy relating the incidents, and apparently liked their jobs. Some of the satisfactions which teachers commonly delight in are very much in evidence in the words of the fourth-grade teacher who sent in the following anecdote:

"It was my practice to read to my pupils from Laura Ingalls Wilder's books during cold or stormy noon hours when they could not be out-of-doors. These are true pioneer stories and always interest the children.

"We often dramatized lessons in reading as a culmination activity and this particular group enjoyed that. One noon it was necessary for me to attend a meeting down the hall and I suggested that they 'act out' the particular chapter I had just read. I told them to 'figure it out' by themselves and that I'd be back soon to witness the result.

"When I tip-toed back a few minutes later to see how things were progressing, two leaders were managing—assigning parts, designing costumes from scarves, etc. They were so interested that I deliberately stayed away longer.

"My principal accompanied me back to my room, to give more importance to their effort. We sat quietly at the back of the room as Laura's story was dramatically unfolded. It was beautifully done—and with no help but their innate understanding of little girls when their much loved pet, because of his advanced age, had to be left behind when the family traveled West. I can still hear the 'dog's' pitiful whimper and Mary's tearful goodbye, as they parted.

"Our principal was impressed and asked our group to present their playlet at P.T.A. the following week. This was done, with nothing added but more costumes. I kept hands-off and it was explained that the offering was entirely the children's own.

"In a small community such as ours was, this was an important event and the children were rewarded by the applause and pride of the parents and friends. Of course they were pleased that I, too, was proud of them."

As this incident shows, the teacher is not always praising or even reacting to his pupils in a responsive environment. In the case of this teacher, her responses undoubtedly had come forth on many occasions before, and it was not necessary for her overtly to encourage or support the children in their activity.

One means whereby teachers can recognize the value of a responsive environment in which children feel psychologically safe in trying out their ideas is to engage in some kind of self-evaluation. The tape recorder or TV camera are very useful instruments in this kind of self-evaluation. The trend toward self-evaluation and mutual evaluation among teachers is growing; and this is probably the most objective means of achieving self-awareness for teachers who are unconsciously stifling their pupils intellectually and spiritually. In a project involving a portable TV camera, Enochs (1964) has demonstrated how teachers can become aware of the ways in which they fail to apply the principles discussed in this chapter.

Making Your Own Summary

Mrs. Porto experienced considerable difficulty in getting her sixth-graders to be enthusiastic about their music period. The boys were at the stage when singing in a classroom somehow produces an unusual amount of self-consciousness and embarrassment. There were no strong voices among the girls, and so the songs she asked the children to sing were rendered without skill or enjoyment. Mrs. Porto had taken a course in how to teach music to elementary pupils when she was in college, and she played the piano fairly well. Moreover, Mrs. Porto was very fond of music. But she could not get her pupils to share her love for it—at least audibly.

Then one day she realized that there was more to music than two-part singing. She remembered that several of her pupils were taking piano and violin lessons. It was just possible, she thought, that many of her pupils were getting enough music during the week. The others, however, were not getting enough *out* of their music instruction. Suddenly, she had an inspiration. Why not have the children who played instruments perform for the class? It might provide the spark which was badly needed to engender some enthusiasm about music. And why not invite those who did not play instruments to make up musical skits—with popular songs instead of the classics and folk songs in the textbook? They could present the whole thing as a kind of amateur hour every Friday.

The following day she asked for volunteers for a "Friday Fling," and was pleasantly surprised by having more children volunteer than could be accommodated by a single program. The volunteers drew straws to determine who would be on the first program (which Mrs. Porto typed up and duplicated so that each pupil could have a copy). Those who drew short straws were scheduled for the following Friday. The performers asked if they might use the classroom and the cafetorium to practice their "acts," and for three days they worked to polish their performances. Here is the program that Mrs. Porto hoped would put new life into what had been a deadly music period.

Mrs. Porto's Sixth-Grade Class
January 17, 1968

Vocal Solo. . . . . .Selected

    Shelley

Vocal Solo. . . . . "Kisses Sweeter Than Wine"

    David   (Folk Tune)

Piano Solo. . . . . "Sonatina in G"   Beethoven

    Fritz

Piano Duet . . . . "Galloping"   Kleeman

    Alice and Gail   (original)

"Surprise". . . . .

    Maddy

Piano Solo. . . . . "I, IV, I, V"   Wattenberg

    Ann   (original)

Comedy Act. . . . .

    John and Peter

Vocal Duet . . . . "Strolling through the Park"

    Christy and Lucy   (original words)

"Special Surprise". . . . . Medley

   Gail

Comedy Act. . . . .

   Queenston Trio: Fern, Claire, and Margaret

Do you think Mrs. Porto's plan worked? If the children did become excited about their Friday music program, would it be likely that they would learn more about music as a result of their activities relating to the program? How long would you expect that they would be enthusiastic about learning musical compositions and creating them? By encouraging her pupils to sing and play popular songs, was Mrs. Porto sacrificing too many of the skills and understandings which she had previously tried to develop? Which of the principles discussed in this chapter were put into action by Mrs. Porto?

REFERENCES

Bradford, L. P., J. R. Gibb, and K. D. Benne (eds.). *T-Group Theory and Laboratory Method.* New York: John Wiley & Sons, 1964.

Enochs, P. D. "An Experimental Study of a Method for Developing Creative Thinking in Fifth Grade Children." Doctoral dissertation, University of Missouri, Columbia, 1964.

Lewin, K. "Frontiers in Group Dynamics." *Human Relations,* 1947, **1**, 5–41.

Torrance, E. P. and Staff. *Role of Evaluation in Creative Thinking.* Final Report on USOE Project 725. Minneapolis: Bureau of Educational Research, University of Minnesota, 1964.

CHAPTER 12

GUIDING

PLANNED SEQUENCES

OF CREATIVE ACTIVITIES

Guiding
Youthful climbers,
Hurtling inaccessible mountains,
Tripping on pebbles of self-doubt,
Trusting.

The Problem

Mrs. Jorgenson's third-graders often asked questions that were difficult to answer. Mrs. Jorgenson also encouraged her pupils to find the answers on their own; but, lacking the reading skills of the older children, they were unable to make use of books very extensively in seeking solutions to their problems. Whenever a question arose which particularly interested the children, however, Mrs. Jorgenson encouraged the children to record their findings in a booklet which they themselves created. She felt that, by involving the children in a project which required writing their own words, they would take a greater interest in printing legibly and attractively.

One day a girl noticed that the two fish in the aquarium seemed to be biting at the ends of an aquatic plant which had been placed in the aquarium the previous day. A few days later, when a boy announced excitedly that the new plant had disappeared, the girl declared that "the fish must have eaten it up." Another young man, thoroughly imbued with the scientific spirit, suggested that the class obtain another plant and then observe what would happen to it. He believed that the observations should be made hourly, but the class pointed out that it would not be possible to see what went on in the aquarium at night when no one was in the building; and so it was agreed that a committee should be elected which would make official observations in the morning when the class convened and again just before class was dismissed in the afternoon. Mrs. Jorgenson suggested that the results of the experiment be made into a booklet complete with cover and illustrations.

One of Mrs. Jorgenson's principal goals in encouraging her pupils to make booklets about their activities was to cause them to take more pride in their printing.

Might she have been more effective in achieving this objective if she had asked her pupils to make their own individual booklets instead of cooperating in the construction of a class booklet?

Mrs. Jorgenson realized that neither her goal of improved handwriting nor her goals of scientific observation and problem-solving skills would be accomplished by this single activity: her pupils must engage in a number of sequences of creative-thinking activities and these activities must be planned and guided.

Does her method of group problem-solving research defeat her purposes? Under these conditions can she plan and guide the learning experiences? Can children this age use successfully such research methods?

Role of Guided, Planned Learning

For centuries, educators have struggled with the problem of how learning experiences should be guided and planned. At one extreme are those who favor what virtually amounts to "coerced" learning (i.e., learning by authority, overdirection, force, or imitation of a compulsive type). At the other extreme, are those who favor "unguided" and "unplanned" or "laissez-faire" learning with its lack of discipline, direction, and guides to behavior. In our opinion, one or the other of these extremes tends to characterize most teaching today and in the past. Guided, planned learning demands teachers with more training, skill, and imagination than do these two extreme approaches. Its implementation also requires more intellectual and emotional energy. It also emphasizes man's self-acting and creative nature rather than his receptive nature.

Ojemann (1948, 1966), a strong advocate of the concept of guided, planned learning, has called attention to this approach through his criticisms of some of the common misinterpretations of the research of Jean Piaget (1951). Ojemann argues that the developmental studies of Piaget and others tell us only how children develop when exposed to the learning experiences that the environment just happens to provide. They do not tell us anything about optimal and maximal development. Ojemann and Pritchett (1963) and Ojemann, Maxey, and Snider (1965) have conducted experiments to demonstrate that when children are exposed to guided, planned sequences of learning experiences, the development of concepts can be quite different from what is usually found. In one of these experiments (Ojemann and Pritchett, 1963), it was shown that by engaging in an interesting series of such experiences, five-year-olds attained concepts about gravity that characterize twelve-year-olds. In another (Ojemann, Maxey, and Snider, 1965), third-graders attained probability concepts usually reserved for college students. We (Torrance and Myers, 1962) have also shown that sixth-grade pupils, through guided, planned experiences, can attain understanding of research concepts not usually taught until graduate status is reached.

A number of studies have been reported concerning the use of specially constructed instructional materials for stimulating creative expression and growth. Films have been seen by a number of investigators as offering potentialities for stimulating creative expression and contributing to creative growth. Witty (1956) has reported results obtained by showing "The Hunter and the Forest," a story without words. Creative productions by students were evaluated according to the following criteria: the expression of genuine feeling; sensitivity on the part of students to the value of particular words, phrases, and larger language units in expressing their feelings; the materials and symbols presented; and use of correct and appropriate English.

Studies by Neal (1957) and Hutchinson (1963) in actual classrooms indicate that planned, guided experiences can contribute to creative development in significant ways. Neal's study involved the selection and testing of teaching techniques for developing methods of scientific inquiry in grades one through six. She found that children can be aided through direct teaching procedures in identifying and stating problems, in formulating plans to collect and evaluate data from a number of sources, in formulating hypotheses and concepts, and in applying concepts and methods to new situations. Test data indicated a consistent pattern of growth for each method of scientific inquiry from grades four through six.

Hutchinson's (1963) study was in junior high school social studies. The control group received what might be termed unplanned experiences and apparently was concerned primarily with the acquisition of information. The experimental group received planned, guided experiences which involved opportunities for using divergent thinking and evaluative abilities in acquiring information and skills. In the experimental classes where the methods were geared to the full range of mental abilities (memory, logical reasoning, ideational fluency, spontaneous flexibility, originality, elaboration, redefinition, sensitivity to problems, judgment, and the like) and not just to those abilities assessed by intelligence tests (primarily memory, recognition, logical reasoning, and the like), new productive and creative stars emerged. The relationships (coefficients of correlation) between measures of achievement and measures of creative thinking were higher in the experimental classes than in the comparison classes. In one of the experimental groups, three of the students in the lowest quartile on mental age were the creative and productive stars.

The most obvious problem in constructing planned experiences in creative thinking is to provide materials which can be taught by ordinary teachers without special instruction to ordinary students. These materials must, at the same time, select the best that is known about creativity and the basic or underlying principles of the various curricular areas such as reading, language arts, social studies, mathematics, science, music, art, and others. In this chapter, we will attempt to describe in some detail one set of planned experiences which have been developed and how they were received by teachers and pupils in a variety of educational settings.

Imagi/Craft: Guided, Planned Experiences in Creative Thinking

After several rather unsuccessful experiences in trying to help teachers acquire skills in encouraging creative growth through inservice education, we turned our attention to the development of instructional materials that apply the concept of guided, planned sequences of learning experiences. These materials represented an attempt to avoid some of the failures due apparently to inhibiting attitudes, lack of spontaneity, lack of time for preparation and planning, and perhaps lack of boldness or courage among many elementary teachers.

First, we developed several sets of exercises that were later combined into workbooks or ideabooks entitled *Can You Imagine?* (1965a), *Invitations to Thinking and Doing* (1964), and *Invitations to Writing and Speaking Creatively* (1965b). Then B. F. Cunnington came forth with the idea for *Imagi/Craft* (Cunnington and Torrance, 1965a), sets of recorded materials which provide flexible sequences of guided experiences in creative thinking. These materials were designed to bolster the teacher's courage and spontaneity and to grip the imagination of children. Since it had been shown (Torrance, 1962) that children in most schools in the United States show drops in creative functioning at about the fourth grade, it was decided to develop a set of materials suited to most fourth-grade curricula.

THE IMAGI/CRAFT MATERIALS

Having convinced ourselves that the fourth-grade slump in creative thinking is not an unalterable developmental phenomenon, we determined to find out if Cunnington's idea of dramatized recordings for use as key elements in guided, planned sequences of creative thinking might be used successfully in offsetting the influences responsible for the fourth-grade slump in creative functioning. Although we believed that much of the answer lay in teacher-pupil relationships and in the manifestation of values favoring creative growth, we realized that changes in these areas of human behavior are indeed difficult to achieve. We believed further that the best solution to this problem would come from experimentation with instructional materials providing guided, planned experiences in creative thinking. An attempt was made to build into these materials the best that we and our associates knew about the creative-thinking process from research and experience, as well as what we knew about the nature, interests, abilities, and problems of fourth-grade children.

An analysis of the nature of the task suggested that emphasis be given to the following five major objectives:

1. To discover, motivate, and develop creative awareness.
2. To develop an understanding of the nature and value of creative thinking and creative achievement.
3. To provide provocative data in the form of dramatized supplements to the curriculum in the fields of science, history, geography, and the language arts.
4. To stimulate and guide creative behavior.
5. To create an awareness of the value of one's own ideas.

It was desired that the bulk of the instructional materials correlate with the usual curriculum of the fourth grade. Thus, it was decided that one-fourth of the materials would deal with great moments of scientific discovery and invention; one-fourth with great moments in historical achievement; one-fourth with great moments in geographical discovery; and one-fourth—related largely to language arts—with fantasy. In spite of this division, however, it was intended that any single planned sequence of experiences might take the learner into several curricular fields. For example, one of the records in the Great Moments in Scientific Discovery series might lead directly to art and creative-writing experiences. These in turn might lead to activities in reading, history, music, arithmetic, character education, psychology, economics, government, and other areas.

The titles finally used in the field tests were:

Science
   Trailblazer to the Stars (Robert Goddard)
   All-Around American (Benjamin Franklin)
   Master of Miracles (Thomas Edison)
History
   Eyes at Their Fingertips (Louis Braille)
   Wizard on Wheels (Henry Ford)
   Wings for the World (Wright Brothers)
Geography
   Captains of Courage (Lewis and Clark)
   Polar Pilot (Richard Byrd)
Fantasy
   The Dog They Named King
   Giovanni and the Giant
   Christmas Minstrel
   Sounds and Images

This selection of titles was based on data from a national survey of common elements in the elementary school curriculum in the United States and the opinions and preferences of many teachers and curriculum specialists. Since these titles reflect the curriculum of the early 1960's, there is no reference to minority group members and creative women. However, there is a variety of useful material available concerning disadvantaged groups such as Negroes, American Indians, Mexican-Americans, Puerto Ricans, and the like. Since we think it is tremendously important that children in these groups be able to find themselves in their books and other instructional materials, a list of suggested materials has been placed at the end of this chapter.

DESCRIPTION OF THE MATERIALS

In producing the recorded dramas, an effort was made to give pupils intimate insights into the thought processes that enabled men such as Edison, Franklin, and the Wright brothers to make important creative contributions. Much care was exercised to make the science, history, and geography stories and the teacher's guides as accurate as possible.

A variety of production techniques was used in developing the records. Some of the units make use of the "stop" device, whereby a teacher may shut off the record player at one of the more climactic moments and then request the class to provide possible solutions to the problem being encountered in the drama. After the class has responded, the story may proceed to the conclusion, thus allowing the pupils to compare their responses with the recorded solution. In most of the recordings, the introduction is designed to heighten anticipation and expectation. In some, the listener is instructed to listen with a particular viewpoint or to process the information in a particular way. In several of the recordings, the listener is instructed to make some creative response to a stimulus and then to produce something based on this creative response.

The recordings based on science, history, and geography content were designed initially to acquaint fourth-grade children with the nature of the creative process and the value of original ideas and to motivate them to behave in creative ways. The inclusion of the fantasy material was based on the rationale that fantasy needs to be kept alive among children. Its inclusion represents an attempt to help offset an excessive quest for certainty, safety, and objectivity common among many fourth-graders.

INSTRUMENTS USED IN EVALUATING OUTCOMES

An attempt was made to select instruments which would come closest to assessing the hypothesized outcomes of the experimental conditions resulting from the use of the guided, planned experiences in creative thinking which revolved about the records. It was hypothesized that fourth-grade pupils under the experimental conditions compared with those under control conditions would:

1. Show greater growth as measured by a set of pre- and post-tests of creative thinking.
2. Like school better and find it more exciting.
3. Participate in more creative activities on their own.
4. Show as much growth in basic educational skills, as measured by a battery of standardized achievement tests at the beginning and at the end of the experimental period, as in creative thinking.

The following tests or other data-collection devices were used for obtaining the data with which to test the hypotheses:

1. *Abbreviated Form VII of the Minnesota Tests of Creative Thinking* (Torrance, 1963). This form was adapted for use in this study from earlier tests developed by Torrance and includes the following four tasks: incomplete figures, circles, product improvement, and unusual uses. Each task yields scores on fluency, flexibility, originality, and elaboration. Each task attempts to sample different aspects of creative thinking.
2. *Sounds and Images Test of Originality.* The *Sounds and Images* (Cunnington and Torrance, 1965) recording consists of four sound effects, each of which is repeated in sequence three times. The sound effects range from simple to complex, from commonplace and familiar to unusual or strange. Each repetition of a sound effect is followed by a brief pause for the subject to record in the appropriate place the word picture of the image each sound effect suggests. Responses are evaluated on criteria that yield a measure of originality (uncommonness of response).
3. *Imaginative Stories Test.* Each form of the Imaginative Stories Test (Torrance, 1965, pp. 279–288) consists of a suggested list of ten titles. Subjects are asked to select one of them, or make up a similar one, and to compose the most interesting and exciting story they can about the topic within a time limit of twenty minutes. All of the titles involve animals or persons who possess some divergent characteristic or manifest some

kind of divergent behavior. The stories were evaluated according to criteria which provide measures of originality and interest. The following nine characteristics were considered in evaluating originality:

a. Picturesqueness, power to excite images that are colorful, strikingly graphic, etc.
b. Vividness, liveliness, intenseness, emotionally stirring, vigorous, fresh, alive, spirited, etc.
c. Flavor, possessing a characteristic element or taste, or appeals to sense of taste, smell, touch, or feel.
d. Personal element, involvement of the author in the account or expression of personal feelings about the events described.
e. Original solution or ending, surprising, has a punch line.
f. Original setting or plot; unusual, unconventional, or new setting, theme, or plot.
g. Humor, portrays comical, funny, amusing; brings together incongruities.
h. Invented words or names.
i. Other unusual twists in style or content.

4. *"How-I-Like-School" Inventory.* The "How-I-Like-School" Inventory, developed by Cyril J. Hoyt of the University of Minnesota, consists of fifty rather straightforward questions concerning liking or disliking for school. A score was obtained by adding all of the responses indicating a favorable attitude about school. In addition, analyses were made of items especially relevant to the aims of the study. The following are sample items:

Is most schoolwork interesting?	YES	NO
Do you feel important in school?	YES	NO
Do you feel you lose out if you miss school?	YES	NO
Do you hate school?	YES	NO
Do you enjoy school?	YES	NO

5. *Creative Activities Checklists.* Two checklists of creative activities were developed for use in this study. One of these was especially directed at ascertaining what creative activities were initiated by the subjects of the study during Christmas vacation; the other, for activities initiated during the summer vacation follow-

ing the use of the experimental materials. The following are examples of the activities listed:

_____Made up puzzles (crossword, jigsaw, anagrams, etc.).
_____Tried to figure out how to hold breath longer.
_____Made a rocket.
_____Made up a joke.
_____Made up a guessing game.

6. *Achievement Tests.* Pre- and post-training data were obtained concerning performances on the achievement test routinely given by the three school systems which participated in the study. Two of the school systems used the Iowa Tests of Basic Skills and the other used the California Achievement Tests.

7. *Teacher Reports on Recorded Materials and Teacher Guides.* Teachers using the experimental materials were asked to prepare a reaction report on each record following the completion of the unit in which it was used. It consisted of the following questions:

How did your pupils react to the story?
Which single pupil seemed to show the greatest interest? In what way?
What did you feel was the effective element in the dramatization?
How did your pupils react to the lesson which followed the dramatization?
Was the lesson suitable for your pupils in both lesson content and level of difficulty?
What kinds of learning experiences or activities resulted, directly or indirectly, from the playing of the records?
Do you have any suggestions as to how the record might be made more educative for your class?

EXPERIMENTAL PROCEDURES

The subjects of the study included thirty fourth-grade classes in the Richfield, Minnesota, Public School System totaling 800 pupils; six fourth-grade classes in Sioux Falls, South Dakota, totaling 155 pupils; and six fourth-grade classes in Brunswick, Georgia, totaling 182 pupils. Teachers in the Richfield and Brunswick studies were assigned randomly to the experimental and control conditions.

In Sioux Falls, the experimentals were in one school, and the fourth grades in similar schools served as the controls. The teachers in the experimental groups agreed to use the experimental recordings, and those in the control groups were instructed to go ahead with whatever plans they had already formulated for their classes. Some of them had already worked out rather detailed plans for encouraging creative development in their pupils.

Details of the procedures are set forth in other sources (Torrance and Gupta, 1964; Torrance, 1965). A unit of the experimental materials was scheduled every two weeks during the period between the pre- and post-testing.

EXAMPLE OF EXPERIMENTAL MATERIAL

To provide the reader with a rough idea of the kind of sequences of creative activities that a teacher could plan from the experimental materials, some brief examples will be given from Cunnington and Buckland's *Eyes at Their Fingertips* (*The Louis Braille Story*) (1962).

Accompanying each recorded drama and lesson in the Imagi/Craft series was a teacher's guide prepared by experienced teachers and subject-matter specialists under our guidance. Much care was exercised to make each guide a rich source of ideas for guiding and planning sequences of creative-thinking experiences. Each guide contained sections devoted to the drama itself (possible outcomes, readiness for listening, interpreting the drama, and creative activities) and the correlated lesson (possible outcomes, materials needed, readiness for listening, and interpreting the dramatization, and creative activities). In addition, the teacher was provided with suggested readings for himself and his pupils, as well as the script for both the drama and the lesson.

Here is an excerpt from the guide for *Eyes at Their Fingertips* (*The Story of Louis Braille*) (1962).

ACTIVITIES WHICH COULD BE DONE BY THE INDIVIDUAL PUPIL

Engaging in recreative activities such as investigating, using, and improving the Morse Code or the Boy Scout Code.

Creating a new code and putting it on a mimeographed sheet for others to puzzle over.

Proposing an invention, writing about it, diagramming it, or making a model of it.

Investigating topics of interest such as: Famous Blind Men and Women, Ways Our School Helps the Blind, France in the 1800's.

ACTIVITIES WHICH COULD BE DONE BY THE WHOLE GROUP

Tracing the development of an invention of interest to individuals or a small group.

Creatively dramatizing moments of discovery.

Making a booklet, mural, or movie concerned with real or imaginary inventions.

Participating in a free "brainstorming" period, playing around with ideas such as "Why don't they invent . . . ?" or "I wish they'd invent . . . ," expressing them by writing, drawing, or in any chosen manner.

Do you believe that a majority of the experimental teachers were able to use one or more of these suggestions? If you had been one of the experimental teachers, would you have been likely to take seriously some of the suggestions given in the teacher's guide?

An Example of an Exercise to Follow a Recorded Dramatization

The following exercise created by Torrance was one of the many suggested for the pupils who listened to *Eyes at Their Fingertips:*

One of the big reasons why Louis Braille, himself a blind boy, thought of and worked out a way for blind people to read and write better was that the old way really bothered him. It really got under his skin that little blind children had to read out of books that were so big that they couldn't carry them around. And besides, reading raised or embossed writing wasn't very accurate. Try to think of as many things as you can that really bother you and get on your nerves—things that bother you so much that you would like to change them or invent something new to make them less annoying. List as many of them as you can in the space below. . . .

Of all the things you listed on the first page, what bothers you most? What really gets you down? Is there any one of the things you listed on the first page that towers over all of the others and makes them seem small? Pick out one of the things you have just listed and write it in the blank below. . . .

Now, think of all of the things you can about this annoyance or "thorn in your flesh" that make it annoying and list them below. What is there about it that bothers you? . . .

In the spaces below list as many things as you can think of that would make it less annoying or remove the annoyance from your life. It doesn't have to be something that is now possible. Play being a magician and list all of the things that make it ideal. . . .

Now, think of something you could invent or some plan that would remove some of the things that bother you about this annoyance and would have as many as possible of the characteristics you listed at the bottom of the last page. . . .

Louis Braille was helped in developing this kind of writing because he was familiar with sonography, which had proved unsuccessful. Do you know of any unsuccessful attempts to solve the problem you selected? If you do, write them below. If you don't know of any, how could you find out if there have been any? Write your answer below. . . .

If you thought of some unsuccessful attempt to solve your problem, what would have to be changed about it to make it successful? . . . Can you draw a picture or a diagram of the invention or plan which you have in mind? Sketch it below. If not, describe it as fully as possible. . . .

If you were to succeed with your invention or plan, it would change many things. Think of as many things as you can that would probably be changed if your plan or invention became successful. List them below. . . .

How could you adapt this exercise to a unit of study that your class is currently engaged in?

RESULTS OF FIELD EVALUATION

Through the rather extensive program of pre- and post-testing, the growth of the children exposed to the experimental materials was compared with that of subjects in the control groups through the use of appropriate statistical tests of significance.

In the school system involving fifteen experimental and fifteen control teachers, the control subjects showed losses rather than gains on four of the ten measures of creative thinking while the experimentals showed gains on all ten (eight statistically significant). In the second system (three controls and three experimentals), both controls and experimentals showed statistically significant gains, but the experimentals showed superior growth on three variables and the controls on one, when post-test scores were corrected for pre-test scores. In the third system (three experimentals and two controls), the experimentals showed gains on all ten variables while the controls showed losses on two of them and no gains on the others. Thus, in spite of the fact that the control teachers did many things to encourage creative growth, the evidence is in favor of the experimental classes using the records and auxiliary materials.

In all three school systems, a smaller proportion of the experimentals than the controls indicated that they "hated school." During the Christmas vacation, the experimentals reported having engaged in a larger number of creative activities on their own in two of the school systems. During the summer vacation, the experimentals in one system reported a larger number of creative activities than their controls. In all other cases, the differences were not statistically significant.

In one school system, the use of the materials seems to have facilitated traditional kinds of educational achievement. In the second and third it seems to have made no difference.

Thus, the weight of the evidence seems to indicate that planned, guided experiences in creative thinking can facilitate creative growth at the fourth-grade level and tend not to interfere with usual kinds of achievement.

The reaction reports of the teachers indicated that most of them improved gradually in their ability to use the recordings effectively. Some of them achieved outstanding success almost from the beginning. Some were resistant to using the materials throughout and it is clear that a few of them did little more than play the records to their classes. In almost all classes, the recorded dramas seemed to grip the imagination of the pupils. Response seems to have been especially good among boys, gifted boys and girls, and children who tend to be isolated and nonconforming. Response to the recorded lessons was also generally enthusiastic except in cases where the pupils had not been prepared in advance for the lesson and where motivation conditions were generally rather poor. A number of teachers indicated that some pupils who were not ordinarily motivated became enthusiastic about some of the lessons.

Ideabooks as Guided, Planned Sequences

RATIONALE FOR THE IDEABOOK

Although we have never believed that it is possible to "program" creative thinking in the same way that facts and principles are programmed in teaching machines and programmed textbooks, we have felt that, when individuals become involved in a subject or activity that interests them, their creative ideas can be fostered by planned sequences that allow the creative process to evolve naturally. In devising materials that encourage original thinking, we have kept a model of the creative process before us. The model is based upon the notion that creative thinking derives from the individual's interaction with his environment when he becomes sensitive to problems, deficiencies, gaps in knowledge, missing elements, and disharmonies; identifies the difficulty or difficulties; searches for solutions, makes guesses, or formulates hypotheses; tests and retests his hypotheses or solutions and assesses them according to appropriate criteria; and then communicates the results.

There are several elements in the creative process that can be emphasized when a teacher wishes to nurture productive thinking in his pupils. Perhaps the first factor to be considered is that creative thinking requires time. There must be time for the individual to become familiar with the materials he is dealing with; he must become comfortable in his surroundings; and he must become aware of his own reactions to the materials or subject matter. It has been observed that artists and scientists who have contributed significantly to our culture have immersed themselves in their subjects or media. This takes time. Ideas occur spontaneously, of course, but there must have been some preparation for their birth—one must have done considerable thinking about the problem and similar problems and struggled consciously to come up with a solution before the spontaneous idea occurred. Therefore, a warming-up phase in which the individual has an opportunity to play around with ideas without worrying about time factors has been a feature of the exercises of *Invitations to Thinking and Doing* (1964) and the other Ideabooks. The warming-up activity can take many forms—from elaborating upon a few wiggly lines to imagining what you would do if you were bequeathed an assortment of bizarre items by an eccentric aunt—but it always permits the pupils to become involved in thinking about something without worrying about time. The emphasis is upon ideation.

Many investigators have also noted that people have highly original ideas when they allow one thing to lead to another naturally, when they are able to follow lines of inquiry in a natural manner. This feature of allowing one thing to lead to another was also built into the Ideabooks. For example, in "What's in a Name?", an exercise which involved the pupil in providing names for people, animals, businesses, gadgets, and television programs, the pupil is asked (a) to think about the role that names play in the successes and failures of people and products; (b) to produce appropriate names for various things (such as a man who never loses his temper and an automobile with five wheels); (c) to recall unusual names of people he has encountered; (d) to react to the names of three men or boys; and then (e) to write a story which suggests itself to him when he thinks of some unusual name (perhaps one of the three names given).

The sequence of activities of this exercise is designed to involve the pupil more deeply in thinking about names. Actually, there are three levels of involvement if he accepts the invitations offered in the exercise. At the first level, he is engaged in a task which can be thought of as the initiating or warming-up phase. This part of the exercise is usually administered as a group activity for a class. At the second level, the pupil is put on his own. He is presented with an activity that is intended to capitalize upon the interest engendered by the warming-up activity. When the pupil reaches the third level of involvement, he is invited to probe more deeply into the subject or to launch some project that he has conceived during the progress of the exercise. The activities of the exercise apparently follow one another in a logical order, but creative thinking is often characterized by mental leaps and by irrational thinking; and so teachers and pupils are advised to omit any of the activities if they wish or to substitute others which may be more felicitous.

Two versions of the "idea trap" were incorporated into the first Ideabook, *Invitations to Thinking and Doing*. Wide margins were used to encourage the pupil to jot down his reactions to the exercises as they occurred to him, or just to doodle. At the top of the margins were headings such as "Notes, Comments, and Doodles" and "For Notes and Doodles." Each lesson ended with a space called "The Idea Box." If the pupil had an inspiration during the time he was engaged in the exercise or at any time during the school day, he was to record the idea in this space. We believed that by providing space for the pupil's private "brainstorms" he would be more likely to feel that his ideas were worthwhile.

All of the exercises were written to convey our conviction that learning and thinking are continuous and personal. For instance, the second-level activity for "You, the Magician" (Unit 4 of *Invitations to Thinking and Doing*) invites the pupil to describe how *his* life might be changed if he were able to make something louder so that it would be more pleasant, to make something go backwards in order that it be improved, and other transformations. At the end of the exercise (and at the end of the other exercises in the booklet), the pupil is invited to list some of the things about which he wants to know more. These matters may or may not be related to the exercise. By providing a place for noting interesting or puzzling subjects at the conclusion of each exercise, we intended to indicate that there are a multitude of topics that intermediate-grade pupils might investigate. Since to engage in creative thinking is to rely principally upon one's own resources, it follows that the individual pupil must have *practice* in expressing himself. The principal function of the Ideabooks is to provide opportunities for pupils of widely varying talents and backgrounds to have regular experiences in thinking for themselves in a classroom setting.

Although the theoretical underpinnings of the Ideabooks seemed sound to us, there was only one way at the beginning to find out if these materials were effective in releasing and nurturing creative abilities. They had to be tested in the field. We wanted to know if materials that were based upon proven principles for fostering creative growth could be used by teachers who had not received training in nurturing creativity.

AN EXPERIMENT IN ENCOURAGING SIXTH-GRADERS TO THINK CREATIVELY

This same question occurred to R. J. Britton (1967), Director of Research for the Henrico County Public Schools of Virginia, approximately a year after the Ideabooks were conceived. When a challenge was presented to the teachers of the school district "to provide more situations in their classrooms where children could think more creatively and work with more integrity," it became apparent that the majority of teachers could not provide experiences in their classrooms which would excite the minds of their pupils. This was the result, according to the teachers, of a lack of understanding of the concept of creativity and a reluctance to venture away from "normal teaching." However, the teachers and administrators of Henrico County had been inspired by Dr. Louis Armstrong to engage in a School Improvement Program which emphasized the idea that a "spirit of adventure is essential to improved teaching and learning." They had assumed that "teachers who teach the same way, or virtually the same way, year after year destroy not only their own intellectual curiosity but that of their pupils as well." Hence, the strategy of the School Improvement Program was one of having each teacher:

1. Try something new each year;
2. Let the something he tried make sense and offer real promise of improving what he is doing;
3. Tell his fellow teachers about his efforts to improve and to get their advice and help;
4. Let the something he tried be within the context of his present way of teaching, and change old ways of teaching only as new ways prove their worth; and
5. Report in writing what he does.

While he felt that the program was achieving good results throughout the district, Britton believed that there should be some measurable evidence of the kind of changes which occur when teachers try out their ideas and when children learn creatively. Accordingly, he launched an experiment in which seven classes of sixth-grade pupils (the experimental group) were given creative-thinking exercises regularly. *Invitations to Thinking and Doing* was chosen as the set of creative-thinking exercises to be used in the experimental classrooms. An equal number of children in this same grade (the control group) were to have similar curricular experiences but not engage in the activities suggested by the exercises in *Invitations to Thinking and Doing.* In October, fourteen of the ninety sixth-grade classes in the district were randomly selected to constitute the experimental and control groups. The names of the fourteen teachers of those classes were placed in a box, and seven were withdrawn and designated as teachers of the experimental pupils. The remaining seven were to be the teachers of the control pupils. All fourteen teachers, with their principals, were called together and the study was explained. They were asked to cooperate, but each teacher was free to withdraw if he so desired. All of the teachers agreed to take part in the experiment.

After all of the teachers had been interviewed, the experimental teachers were called for their first conference in November. The experiment was explained in detail, and each teacher was given published, professional material to read and study. In December, they were called together again for a discussion of the professional material that had been given to them. At that meeting each teacher in the experimental group was given a single copy of *Invitations to Thinking and Doing.* During December and a part of January three sessions were held with the teachers in the experimental group. A careful check was made to guard against the booklet's falling into the hands of anyone other than the experimental teachers. No one was told of the experiment except the teachers and principals involved.

During the last week in January, Minnesota Tests of Creativity were made available to the teachers of both the experimental and control groups two days prior to the testing. All children were tested at the same hour on the same day, and all test material was collected on the same day. (Forms VA and NVA were used for both the pre-test and post-test.) Agreement was reached by all concerned to use all of the exercises and activities in the booklet. It was agreed that the children would be introduced to the experiences on the same day for four weeks. At the end of February the experimental teachers met again to discuss the progress of the experiment. It was agreed at this meeting to increase experiences to two a week on identical days, Tuesday and Thursday. At the end of March the experimental group met once more to discuss their experiences. From then until the end of the second week of May, all of the experimental teachers agreed to follow the plan of two experiences a week until the booklet was completed. The following week all of the teachers involved in the experiment gave the post-test.

When the data from the tests were analyzed, it was found that significant differences existed in both total verbal and total nonverbal areas of creativity in favor of the experimental group.

Inasmuch as all of the teachers of the district had been urged for over two years to encourage their pupils to think originally and independently, Britton and his staff assumed that the control teachers would do their "regular" teaching and that it would emphasize creative thinking to some extent. The experimental teachers, on the other hand, were not instructed as to how the exercises were to be administered; no specific teaching techniques were recommended. They were given complete freedom to follow the guide for the booklet in their own ways. If the differences in test scores are indicative of genuine differences in creative growth, we might suppose that giving pupils the opportunity to use their imaginations and to express themselves *on a rather frequent basis* facilitates the development of creative power.

During the course of the experiment, Britton noted some interesting reactions by some of the experimental teachers. Of the seven, two experienced personal difficulty in deviating from traditional patterns of teaching. Four of the teachers had no trouble expanding the experiences their pupils had with the exercises and activities of the booklet into other areas of the curriculum. One teacher frankly admitted that the experiences with creative thinking had done more for her as a teacher than they had done for the children.

The reactions of the pupils in the experimental group to the exercises were especially interesting. It was noted that they had difficulty in becoming adjusted to the exercises in *Invitations to*

Thinking and Doing at the start; in fact, the experiment was in its fifth week before real interest became observable. By the eighth week, however, "almost all of the pupils were actively and enthusiastically engaged in the experiences."

Probably the most important results of the experiment can be found in the effects upon the children. Many children who had not been successful during their six years in school gained recognition and self-confidence as a result of engaging in the creative-thinking activities. One boy, in particular, seemed to benefit directly from the experiment. A complete rejectee with physical abnormalities, he emerged as the leader of his group. His wealthy parents had spent thousands of dollars working with psychiatrists, psychologists, and neurosurgeons trying to bring the child out of his shell. By the end of Britton's study, he had written a highly original three-part play dealing with a vital moral problem and was able to act out all three parts exceptionally well. The boy's parents attributed his tremendous improvement to the experiences he had enjoyed during the course of the experiment.

A second child whose behavior showed a marked improvement was a young girl who was also a rejectee. She was tremendously overweight and had a personal hygiene problem. During the course of the study, it was discovered that this child had an excellent singing voice. The group of children in her class rewrote the opera *Carmen,* and the girl was selected by her classmates to take the lead role. In the process, her personal hygiene problem disappeared.

Another child who especially benefited from the experiment was a boy who showed very little interest in school. Throughout his school life, he had barely met the promotion requirements from grade to grade. During the study he was given a brick with twelve holes in it and asked to find out how many uses he could make of the brick. He presented the brick with two additional bricks similar to it as a proposed apartment unit for the future. The holes in the brick were to be utilized as heating, air conditioning, ventilating, and smog catching devices. The two additional bricks were used to fashion a cantilever structure. In sharp contrast to his usual reactions to school activities, the boy did a tremendous amount of research in order to develop his ideas.

Many other children were identified as responding positively to school for the first time. Among them was a boy who, spurred on by the creative-thinking exercises to spend a great deal of his time working in a television shop, has since become an outstanding student of electronics.

A TWO-WEEK TRAINING PERIOD

An experiment similar to Britton's, but on a much smaller scale, was conducted within a sixth-grade class by Ann M. Casey (1965). Exercises from *Invitations to Thinking and Doing* were taught one half-hour every day for two weeks to the experimental group by the experimenter while the control group was given assignments in a reader and its accompanying workbook by the classroom teacher. At the end of this brief period, the Ask-and-Guess Test was administered to both groups and the tests were scored for fluency, flexibility, and originality. Casey found that the experimental group was significantly more fluent, more flexible, and more original than the control group.

Making Your Own Summary

You have been reading about materials that are designed to lead pupils through a series of steps to a point where they have grasped a concept or generalization and are able to demonstrate their understanding of the concept. Since you are somewhat dissatisfied with the many misconceptions that your second-graders have been coming up with recently, you decide to devise your own materials and activities in teaching a unit about the American family. In order to do so, you decide to use some materials about families that differ dramatically from those your pupils are familiar with. Because there are some good photographs and books about primitive peoples in the instructional materials center of your district, you choose an illustration of an Arunta family in central Australia. You plan to ask a series of questions about the illustration and engage your pupils in one or two activities in order that they obtain important insights about their own way of life. You study the illustration and books and jot down these questions:

Figure 7. An Arunta Family on the Move. The Arunta are nomadic hunters and gatherers. They carry the few tools which they use with them. (Reprinted by permission from *The Arunta,* Publication No. 6, Anthropology Curriculum Project, University of Georgia, Athens, 1965.)

How would you compare these people with those you know here?

What do you suppose they are doing?

How can we find out more about them?

What can you tell about the place in which they live? Where is it?

Why don't we make up a story or a song about these people? Let's give them a name. What would be a good name for them?

What are some of the important things we can't find out by looking at his picture?

Could they live anywhere near us? Are you sure? Why?

What is the man carrying? What is the boy carrying?

Can you figure out some of the things that the woman is carrying?

Which one is the father? How do you know? (Do fathers usually carry their children? In this way?)

Arrange the questions in a sequence which will enable the children to arrive at some reasonable generalizations about the Arunta family and their own families and environments.

What are some of the major stages in this plan? What are the disadvantages of teaching your pupils in this manner? What are some of the advantages of this technique?

REFERENCES

Britton, R. J. "A Study of Creativity in Selected Sixth Grade Groups." Doctoral dissertation, University of Virginia, Charlottesville, 1967.

Casey, A. M. "The Effects of Using a Workbook Approach in Teaching Divergent Thinking in Sixth Grade Pupils." Master's thesis, Cornell University, Ithaca, N. Y., 1965.

Cunnington, B. F. and P. Buckland. *Teacher's Guide for Eyes at Their Fingertips.* Minneapolis: Bureau of Educational Research, University of Minnesota, 1962.

Cunnington, B. F. and E. P. Torrance. *Imagi/Craft.* Boston: Ginn & Co., 1965a.

Cunnington, B. F. and E. P. Torrance. *Sounds and Images.* Boston: Ginn & Co., 1965b.

Hutchinson, W. L. "Creative and Productive Thinking in the Classroom." Doctoral dissertation, University of Utah, Salt Lake City, 1963.

Myers, R. E. and E. P. Torrance. *Invitations to Thinking and Doing.* Boston: Ginn & Co., 1964.

Myers, R. E. and E. P. Torrance. *Can You Imagine?* Boston: Ginn & Co., 1965a.

Myers, R. E. and E. P. Torrance. *Invitations to Speaking and Writing Creatively.* Boston: Ginn & Co., 1965b.

Myers, R. E. and E. P. Torrance. *For Those Who Wonder.* Boston: Ginn & Co., 1966.

Neal, L. A. "Techniques for Developing Methods of Scientific Inquiry in Children in Grades 1–6." Unpublished doctoral dissertation, Colorado State College, 1957.

Ojemann, R. H. "Research in Planned Learning Programs and the Science of Behavior." *Journal of Educational Research,* 1948, **42,** 96–104.

Ojemann, R. H. "Purpose of Conference on Guided Learning." In R. H. Ojemann and K. Pritchett (eds.). *Giving Emphasis to Guided Learning.* Cleveland, Ohio: Educational Research Council of Greater Cleveland, 1966. Pp. 1–4.

Ojemann, R. H., E. J. Maxey, B. C. Snider. "The Effect of a Program of Guided Learning Experiences in Developing Probability Concepts at the Third Grade Level." *Journal of Experimental Education,* 1965, **33,** 321–330.

Ojemann, R. H. and K. Pritchett. "Piaget and the Role of Guided Experiences in Human Development." *Perceptual and Motor Skills,* 1963, **17,** 927–939.

Piaget, J. *The Child's Conception of Physical Causality.* New York: Humanities Press, 1951.

Torrance, E. P. *Guiding Creative Talent.* Englewood Cliffs, N.J.: Prentice-Hall, Inc., 1962.

Torrance, E. P. and R. E. Myers. *Teaching Gifted Elementary Pupils How to Do Research.* Minneapolis: Perceptive Publishing Co., 1962.

Torrance, E. P. *Scoring Guide for Abbreviated Form VII of the Minnesota Tests of Creative Thinking.* Minneapolis: Bureau of Educational Research, University of Minnesota, 1963. Mimeographed.

Torrance, E. P. *Rewarding Creative Behavior.* Englewood Cliffs, N.J.: Prentice-Hall, Inc., 1965.

Torrance, E. P. and R. Gupta. *Development and Evaluation of Recorded Programmed Experiences in Creative Thinking in the Fourth Grade.* Minneapolis: Bureau of Educational Research, 1964.

Torrance, E. P. and R. E. Myers. *Teaching Gifted Elementary Pupils How to Do Research.* Athens, Ga.: Georgia Studies of Creative Behavior, 1962.

Witty, P. "The Use of Films in Stimulating Creative Expression in Identifying Talented Pupils." *Elementary English,* 1956, **33,** 341–344.

INSTRUCTIONAL MATERIALS DEALING WITH CREATIVE ACHIEVEMENTS OF MAJOR DISADVANTAGED AND MINORITY GROUPS IN THE UNITED STATES

The selected list of materials which follows focuses on such disadvantaged and minority groups as Negroes, American Indians, Mexican-Americans, Puerto Ricans, and the like. In the past, the instructional materials used in schools in the United States have given little attention to the creative achievements of these groups. Children in these groups have been unable to identify with the personalities encountered in their reading, history, art, music, or other books. Now, it is rather generally recognized that it is important that children be able to find themselves and their cultural heroes in their books. This seems to be necessary in the achievement of favorable and realistic self-images. In our opinion, disadvantaged and minority group children can learn creative behavior by encountering stories and other accounts of the creative behaviors of members of their own ethnic and culture groups. The materials included in this list have been chosen with this objective in mind. No attempt has been made to offer a comprehensive list. The books feature creative behavior in everyday life as well as in outstanding achievement.

PART I. MATERIALS ON NEGROES

BOOKS

Adams, R. L. *Great Negroes Past and Present.* Chicago: Afro. Am. Publishing Company, 1964.

Adoff, A. *I am the Darker Brother.* New York: The Macmillan Company, 1968.

Baldwin, J. *Nobody Knows My Name.* New York: Dial Press, 1961.

Baldwin, J. *Notes of a Native Son.* New York: Dial Press, 1961.

Barrett, W. E. *Lilies of the Field.* New York: Popular Library, 1963.

Blanton, C. *Hold Fast to Your Dreams.* New York: Julian Messner, 1964.

Bontemps, A. *Famous Negro Athletes.* New York: Dodd, Mead & Company, 1964.

Douglass, F. *Narrative of the Life of Frederick Douglass, an American Slave.* Cambridge, Mass.: Harvard University Press, 1960.

Dunbar, P. L. *Little Brown Baby.* New York: Dodd, Mead & Company, 1940.

Durham, P. and E. L. Jones. *The Adventures of the Negro Cowboys.* New York: Dodd, Mead & Company, 1966.

Einstein, C. *Willie Mays: Coast to Coast Giant.* New York: G. P. Putnam's Sons, 1963.

Elliott, L. *George Washington Carver: The Man Who Overcame.* Englewood Cliffs, N. J.: Prentice-Hall, Inc., 1966.

Erwin, B. K. *Behind the Magic Line.* Boston: Little, Brown and Company, 1969.

Felton, H. *Edward Rose, Negro Trail Blazer.* New York: Dodd, Mead & Company, 1967.

Felton, H. *Nat Love, Negro Cowboy.* New York: Dodd, Mead & Company, 1969.

Gibson, B. with P. Pepe. *From Ghetto to Glory.* Englewood Cliffs, N. J.: Prentice-Hall, Inc., 1968.

Gould, J. *That Dunbar Boy.* New York: Dodd, Mead & Company, 1959.

Graham, S. *The Story of Phyllis Wheatley.* New York: Julian Messner, 1957.

Gregory, D. with R. Lipsyte. *Nigger: An Autobiography.* New York: E. P. Dutton & Co., 1964.

Hughes, L. *Famous American Negroes.* New York: Dodd, Mead & Company, 1954.

Hughes, L. *The First Book of Jazz.* New York: Franklin Watts, 1955.

Hughes, L. *Famous Negro Music Makers.* New York: Dodd, Mead & Company, 1955.

Hughes, L. *Famous Negro Heroes of America.* New York: Dodd, Mead & Company, 1958.

Hughes, L. *New Negro Poets: USA.* Bloomington, Ind.: Indiana University Press, 1965.

Hughes, L. and A. Bontemps (eds.). *The Book of Negro Folklore.* New York: Dodd, Mead & Company, 1958.

Jackson, J. *Anchor Man*. New York: Harper & Row, 1957.

Jackson, J. *Tessie*. New York: Harper & Row, 1968.

Johnston, J. *A Special Bravery*. New York: Dodd, Mead & Company, 1967.

Kirkeby, E. *Ain't Misbehavin': The Story of Fats Waller*. New York: Dodd, Mead & Company, 1966.

Kugelmass, J. A. *Ralph J. Bunche, Fighter for the Peace*. New York: Julian Messner, 1952.

Lee, I. H. *Negro Medal of Honor Men*. New York: Dodd, Mead & Company, 1967.

Meltzer, M. (ed.). *In Their Own Words: A History of the American Negro, 1619–1865*. New York: Thomas Y. Crowell Company, 1964.

Meltzer, M. (ed.). *In Their Own Words: A History of the American Negro, 1865–1916*. New York: Thomas Y. Crowell Company, 1965.

Meltzer, M. (ed.). *In Their Own Words: A History of the American Negro, 1916–1966*. New York: Thomas Y. Crowell Company, 1967.

Patterson, F. (with M. Cross) *Victory Over Myself*. New York: Scholastic Book Services, 1962.

Ploski, H. A. and Brown. *The Negro Almanac*. New York: Bellweather Company, 1968.

Price, A. *Haunted by a Paintbrush*. Chicago: Children's Press, 1968.

Robinson, W. H. *Black American Poets of the 18th and 19th Centuries*. Dubuque, Iowa: W. C. Brown, 1969.

Rollins, C. M. *They Showed the Way: Forty American Negro Leaders*. New York: Thomas Y. Crowell Company, 1964.

Rollins, C. M. *Famous American Negro Poets*. New York: Dodd, Mead & Company, 1965.

Rollins, C. M. *Famous Negro Entertainers of Stage, Screen, and TV*. New York: Dodd, Mead & Company, 1967.

Romero, P. *In Black America*. Washington, D. C.: United Publishing Company, 1969.

Scott, R. *Big City Rodeo Rider*. Chicago: Children's Press, 1968.

Shapiro, M. J. *Jackie Robinson of the Brooklyn Dodgers*. New York: Julian Messner, 1957.

Shotwell, L. *Roosevelt Grady*. New York: Grossett & Dunlap, 1964.

Stevenson, A. *George Carver, Boy Scientist*. Indianapolis, Ind.: Bobbs-Merrill, 1959.

Stevenson, A. *Booker T. Washington, Ambitious Boy*. Indianapolis, Ind.: Bobbs-Merrill, 1960.

Williams, G. W. *History of the Negro Race in America*. New York: Bergman Publishers, 1968.

Yates, E. *Amos Fortune, Free Man*. New York: E. P. Dutton & Co., 1950.

FILMS

Booker T. Washington, color, Vignette Film. Order from Bailey Films, Inc., 6509 DeLongpre Ave., Hollywood, Calif. 90028.

Duke Thomas, Mailman, color or black and white. Primary and Intermediate. Dimension Film. Order from Churchill Films, 662 North Robertson Blvd., Hollywood, Calif. 90069.

George Washington Carver, black and white, Vignette Film. Order from Bailey Films, Inc., 6509 DeLongpre Ave., Hollywood, Calif. 90028.

Martin Luther King, Jr., a Man of Peace, black and white. Order from Journal Films, 909 West Diversey Parkway, Chicago, Ill. 60614.

Negro Heroes from American History, color. Order from Bailey Films, Inc., 6509 DeLongpre Ave., Hollywood, Calif. 90028.

Paul Laurence Dunbar: American Poet, color, Vignette Film. Order from Film Associates of California, 11559 Santa Monica Blvd., Los Angeles, Calif. 90025.

W. C. Handy, color, Vignette Film. Order from Bailey Films, Inc., 6509 DeLongpre Ave., Hollywood, Calif. 90028.

BIOGRAPHICAL AV

American Negro Pathfinders (Bethune, Marshall, Randolph, Bunche, King, Davis), 6 filmstrips. Film Associates of California, 11559 Santa Monica Blvd., Los Angeles, Calif. 90025.

Great Negro Americans (Bunche, Anderson, Bethune, Owens, Williams, Armstrong), LP album, teacher's guide. Alan Sands Productions, 565 Fifth Avenue, New York, N. Y. 10017.

Leading American Negroes (Bethune, Carver, Smalls, Douglass, Tubman, Banneker), filmstrip, color, sound on records. Society for Visual Education, Inc., 1345 Diversey Parkway, Chicago, Ill. 60614.

Negro Heroes from American History (Attucks, Du Sable, Beckwourth, Tubman, Smalls, Henson, Johnson, Miller), Super 8mm, International Communications Films, 1371 Reynolds Ave., Santa Ana, Calif. 92705.

The Quest for Freedom, 12 tapes, presenting Negroes in these categories: adventure, sports, abolition, military life, scientists, inventors, music, stage, screen, education, government, business. Tapes Unlimited, 13113 Puritan Ave., Detroit, Mich. 48227.

PART II. MATERIALS ON AMERICAN INDIANS

BOOKS

Bleeker, S. *The Seminole Indians.* New York: William Morrow & Company, 1954.

Brown, J. E. *The Sacred Pipe of the Oglala Sioux.* Norman, Okla.: University of Oklahoma Press, 1953.

Bureau of Indian Affairs. *Indians, Eskimos and Aleuts of Alaska.* Washington, D. C.: Superintendent of Documents, U. S. Government Printing Office, 1966. (This is one of a series and includes: *Indians of California, Indians of the Central Plains, Indians of the Dakotas, Indians of the Great Lakes, Indians of Montana-Wyoming, Indians of the Northwest,* and *Indians of Oklahoma.*)

Clark, A. N. *Little Navajo Bluebird.* New York: Viking Press, 1943.

Clark, E. E. *Indian Legends from the Northern Rockies.* Norman, Okla.: University of Oklahoma Press, 1966.

Cohoe, W. *A Cheyenne Sketchbook.* Norman, Okla.: University of Oklahoma Press, 1964.

Custer, E. B. *Following the Guidon.* Norman, Okla.: University of Oklahoma Press, 1966.

Douglas, M. S. *Freedom River.* New York: Charles Scribner's Sons, 1953.

Drucker, P. *Cultures of the North Pacific.* San Francisco: Chandler Publishing Company, 1965.

Grinnell, G. B. *Pawnee Hero Stories and Folk Tales.* Lincoln, Neb.: University of Nebraska Press, 1961.

Grinnell, G. B. *By Cheyenne Campfires*. New Haven, Conn.: Yale University Press, 1962.

Grinnell, G. B. *The Cheyenne Indians*. New York: Cooper Square Publishers, 1962.

Key, A. *Cherokee Boy*. Philadelphia: Westminster Press, 1964.

Kilpatrick, J. F. and A. G. Kilpatrick. *Friends of Thunder*. Dallas, Tex.: Southern Methodist University Press, 1964.

Kilpatrick, J. F. and A. G. Kilpatrick. *The Shadow of Sequoyah*. Norman, Okla.: University of Oklahoma Press, 1965.

Kilpatrick, J. F. and A. G. Kilpatrick. *Walk in Your Soul*. Dallas, Tex.: Southern Methodist University Press, 1965.

Kilpatrick, J. F. and A. G. Kilpatrick. *Run Toward the Nightland*. Dallas, Tex.: Southern Methodist University Press, 1967.

Klaussen, D. D. *Pueblo Indians*. Columbus, Ohio: Charles E. Merrill, 1952.

Lee, D. *Freedom and Culture*. Englewood Cliffs, N. J.: Prentice-Hall, Inc.: 1959.

Marriott, A. *Winter-Telling Stories*. New York: Thomas Y. Crowell Company, 1947.

Marriott, A. *Maria: The Potter of Ildefonso*. Norman, Okla.: University of Oklahoma Press, 1948.

Marriott, A. *Indians of the Four Corners*. New York: Thomas Y. Crowell Company, 1952.

Marriott, A. *Saynday's People*. Lincoln, Neb.: University of Nebraska Press, 1963.

Marriott, A. and C. K. Rachlin. *American Indian Mythology*. New York: Thomas Y. Crowell Company, 1968.

Mathews, J. J. *The Osages*. Norman, Okla.: University of Oklahoma Press, 1963.

Roediger, V. M. *Ceremonial Costumes of the Pueblo Indians*. Berkeley, Calif.: University of California Press, 1961.

Scheer, G. F. *Cherokee Animal Tales*. New York: Holiday House, 1968.

Shepard, B. *Mountain Man, Indian Chief*. New York: Harcourt, Brace & World, 1968.

Starr, S. and J. B. Wertz. *Pueblo Boy: An Indian Picture Book*. New York: David McKay Company, 1938.

Velarde, P. *Old Father, the Story Teller.* Globe, Ariz.: Dale Stuart King, 1960.

Vogt, E. Z. and E. M. Albert (eds.). *People of Rimrock.* Cambridge, Mass.: Harvard University Press, 1966.

Weltfish, G. *Lost Universe.* New York: Basic Books, 1965.

Wharton, V. *The Coming of Flame.* New York: Dell Publishing Company, 1963.

White, E. Q. *No Turning Back.* Albuquerque, N.M.: University of New Mexico Press, 1964.

PART III. MATERIALS ON MEXICAN-AMERICANS AND PUERTO RICANS

BOOKS

Baker, N. B. *Juarez, Hero of Mexico.* St. Louis, Mo.: Webster Publishing Company, 1949.

Barry, R. *The Musical Palm Tree.* New York: McGraw-Hill Book Company, 1965. (Puerto Rico).

Beiler, E. *Tres Casas, Tres Familias.* New York: Friendship Press, 1964. (Cuban, Puerto Rican, Mexican).

Bronson, W. S. *Pinto's Journey.* New York: Julian Messner, 1948. (Mexican).

Colorado, A. J. *The First Book of Puerto Rico.* New York: H. W. Wilson Co., 1965.

Colman, J. *The Girl from Puerto Rico.* New York: William Morrow & Company, 1961.

Edell, C. *A Present from Rosita.* New York: Julian Messner, 1960.

Heuman, W. *City High Five.* New York: Dodd, Mead & Company, 1964. (Puerto Rican).

Hull, E. *Moncho and the Duke.* New York: Friendship Press, 1964. (Puerto Rican)

Krumgold, J. *. . . . and Now Miguel.* New York: Thomas Y. Crowell Company, 1953. (Mexican)

Lewiton, M. *Candita's Choice.* New York: Harper & Row, 1959.

McFadden, D. L. *Growing Up in Puerto Rico.* Morristown, N. J.: Silver Burdett Company, 1958.

Morgan, C. M. *A New Home for Pablo.* New York: Abelard-Schuman, 1955. (Puerto Rican)

Mulcahy, L. *Pita.* New York: Coward-McCann, 1954. (Spanish-American)

Plenn, D. T. *The Green Song.* New York: David McKay Company, 1954. (Puerto Rican)

Plenn, D. T. *The Violet Tree.* New York: Farrar, Straus & Giroux, 1962.

Politi, L. *Pedro, the Angel of Olvera Street.* New York: Charles Scribner's Sons, 1946. (Mexican)

Politi, L. *Juanita.* New York: Charles Scribner's Sons, 1949. (Mexican)

Vavara, R. *Pizorro.* New York: Harcourt, Brace & World, 1968. (Mexican)

PART IV. MATERIALS ON MIXED AND OTHER DISADVANTAGED GROUPS

BOOKS

Adrian, M. *Refugee Hero.* New York: Hastings House, 1957.

Baez, J. *The Joan Baez Songbook,* arrangements and introduction by E. Liegmeister. New York: Ryerson Music Publishers, 1964.

Bikel, T. *Folksongs and Footnotes.* New York: World Publishing Company, 1960.

Carroll, R. and L. Carroll. *Tough Enough and Sassy.* New York: Henry Z. Walck and Company, 1958.

Cavanah, F. *We Came to America.* Philadelphia: McRae Smith Company, 1954.

Corbin, W. *High Road Home.* New York: Grossett & Dunlap, 1954.

Crane, F. *Gypsy Secret.* New York: Grossett & Dunlap, 1963.

Estes, E. *Two Hundred Dresses.* New York: Harcourt, Brace & World, 1944.

Forbes, K. *Mama's Bank Account.* New York: Harcourt, Brace & World, 1943.

Friedman, F. *The Janitor's Girl.* New York: Scholastic Book Services, 1964.

Gates, D. *Blue Willow.* New York: Scholastic Book Services, 1963.

Holland, J. (ed.). *The Way It Is.* New York: Harcourt, Brace & World, 1969.

Lee, M. *The Rock and the Willow.* New York: Lothrop, Lee and Shepard, 1963.

Lens, S. *Poverty: America's Enduring Paradox.* New York: Thomas Y. Crowell Company, 1969.

Lenski, L. *San Francisco Boy.* Philadelphia: J. B. Lippincott Company, 1955.

MacIntyre, E. *Ninji's Magic.* New York: Alfred A. Knopf, 1966.

McClosky, R. *Homer Price.* New York: Scholastic Book Services, 1962.

Reesink, M. *The Fisherman's Family.* New York: Harcourt, Brace and World, 1968.

Ritchie, J. *Folksongs of the Southern Appalachians as Sung by Jean Ritchie.* New York: Oak Publications, 1965.

Ruth, B. as told to Bob Considine. *The Babe Ruth Story.* New York: Scholastic Book Services, 1963.

Sandburg, C. *The American Songbook.* New York: Harcourt, Brace & World, 1942.

Seredy, K. *The Tenement Tree.* New York: Viking Press, 1959.

Smiley, M. B., D. Paterno, and B. Kaufman. *Who Am I?* New York: The Macmillan Company, 1966.

Smiley, M. B., R. Corbin, and J. J. Marcatante. *Stories in Song and Verse.* New York: The Macmillan Company, 1966.

Smiley, M. B., F. B. Freedman, J. Tilles, and J. J. Marcatante. *Coping.* New York: The Macmillan Company, 1966.

Smiley, M. B., F. B. Freedman, and J. J. Marcatante. *A Family Is a Way of Feeling.* New York: The Macmillan Company, 1966.

Smith, G. H. *Bayou Boy.* Chicago: Follett Publishing Company, 1965.

Speigler, C. G. *Courage Under Fire and Against the Odds.* Columbus, Ohio: Charles E. Merrill, 1967.

Steichen, E. *The Family of Man.* New York: Museum of Modern Art, 1955.

Sterling, D. *Tender Warriors.* New York: Hill and Wang, 1962.

Vogel, R. *The Other City.* New York: David White Company, 1969.

CHAPTER 13

BECOMING
A BETTER,
MORE CREATIVE TEACHER

Challenge—
Daily delight
Rising to occasions
Demanding a sensitive touch
Pupils.

The Problem

Miss Barr was in her first year of teaching and was undergoing painful conflict about her teaching. Her father, now retired, had been an elementary school principal in a small town for twenty-three years. Before that, he had taught fourth, fifth, sixth, seventh, and eighth grades—at first simultaneously. He had also driven the school bus and served as an unpaid coach at the high school. His influence upon his daughter toward school and children had been strong. Miss Barr believed that children should have opportunities to explore and to experiment, to make honest mistakes, and in so doing to discover and develop their potentialitites. These had been her father's ways of teaching.

Now in her third month of teaching, Miss Barr was not sure that her father's ways were right for her. Her second-grade classroom apparently was conducted too loosely as far as the other primary teachers on her wing of the newly-constructed school building were concerned. The children were not as orderly as they should be. Her classroom was not as tidy as were the rooms of her associates. No one criticized Miss Barr to her face, but she was given numerous tips by the old hands about how to maintain control of her class and how to decorate her room. Mr. Muir, the principal, remained in the background. He was cordial but almost disinterested. Miss Barr did not know whether he was simply letting her find herself as a teacher or ignoring her. She wanted him to observe her teaching and then to comment upon the learning environment, but she was afraid to approach him and frightened of the possibility of his negative evaluation.

By the time Christmas vacation had ended, Miss Barr had made up her mind. She would make a genuine effort to conform to the standards of the other primary teachers. Even though she was sure that her pupils were acquiring skills and information as rapidly and as thoroughly as the children in the other two second-grade classrooms, she decided to reduce their freedom of movement and restrict the amount of conversation in the room. Within two weeks, Miss Barr had succeeded in each of her new goals. Her class-room was not as noisy as it had been, and she felt that the other teachers were more approving of her.

Still, Miss Barr felt uneasy. She was not at all certain that she was doing the right thing. The atmosphere was far more austere than she liked to have it. Learning did not seem to be the joyous thing that it had been earlier. On the other hand, the children, after expressing surprise and disappointment, were adjusting to less autonomy and more admonitions. In spite of the rise of her stock in the faculty exchange, Miss Barr wondered if she had let both herself and her father down.

Should Miss Barr model herself after her father? Should she model her teaching behavior according to the expectations of the other teachers in her building? How can she invent her own way of teaching, a way of teaching that is uniquely suited to her strongest assets as a person and as a teacher?

One's Way of Teaching, a Unique Invention

Miss Barr's problem is every teacher's problem—inventing his way of teaching. It is an invention that is never finished. It is al-ways in process. The real problem is one of becoming a "better, more creative teacher." You will note that we did not entitle this chapter "Becoming an Ideal Teacher" or "Becoming a Great Teacher." The emphasis on "becoming a better, more creative teacher" is likely to be more satisfying, more realistic, and more constructive than striving to be an "ideal" teacher or even a "great" teacher.

In Chapter 5, we described the process by which a teacher can invent that way of teaching which is best suited to him and his teaching goals, as well as to his pupils and their learning needs and goals. We hope that by now you understand this invention process better than you did when you read Chapter 5 and that you are al-ready mastering the skills necessary to facilitate the successful opera-tion of the process.

Like Miss Barr, you might want to consider various models of ideal or great teachers. Miss Barr's first model was her father, but she was disappointed when she discovered that she did not possess the skill and artistry that had taken her father many years to achieve. Then she found unsatisfying and unworthy the models provided by her fellow teachers. It is quite useful to consider the models provided by the most outstanding teachers one has known. However, these models may not fit. And, furthermore, it takes practice, imagination, and plain hard work to acquire the abilities and skills possessed by these teachers. It is useful to read the accounts of great teachers such as those collected by Peterson (1946) and Ernst (1967). Such models are excellent sources of ideas for one's own unique invention if you keep in mind that no one else's model is likely to fit you exactly.

"Ideal" Teacher Checklist

In spite of the foregoing remarks and the position taken in Chapter 5, we readily concede that there are undoubtedly certain characteristics common to all really effective teachers. Moreover, we feel that if these characteristics could be identified, they would provide useful guides in the process of becoming a better, more creative teacher.

In order to obtain some clues about the personality variables that have enabled men and women to become recognized as outstanding teachers, we conducted an informal analysis of two dozen teachers who were acclaimed by fellow teachers, pupils, administrators, and parents as "master" teachers. By studying the responses of these teachers to several questions about their work with young people, we were able to identify a score of characteristics that these outstanding teachers seemed to have in common and which probably contributed to their effectiveness in the classroom. With the addition of some items that reflected our own biases and of several traits that are commonly regarded in the literature and folklore of American education as being critical to teaching effectiveness, a checklist of 66 predicates was compiled. Although many such lists have been compiled in the past sixty years, no attempt was made to make this checklist a combination of them. The Ideal Teacher Checklist is simply a collection of predicates concerning the personal qualities of teachers and their functions in the classroom.

Of the several groups of teachers, administrators, supervisors, and pupils who have responded to the checklist, only four will be considered here: 463 pupils in the fourth, fifth, sixth, seventh, and eighth grades of a Midwestern suburb; 72 pupils in the fourth, fifth, and sixth grades of a West Coast logging community; 105 pupils in a rapidly growing Northwestern town; and 73 students in a Western university whose enrollment at the time the checklist was completed was about 10,000. The respondents provided information regarding their school, sex, age, and grade but did not reveal their identities. They were asked to check and double-check the characteristics they would expect to find in an "ideal" teacher and to cross out those characteristics which they would never expect to find in such a teacher.

A score was obtained for each characteristic by awarding two points for each double check (strongly characteristic or highly essential to the ideal teacher), one point for single checks (highly desirable characteristics of such a teacher), and minus one for each crossout (undesirable characteristics). In each group of respondents, the points were added for each characteristic and then the characteristics were ranked from most to least desirable. The following results were obtained:

IDEAL TEACHER CHECKLIST RESULTS

	Ranks of Characteristics			
Characteristic	*Grades 4–6 N=72*	*Grades 4–8 N=463*	*Grades 10 & 12 N=105*	*University N=73*
Administers punishment fairly	1	3	9	17
Is affectionate	44	54	61	58
Avoids controversy in class	59	49	62.5	63
Is broad-minded	35	39	10	24
Is careful not to make mistakes	28	37	42	49
Causes me to be curious	45	28	20	4
Is cheerful	4	6.5	22	30

Characteristic	Grades 4–6	Grades 4–8	Grades 10 & 12	University
Is confident of his abilities	46	36	23	27
Is critical of my mistakes	65.5	57	53	64
Doesn't stand for any foolishness in class	32.5	42	50	54.5
Doesn't talk too much	56	56	56	41
Dresses neatly	5.5	18.5	25	32
Is eager to help when I need it	2.5	1	8	13.5
Is easy to talk with	16.5	10.5	14.5	17
Encourages me to think	23	21	2	1
Is energetic	20.5	30	35	33
Enjoys life and is full of fun	31	20	30	34.5
Enjoys being with young people	2.5	4	7	6
Is excited about learning	25.5	38	32.5	8
Expresses himself clearly	8	12	4	23
Is exuberant (often enthusiastic)	43	45	38.5	37
Is firm	32.5	32	27	30
Is forward-looking	42	29	38.5	39
Frequently reveals his emotions	61	64	64	65
Is generous with praise	40.5	44	54	44
Gives everyone a chance to express himself	19	14	11.5	7
Has a good sense of humor	5.5	16	14.5	15
Has no favorites	38.5	26	26	36
Insists upon a quiet classroom	35	46	60	57
Is intellectually brilliant	52	51	47	53

IDEAL TEACHER CHECKLIST RESULTS (*continued*)

Characteristic	Grades 4–6	Grades 4–8	Grades 10 & 12	University
Knows the subjects he teaches	14.5	9	1	2
Is keenly aware of what is happening in the classroom	27	31	36	17
Is entertaining	50	50	43	51
Trusts his students	14.5	2	11.5	20.5
Is generally serious	40.5	41	49	49
Likes to tell jokes	48.5	43	41	56
Has a lively imagination	22	25	37	38
Maintains a proper distance from his students	47	58	45	43
Makes interesting assignments	18	6.5	16	20.5
Makes me work hard	48.5	52	40	34.5
Has many interests	25.5	24	32.5	25.5
Is mild-mannered	37	40	44	42
Only praises if something is really outstanding	63.5	62	48	59
Is open-minded	35	27	5	11
Is opinionated	63.5	61	62	62
Respects my ideas	29	17	13	11
Is self-centered	65.5	66	66	66
Is strict	58	63	59	54.5
Has strong convictions	55	47	52	46.5
Is tactful and considerate	20.5	23	21	13.5
Is talkative	62	60	55	60
Is tolerant	38.5	34	31	30
Thinks all of his pupils are important individuals	7	13	3	3
Takes pride in the accomplishments of his pupils	12.5	18.5	18	20.5

Characteristic	Grades 4–6	Grades 4–8	Grades 10 & 12	University
Has traveled extensively	53.5	59	51	45
Tries to understand the behavior of his students	9	22	29	5
Usually can make difficult points clear	10.5	5	28	9
Is well-read	24	35	24	28
Has a warm, friendly personality	16.5	10.5	19	25.5
Will fight for the rights of his students	30	33	34	40
Never gets upset or becomes angry	57	53	58	52
Never changes his mind	60	65	65	61
Will admit his mistakes	12.5	15	6	11
Never raises his voice or shouts	53.5	55	57	46.5
Is patient	10.5	8	17	20.5
Is physically attractive	51	48	46	49

ONE PICTURE OF THE IDEAL TEACHER

There was striking agreement among the respondents with regard to some of the items of the checklist. These items might be noted particularly because it would be expected that pupils' perceptions of school change with age and experience; and, in general, the data support this assumption. However, the elementary pupils, the high school pupils, and the university students seemed to agree on almost half of the items. Here, in order of their importance to the respondents, are the characteristics upon which there was most agreement:

VERY IMPORTANT

Enjoys being with young people
Thinks all his pupils are important individuals
Is eager to help when I need it
Will admit his mistakes
Trusts his pupils

QUITE IMPORTANT

Has a good sense of humor
Is patient
Is easy to talk with
Takes pride in the accomplishments of his pupils
Has a warm, friendly personality
Is tactful and considerate
Expresses himself clearly
Has many interests

FAIRLY IMPORTANT

Is firm
Is tolerant
Will fight for the rights of his students

NOT VERY IMPORTANT

Is exuberant (often enthusiastic)
Is mild-mannered
Is generally serious
Is physically attractive
Is entertaining
Is intellectually brilliant
Has strong convictions
Doesn't talk too much
Never raises his voice or shouts

REJECTED

Never gets upset or becomes angry
Is strict
Is talkative
Is opinionated
Frequently reveals his emotions
Never changes his mind
Is self-centered

TEACHERS SHOULD CARE ABOUT THEIR PUPILS

Even though the list of thirty-two items above does not provide a complete picture of the way the respondents saw their "ideal" teacher, you can obtain a good idea of what was sought and what was rejected. If these data can be regarded as indicative of the way young people perceive teachers, the respondents in this study might have a few suggestions about the way would-be teachers should be selected and trained. For instance, it was not at all important to the respondents that their teachers be highly intelligent; nor was it important that they be good looking (although it was important that the teachers dress neatly). On the other hand, it was very important that teachers be interested in young people and help them to acquire information and skills. The respondents expressed a desire to obtain from their teachers assistance and guidance—even at the college level.

TEACHERS SHOULD BE HONEST

One of the biggest surprises to us was the great importance placed by the respondents upon honesty, as expressed in their reaction to the item "Will admit his mistakes." It is near the top of the list of most-agreed-upon characteristics. In spite of the co-experiencing or co-learning which has become more and more evident during the last decade or so, pupils apparently still see teachers as bluffing and covering up their lack of knowledge. If indeed teachers are still trying to pose as infallible experts, their attempts might be the result of their seeing themselves primarily as repositories and dispensers of information. But it is unlikely that young people want encyclopedists as their teachers. In reacting to the checklist, the respondents showed unmistakably that they did not look for intellectual brilliance in their teachers, nor were they concerned very much about their teachers' accuracy.

TEACHERS DO NOT HAVE TO BE STRICT

The respondents shattered another belief which is prevalent not only among teachers but among pupils as well, namely, that the best teacher is the one who "runs a tight ship." Of the 66 characteristics, "Is strict" was one of the most consistently rejected, ranking 58 and 63 with the elementary groups, 59 with the high school pupils, and 54.5 with the university students. Moreover, "Is firm" did not rank particularly high with any of the groups. We often hear that pupils really have a greater regard for teachers whose disciplinary methods might be termed "tough," but there was no indication from the way the respondents reacted to either "Is firm" or "Is strict" that toughness is respected and permissiveness scorned. "Insists upon a quiet classroom" ranked 35 and 46 for the elementary groups, 60 for the high school pupils, and 57 for the university students; so it is doubtful that the teacher who manages to keep his pupils quiet most of the time is the person the respondents had in mind when they thought about an ideal teacher. Since "Is strict" was ranked so low by all of the groups, our hunch is that it is likely that the respondents found punitive connotations in that predicate.

TEACHERS SHOULD TRUST THEIR PUPILS

It may surprise some readers to discover that children want teachers who trust them. At least the respondents to the checklist leave no doubt about this point. The larger elementary group (grades four through eight) ranked "Trusts his students" second; and, while the other groups did not stress this quality so much, it is clear that it was important to them also. Again, we can only conjecture about the significance of the data. It may well be that pupils realize that adults must have confidence in their ability to act responsibly before the young people can grow emotionally, intellectually, and spiritually. Perhaps the trust which they need is not being offered to them.

Trends by Educational Level

When viewed according to age or educational level, the data presented in this chapter reveal many interesting trends. As might be expected, the responses of the younger pupils indicate that they are more accepting of affection from their teachers and older ones are more rejecting. With maturity, intellectual stimulation becomes more important. Increasingly greater value is placed on the teacher who causes one to think, is excited about learning, encourages thinking, and respects one's ideas. With maturity, physical appearance, orderliness, and accuracy become less important.

Study the data concerning the rankings by each of the groups for the particular educational level with which you are most intimately concerned.

What do you think children at this educational level are trying to say about teachers and schools? In order to meet the expectations of children at this educational level, what kinds of changes would you have to make in your own personality? If you changed in these directions, what effect do you think it would have on your teaching?

THE IDEAL TEACHER

As a group, the respondents saw the ideal teacher essentially as one who values, is concerned about, and helps young people. He is an honest, trusting person who is at ease with them and makes them feel comfortable in his presence. Above all, he is human, a person who makes mistakes and even loses his temper occasionally. He cares about his pupils—each of them is a person worthy of respect. Finally, he provides his pupils with opportunities that enable them to grow. Philosophers and psychologists would probably call the ideal teacher described here a good humanist.

It should be clear by this time that the ideal teacher, in our opinion, is a creative teacher. His own behavior is creative, but even more important, he encourages and facilitates creative development and functioning among his pupils. He is the good humanist described by the respondents in the study sketched above and has to be in order to maintain the kind of relationship that is essential to creative learning and teaching. In the closing section of this final chapter, we will attempt to summarize what we see as the general requirements and orientation for creative learning and teaching, the nature of the creative teacher-pupil relationship, and preparation for this kind of teaching and relationship with children.

GENERAL REQUIREMENTS AND ORIENTATION FOR CREATIVE TEACHING

In creative learning and teaching, a teacher cannot draw his security from following traditional rules, strict schedules, tested and practiced methods, or standard methods of assessment. He must be able to feel security in his pupils' excitement about learning and their progress in becoming human. Successful work in understanding, motivating, and encouraging children in the process of learning creatively requires radical departures from the usual stimulus-response psychology in the direction of the creative or responsive environment. The currently popular methods of behavior modification and shaping will not produce these results.

What we have in mind is far from a directionless kind of guidance. The creation of a responsive environment, as already indicated, actually requires the most alert and sensitive kind of guidance and direction possible. It requires intent listening and responding to what the child is trying to communicate. The creative teacher must be oriented to a psychology of "constructive behavior" rather than to a psychology of adjustment. He must be oriented to potentialities as well as probabilities. He must be able to imagine himself into the thinking and feeling of the child so that he can respond accurately in terms of the child's motivations, abilities, and interests.

In addition to essential information about one's own personality and intellectual functioning, and about personality and intellectual development generally, the above requirements involve such characteristics and skills as psychological openness, aliveness, sensitivity, spontaneity, sense of security, trust in one's own perception of reality, an intuitive and experimental orientation, ability to resist social pressures, tolerance of complexity, ability to grasp new relationships, and tolerance of uncertainty and incompleteness of information.

The Creative Teacher-Pupil Relationship

Moustakas (1959), who has used the concept "creative relationship," sees the creative relationship as essential in growth-facilitating relationships such as teaching and psychotherapy. The creative relationship requires a willingness to embark over untraveled ways. As in creative thinking itself, the teacher must be willing to permit one thing to lead to another, to be ready to get off the beaten track or to break out of the mold, and to relate to the child as a person.

At a very basic level, this relationship is different from most teaching relationships heretofore described. Most current conceptualizations of this relationship are essentially stimulus-response in nature—that is, the teacher stimulates a particular child or group of children, and the child or group of children responds to this stimulus. In almost all of the stimulus-response conceptualizations of teaching, emphasis is on the correctness of the stimulus and the response (method and technique). The creative teacher-pupil relationship involves a co-experiencing, and errors or mistakes in it are virtually irrelevant. It is a matter of *being* rather than one of acting and being acted upon. The child's creative-thinking processes continue uninhibited because the relationship is an open, nonthreatening, creative one.

The relationship that Hughes Mearns (1958) described with his students in creative writing comes close to what we have in mind and have called the creative-teaching relationship. Mearns found that after this relationship had "happened," it did not matter that he criticized the student's writing. Before this, however, criticism tended to be dangerous. Apparently the creative relationship occurs in much the same way that creative thinking occurs. No matter how much one strains to think of a new idea or how badly he may want to think of one, he may not succeed at all. Then it seems to "just happen." It occurs through the operation of the preconscious on the information, relationships, associations, and the like that had accumulated during the period of conscious striving. It requires an openness to experience and a willingness to participate in the relationship once it occurs.

Preparation for the Creative Relationship

A person in a teacher-education program may learn a great deal about teaching techniques, curricular materials, personality development, tests and measurement, statistics and research design group dynamics, learning theory, and teaching strategies. A teacher in training may even learn a great deal about the creative process, the problems of the creative person, the identification of creative potentialities, and the conditions that facilitate creative development and functioning. All of these together though will not be enough. One has to become the kind of person who can be comfortable in a creative relationship and his ways of teaching must be his own invention.

Although "the unique invention" of the teacher is never fully completed, its basic elements at least can be found in teacher preparation programs. As the teacher in preparation fails or succeeds, he will become aware of his deficiencies, defects in techniques, and gaps in knowledge. Out of the tension that this will produce, the teacher will draw upon his past experiences, reach out for new information, and intensify the search for clues in ongoing experiences. He must then apply creatively the scientifically developed techniques and procedures learned in professional courses and seminars or through reading. Then he reads, studies, and puzzles some more. He now sees things of which he had hitherto been unaware. He formulates hypotheses for improving effectiveness and tests and modifies these hypotheses. In turn, he modifies his behavior and tests its effectiveness. Through the pain and ecstasy that accompany this process, the teacher's personal invention—his way of teaching—occurs.

A Proposed Scheme of Teacher Preparation

Numerous books have described creative teaching (Miel, 1961; Smith, 1966; Shumsky, 1965; Gowan, Demos and Torrance, 1967; Michael, 1968), but little attention has been given to the kind of teacher-education program necessary to develop the insights, abilities, and skills to become a creative learner and teacher. The emphasis has been on doing rather than on becoming. In creative learning and teaching, what a teacher *is* is perhaps far more important than what he *does*. In fact, this seems to be confirmed by the responses to the Ideal Teacher Checklist reported earlier in this chapter.

A pioneering and promising approach to the problem of helping teachers in training become creative teachers emerges in *Identity and Teacher Learning,* an unusual little book by Robert C. Burkhart and Hugh M. Neil (1968). Burkhart and Neil assume the position that the human learner is self-acting and creative, requiring guidance and direction, but not dictation and coercion. They describe a teacher-learning process that recognizes the self-acting and creative nature of the teacher-learner and involves increasing self-awareness and identity as well as co-experiencing with another teacher-learner. Burkhart and Neil, artists themselves, see learning to be a teacher as being like learning an art. They see it as requiring depth of experience for self-reflective understanding and continued development, deep personal involvement, and a series of tangible products through which the teacher-learner can review and see, over time, the pattern of his development and the nature of his individuality. They approach the essence of their method of teacher learning when they write that "teaching begins when we let go of answers and get started with the questions."

We will now suggest what we regard as some of the essential elements of a teacher-preparation program to increase the chances that those who experience the program will become the kind of teachers described in this chapter. The proposed preparation program is not presented in terms of courses, seminars, and internships, though it may take place within such a framework. Rather, it is presented in terms of the kinds of experiences necessary to activate and guide development in the three levels of consciousness involved in the creative process: (1) the conscious, logical level; (2) the preconscious or prelogical level; and (3) the subconscious, emotional, irrational level. It is our thesis that these three levels of consciousness are also involved importantly in creative teaching and learning.

During the creative-thinking process, the thinker is continually drawing from his memory bank and evaluating information through logical processes. The creative leap rarely, if ever, takes place through logical processes. Thus, teacher-education programs must consider each of these three levels of consciousness. Although it may be some time before conceptualizations and methodologies can be perfected for implementing such programs fully, enough progress has been made to permit at least some tentative conceptualizations. This is especially true in the realms of preconscious and subconscious levels. Sensitivity training and T-Group methodology (Bradford, Gibb, and Benne, 1964; Schein and Bennis, 1965); the techniques of the Esalen Institute (Schutz, 1967); the contributions of Burkhart and Neil already mentioned; the work of Moreno (1946), W. J. J. Gordon (1961), and others provide a pool of partially tested ideas from which educators can draw. Humanistic psychologists are now giving serious consideration to the development and testing of educational methodologies that involve all three levels of consciousness.

The 1968 program of the American Association for Humanistic Psychology gave attention to lectures, research papers, and laboratory-type demonstrations on such topics as the Think-Feel Polarity and the Organizational Gap, Microlab Encounter, Zero Distance or Interpersonal Yoga, Techniques of Emotional Release, Becoming More Alive Through Play, the Synanon Approach, Honest Communication Between Races, Psychodrama, Breathing in Relation to Awareness, An Experience in Movement, Boundaries of Behavior, Violent Expressions, The Eye and Ear of the Here and Now, The Emergent Group, The TORI (Trust, Openness, Realization and Interdependence) Experiences, Sensory Awakening, Gestalt Therapy, The Creative Behavior Process, Unconventional Phantasies and Experiences, Peak Joy Method, Deeper Dimensions of Encounter Groups, Self-Actualization Workshop, Auto-Suggestive Techniques for Developing Human Potentials, Sentiency Workshop, and the like. All of these programs dealt in some way with educational methodologies for aiding people in using more fully their potentialities at all three levels of consciousness. It may be that none of these methodologies can be applied at the present time in teacher education programs. They provide a source of ideas, however, and help conceptualize the kind of program that is required.

Schutz (1963, 1967) has attempted to conceptualize each of the three levels of consciousness involved in the creative process in terms of acquisition, association, evaluation, and expression. We will use this conceptualization in sketching our proposed teacher education program.

The Conscious, Logical Level

Most existing educational methods are concerned almost entirely with conscious, logical levels of knowing, and the present formulation adds little that is new in teacher education at this level.

Procedures for *acquisition* would include the usual methods of gaining information and experience. There might be added to the content of most existing programs more complete information on mental, emotional, and spiritual functioning in general; the nature of human intelligence and its growth; the creative processes, the creative-thinking abilities, and methods of assessing creative functioning and achievement; the group dynamics involved in freeing the creative thinking abilities to develop and function; the psychology of stress and its relationship to creative functioning; and the dynamics of constructive behavior in contrast to adaptation and adjustment. The teacher's acquisition of information at the conscious, logical level should enable him to become more aware of a child's creative potentialities, his motivations, and the forces that inhibit his potentialities or free them to develop and function at a high level.

Associative elements at the conscious, logical level are involved in seeing the new combinations or reorganizations of information that produce solutions. In creativity training, a variety of procedures have been developed for the deliberate logical generation of new combinations of information in the search for problem solutions. These procedures are referred to under a variety of labels, including "morphological creativity," "attribute listing," "question checklists," and the like (Parnes, 1962). In all of these procedures, ideas and combinations of elements are generated in a logical fashion and used to trigger original ideas.

Procedures for the *evaluation* of information and new combinations of elements designed to solve problems are usually fairly well represented in teacher-education programs, though resisted strongly by many students, usually as a consequence of interfering emotional blocks. The techniques of critical thinking and the methods of research, experimentation, and statistics are used to subject ideas to rigorous tests to avoid deception.

In *expression* at the conscious level, teacher-education programs have rather generally tended to lag in the development of laboratory experiences prior to the culminating student-teacher experiences. Under our proposal there would be a great variety of experiences prior to student teaching that would involve training in interviewing, communicating test results, writing case reports, and the like. Considerable attention would also be given to the development of skills in working with groups of varying size and in guiding creative problem-solving efforts.

The Preconscious, Prelogical Level

Kubie (1958), Tauber and Green (1959), and others have presented weighty anecdotal evidence that creativity occurs largely at a preconscious, prelogical level. There is reason to suspect that the skills called for in learning and teaching creatively rely quite heavily upon these preconscious processes.

It has been assumed generally that these processes are dependent upon chance.[1] Recent work, however, has introduced the exciting possibility of devising educational procedures for bringing the processes into awareness so that people can be trained deliberately to use them. (Some of the more widely used of these have been described and discussed in Chapter 4.) Before beginning teacher training, under our proposal, many candidates would have experienced the awakening effects of various kinds of T-groups and sensitivity training, sociodrama, and the like. Feelings and intuitions would be relied upon as a way of knowing or acquiring certain kinds of knowledge, especially interpersonal cognitions used as a basis for predicting behavior. Some of these procedures provide ways of getting at knowledge that people are not fully aware that they possess. This is perhaps what is involved when students are advised to guess on examinations (if they have studied). It must also have been involved in the experiences of air crewmen, whom Torrance interviewed in survival training, who said that they saved their lives because they recalled in emergencies information that they did not know that they possessed. The answer on the examination and the response in the emergency situation were apparently based on some information, not quite conscious, but expressing itself from a visceral state. If the information were conscious, it could be verbalized, and the reason for its selection could be stated. If a person can be sensitized to visceral states, he can apparently make use of knowledge that cannot be verbalized.

The use of free associations, role playing and sociodrama, analogies, and projective procedures are known fairly well by today's teachers at a conscious level, but apparently few of them make use

of such procedures in an active way that would involve the preconscious processes. The use of provocative questions rather than factual
ones as described in Chapter 9 is another rarely used procedure
that frequently involves the preconscious. The well-known "why"
question is also effective in involving the preconscious. The use of
analogy and other deliberate ways of associating one part of a person's experience to another is illustrated by the Synectics approach
(Gordon, 1961). It also seems possible to train a person to learn
what his own modes of associating at the preconscious level are and
to capitalize upon them.

Evaluative processes also seem to operate at the preconscious
level and are manifested in bodily states. Some things "feel" right or
wrong for no reason that can be brought readily to the conscious
level. Teacher-education programs should provide opportunities for
developing confidence in one's bodily states, at least to the extent of
being willing to test them rather than automatically accepting the
evaluations of others that are contrary to what the teacher "feels" is
right or wrong.

Although this idea may seem somewhat radical, experiences in
elementary and secondary education would suggest the possibility of
artistic or symbolic expression as ways of becoming aware of preconscious attitudes, motivations, and other information. The use of
semantic differentials in evaluating experiences, color-word association tests, and similar procedures approach what we have in mind.
More directly illustrative are Torrance's experiences with pre-primary school children in getting them to express their feelings and
ideas and their reactions to people and objects, with sounds, movements, and pictures.

The Subconscious, Irrational Level

In the Synectics approach to the facilitation of creative functioning, Gordon (1961) and his associates maintain that in getting
ideas the emotional and irrational components of the personality
are more important than the intellectual and rational aspects. In
teacher preparation, concern at this level should perhaps be with removal of emotional blocks. In the area of *acquisition,* the concern
would be with the recognition and removal of learning blocks, sen-

sory distortions, and feeling aberrations (Schutz, 1963). In the area of *association*, focus would be on the removal of fear and anxiety, unconscious compulsions, and the like. In the sphere of *evaluation*, the concern would be with insecurity, fear of disappointing others, and of not measuring up to expectations. In the *expression* area, emphasis would be on the removal of unconscious tendencies to ridicule, embarrass, coerce, and control.

In counselor-education programs and in the training of others whose professional work involves preconscious and subconscious processes, personal therapy is regarded by many as essential. Generally, however, the mention of psychotherapy or personal counseling in teacher education has been regarded as highly threatening and unacceptable because of its association with unfitness. There is a need, of course, to change this conception to one of psychotherapy and personal counseling as growth experiences.

Schutz (1963) identifies three types of problems in removing emotional blocks that reduce effectiveness: (1) overcoming the fear of exploring and using the unconscious, (2) learning how the unconscious works, and (3) feeling free to use it. The educational methods to deal with these problems should allow a person to select his own medium of expression, should afford him more knowledge of the reality of how other people feel about the same issues and about how they react to his performance, and should counteract original parental discouragement of creative expressive behavior by acceptance and reward. A variety of approaches to what is commonly known as "sensitivity training" may possibly offer methods that can be used in teacher-education programs. In one of the procedures described by Schutz, participants in a group experience are required to produce something creative. It does not matter what, but it has to be unusual and satisfying or effective. Participants are also required to keep a daily log of any experiences they have that are relevant to the class or group activity.

Conclusion

The foregoing suggestions for examining the basic nature of creative learning and teaching in a teacher-education program are offered only as a first tentative attempt to conceptualize the problem. Some of the teacher roles proposed will not be acceptable to many teachers and teacher educators. Many teacher educators do not possess the knowledge and/or skills needed for using successfully the procedures proposed in this chapter. There is also a lack of appropriate curricular materials for implementing these procedures. It is to be hoped that there will at least be an openness to search for constructive responses to the challenge.

Making Your Own Summary

Miss Parsons thought that she was one of the luckiest students in her college class. She had been assigned to Mrs. Berry's fourth-grade classroom for her final student teaching experience. Mrs. Berry was known as a masterful teacher, one whose poise, ingenuity, and understanding marked her as an outstanding member of her profession. It was especially comforting to Miss Parsons to learn, after her preliminary visit to her new school, that Mrs. Berry was eager to help young teachers. She offered the younger woman professional magazines and books at the conclusion of their very first meeting, and Miss Parsons was pleased to note that the materials were both inspiring and practical. The principal had also remarked about her good fortune when he walked her to the front door of the school that day. Miss Parsons was sure, as was everyone she talked to, that the experience in Mrs. Berry's classroom would be the very best kind of preparation for the time when she would have her own class.

At the end of the first day of observing the activities of the class and helping out at recesses, Miss Parsons was dazzled by Mrs. Berry's virtuosity. She was in command of the class at all times without seeming to order the children around. She was sensitive to problems which arose and quick to step out of the picture when her presence would not help a pupil or a group of pupils learn. Mrs. Berry's instructional program was exciting without being overpowering. By Friday Miss Parsons felt that she was beginning to learn how Mrs. Berry handled the class, and she was grateful for the time her mentor allotted each afternoon and morning to explaining patiently the short-range and the long-range plans for the children. Mrs. Berry encouraged Miss Parsons to contribute her ideas to the planning, and Miss Parsons was flattered that one or two of her ideas were incorporated in the plans for the next week.

Unfortunately, her ideas did not turn out to be very effective; and, even though Mrs. Berry reassured her by saying no one can ever be certain that a group of youngsters will take to any material or activity, Miss Parsons was depressed by the thought that had the children just gone ahead with Mrs. Berry's plans, the math and spelling lessons would have been more effective. By the end of her second week with Mrs. Berry, Miss Parsons was becoming discouraged. She had consciously patterned herself after Mrs. Berry, adopting little techniques such as modulating her voice to capture the attention of the class and challenging individual pupils to go to the classroom and school libraries to check up on their own generalizations and the statements of others. The results of her actions were never up to her expectations, however. And they were almost pitiful in comparison with the results Mrs. Berry obtained regularly.

Miss Parsons became reluctant to assume more of the teaching responsibilities that Mrs. Berry gently urged upon her. She was bewildered. More importantly, she feared that she did not have the "stuff" to be a good teacher. For all of her sensitivity to fourth-graders, Mrs. Berry did not seem fully aware of the tribulations of her student teacher and began to become impatient with her excuses about not being ready to handle the more important parts of the instructional program. Very swiftly, an impasse between the seasoned professional and the neophyte developed, and it seemed that Miss Parsons might never have that classroom of her own. She was not sure that she wanted it.

Was Miss Parsons really fortunate in having Mrs. Berry as her cooperating teacher? What advice would you give to Miss Parsons? If you were the principal of the school, what advice would you give to Mrs. Berry? Should we place student teachers in the classroom of outstanding teachers so that they will have excellent models of teaching to refer to consciously and unconsciously when they have their own classrooms?

What experiences do you think would be most useful to Miss Parsons in achieving the invention of her own way of teaching and in becoming the kind of person she must become in order to implement her invention?

REFERENCES

Bradford, L. P., J. R. Gibb, and K. D. Benne (eds.). *T-Group Theory and Laboratory Method.* New York: John Wiley & Sons, 1964.

Burkhart, R. C. and H. M. Neil. *Identity and Teacher Learning.* Scranton, Pa.: International Textbook Company, 1968.

Ernst, M. (ed.). *The Teacher,* Englewood Cliffs, N.J.: Prentice-Hall, Inc., 1967.

Gordon, W. J. J. *Synectics.* New York: Harper & Row, 1961.

Gowan, J. C., G. D. Demos, and E. P. Torrance (eds.). *Creativity: Its Educational Implications.* New York: John Wiley & Sons, 1967.

Kubie, L. S. *Neurotic Distortion of the Creative Process.* Lawrence, Kans.: University of Kansas Press, 1958.

Mearns, H. *Creative Power.* New York: Dover Publications, 1958.

Michael, W. B. (ed.). *Teaching for Creative Endeavor.* Bloomington, Ind.: University of Indiana Press, 1968.

Miel, A. (ed.). *Creativity in Teaching.* Belmont, Calif.: Wadsworth Publishing Company, 1961.

Moreno, J. L. *Psychodrama: Vol. I.* New York: Beacon House, 1946.

Moustakas, C. R. *Psychotherapy with Children.* New York: Harper & Row, 1959.

Parnes, S. J. and H. F. Harding (eds.). *A Sourcebook for Creative Thinking.* New York: Charles Scribner's Sons, 1962.

Peterson, H. *Great Teachers.* New York: Vintage Books, 1946.

Schein, E. H. and W. G. Bennis. *Personal and Organizational Change through Group Methods: The Laboratory Approach.* New York: John Wiley & Sons, 1965.

Schutz, W. C. "Creative Behavior: Training and Theory Development." Berkeley: University of California, 1963. Mimeographed.

Schutz, W. C. *Joy: Expanding Human Awareness.* New York: Grove Press, 1967.

Shumsky, A. *Creative Teaching in the Elementary School.* New York: Appleton-Century-Crofts, 1965.

Smith, J. A. *Setting Conditions for Creative Teaching in the Elementary School.* Boston: Allyn and Bacon, 1966.

Tauber, E. and M. R. Green. *Prelogical Experience.* New York: Basic Books, 1959.

Ended?
I hope never,
This urge to grow better
At sensing what is right for each
Youngster!

APPENDIX

CHARACTERISTICS OF LEARNING EXPERIENCES IN
READING AND LITERATURE THAT CAN BE BUILT
INTO INSTRUCTIONAL MATERIALS TO
FACILITATE CREATIVE BEHAVIOR

I. *Activities Before Reading*
  1. Confrontation with ambiguities and uncertainties.
  2. Anticipation and expectation heightened.
  3. Awareness of problem to be solved, difficulty to be faced, gap in knowledge to be filled, etc.
  4. Building onto the individual's or group's existing knowledge.
  5. Concern about a problem heightened.
  6. Curiosity and wanting to know stimulated.
  7. Familiar made strange or strange made familiar by analogy.
  8. Free from inhibiting sets.
  9. Looking at same material from several different psychological or sociological viewpoints.
  10. Provocative question requiring reader to examine information in a different way.
  11. Predictions from limited information required.
  12. Purposefulness of activity made clear.
  13. Structured only enough to give clues and direction.
  14. Taking the next step beyond what is known.
  15. Warm-up provided in some way (easy to difficult, familiar to unfamiliar, bodily involvement, etc.)

II. *Activities During Reading*
  1. Awareness of problems and difficulties heightened in progress of reading.
  2. Creative and constructive rather than cynical acceptance of limitations.
  3. Creative personality characteristics or predispositions (willing-

ness to attempt the difficult, freedom to conform or nonconform, etc.) encouraged.

4. Creative problem-solving process replicated in stories.
5. Creative processes described and illuminated by the story.
6. Exploration made deliberate and systematic.
7. Incompleteness of knowledge presented.
8. Juxtaposition of apparently irrelevant elements presented.
9. Mysteries explored and examined.
10. Open-endedness preserved.
11. Outcomes not completely predictable.
12. Predictions from limited information required.
13. Reading with imagination (to make it sound like the thing happening).
14. Search for truth facilitated by honesty and realism of material.
15. Skills for finding out identified and encouraged.
16. Surprises heightened and deliberately used.
17. Visualization encouraged.

III. *Activities After Reading*
1. Ambiguities played with.
2. Awareness of problem, difficulty, gap in knowledge, etc.
3. Awareness and acknowledgement by teacher of pupil potentialities.
4. Concern about problems heightened.
5. Constructive response called for (stressing other, better ways rather than defects).
6. Continuity with previously learned skills, information, etc.
7. Creative and constructive, rather than cynical, acceptance of limitations.
8. Digging deeper required, going beneath or beyond the obvious.
9. Divergent thinking made legitimate.
10. Elaborating what is read.
11. Elegant solutions (simplest solutions taking into account the largest number of variables) encouraged.
12. Empathic metaphor to give new feeling or understanding of an object, person, or state.
13. Experimentation required.
14. Familiar made strange or strange made familiar by analogy.
15. Fantasies examined to find solutions to realistic problems.
16. Future projection encouraged.
17. Going beyond what is read.
18. Improbabilities entertained.

19. Irrelevance accepted and entertained.
20. Judgment deferred until pool of ideas has been produced.
21. Knowledge from one field brought to bear on problems in another field.
22. Looking at same material from several different viewpoints encouraged.
23. Manipulation of ideas and objects encouraged.
24. Multiple hypotheses encouraged.
25. One thing permitted to lead to another.
26. Paradoxes confronted and examined.
27. Play in pushing a fundamental law or scientific principle to its limit facilitated.
28. Possible causes and consequences called for.
29. Provocative questions used.
30. Potentialities discovered and tested.
31. Reorganization of information required.
32. Returning to previously acquired skill, information, etc., to see new relationship or returning to an unsolved problem (one posed before reading) encouraged.
33. Self-initiated learning encouraged.
34. Skills for finding out identified and encouraged.
35. Synthesis of different and apparently irrelevant elements facilitated.
36. Systematic testing of hypotheses encouraged.
37. Taking the next step beyond what is known facilitated.
38. Testing and revision of predictions provided.
39. Transforming and rearranging what is read encouraged.

NAME INDEX

SUBJECT INDEX

Froebel 52 — hands

defocus 217

Kirk 216 241

Garner 218 dog month a mile can you imagine
241

mason synthesis? 217
241

little girl 160 responding teacher
214

opportunity teaching?

creative process model
286

106 Use in Verbal summary

229 direction giving rules